Teaching in the Study of Religion and Beyond

ALSO AVAILABLE FROM BLOOMSBURY:

Teaching and Learning Religion: Engaging the Work of Eugene V. Gallagher and Patricia O'Connell Killen, Edited by Davina C. Lopez and Thomas Pearson

Teaching Critical Religious Studies: Pedagogy and Critique in the Classroom, Edited by Jenna Gray-Hildenbrand, Beverley McGuire and Hussein Rashid

Teaching in the Study of Religion and Beyond

A Practical Guide for Undergraduate Classes

**Edited by
RUSSELL T. McCUTCHEON**

BLOOMSBURY ACADEMIC
LONDON • NEW YORK • OXFORD • NEW DELHI • SYDNEY

BLOOMSBURY ACADEMIC
Bloomsbury Publishing Plc
50 Bedford Square, London, WC1B 3DP, UK
1385 Broadway, New York, NY 10018, USA
29 Earlsfort Terrace, Dublin 2, Ireland

BLOOMSBURY, BLOOMSBURY ACADEMIC and the Diana logo are trademarks of
Bloomsbury Publishing Plc

First published in Great Britain 2024

Copyright © Russell T. McCutcheon and contributors, 2024

Russell T. McCutcheon has asserted his right under the Copyright, Designs and Patents Act, 1988, to be identified as Editor of this work.

For legal purposes the Acknowledgments on p. xi constitute an extension of this copyright page.

Cover design by Namkwan Cho
Cover image © Olex Runda/Shutterstock

All rights reserved. No part of this publication may be reproduced or transmitted in any form or by any means, electronic or mechanical, including photocopying, recording, or any information storage or retrieval system, without prior permission in writing from the publishers.

Bloomsbury Publishing Plc does not have any control over, or responsibility for, any third-party websites referred to or in this book. All internet addresses given in this book were correct at the time of going to press. The author and publisher regret any inconvenience caused if addresses have changed or sites have ceased to exist, but can accept no responsibility for any such changes.

A catalogue record for this book is available from the British Library.

Library of Congress Cataloging-in-Publication Data
Names: McCutcheon, Russell T., 1961– editor.
Title: Teaching in the study of religion and beyond : a practical guide for undergraduate classes / edited by Russell T. McCutcheon.
Description: London ; New York : Bloomsbury Academic, 2024. | Includes bibliographical references and index.
Identifiers: LCCN 2023031209 (print) | LCCN 2023031210 (ebook) | ISBN 9781350351073 (hb) | ISBN 9781350351066 (pb) | ISBN 9781350351097 (ebook) | ISBN 9781350351080 (epdf)
Subjects: LCSH: Religion–Study and teaching (Higher)
Classification: LCC BL41 .T425 2024 (print) | LCC BL41 (ebook) | DDC 200.71—dc23/eng/20230815
LC record available at https://lccn.loc.gov/2023031209
LC ebook record available at https://lccn.loc.gov/2023031210

ISBN: HB: 978-1-3503-5107-3
PB: 978-1-3503-5106-6
ePDF: 978-1-3503-5108-0
eBook: 978-1-3503-5109-7

Typeset by RefineCatch Limited, Bungay, Suffolk
Printed and bound in Great Britain

To find out more about our authors and books visit www.bloomsbury.com and sign up for our newsletters

"What we seek to train in college are individuals who know not only that the world is more complex than it first appears, but also that, therefore, interpretative decisions must be made, decisions of judgment which entail real consequences for which one must take responsibility, from which one may not flee by the dodge of disclaiming expertise."

JONATHAN Z. SMITH, "THE INTRODUCTORY COURSE: LESS IS BETTER"

Contents

Acknowledgments xi
About This Book xii

    Introduction 1
    Russell T. McCutcheon
1   Academic Misconduct 8
    Leslie Dorrough Smith
2   Accessibility 14
    Russell T. McCutcheon
3   Accommodations 17
    Rita Lester
4   Assessment 23
    Steven Ramey
5   Assignments 28
    Teemu Taira
6   Attendance 33
    Leslie Dorrough Smith
7   Class Participation 38
    Khurram Hussain
8   Core Curriculum/General Education 43
    Craig Martin
9   Critical Thinking 48
    Emily D. Crews
10 Curriculum 53
    Rita Lester

11　Digital Humanities 58
　　Michael J. Altman
12　Directed Readings/Independent Studies 62
　　Khurram Hussain
13　Diversity, Equity, and Inclusion (DEI) 66
　　K. Merinda Simmons
14　Examples 70
　　Michael J. Altman
15　Experiential Learning 74
　　Emily D. Crews
16　Extra Credit 78
　　Vaia Touna
17　Films 83
　　Khurram Hussain
18　Final Examinations 87
　　Michael J. Altman
19　Grading 91
　　Vaia Touna
20　Group Work 97
　　Teemu Taira
21　High-Impact Practices 102
　　Rita Lester
22　Honors 108
　　K. Merinda Simmons
23　Introduction vs. Survey 112
　　Vaia Touna
24　Large Lectures 117
　　Steven Ramey
25　Learning Management Systems (LMS) 122
　　Russell T. McCutcheon

26 Library Resources 126
Emily D. Crews

27 Office Hours 130
Leslie Dorrough Smith

28 Online/Remote Courses 134
Steffen Führding

29 Peer Tutors 140
Russell T. McCutcheon

30 Prerequisites 144
Steffen Führding

31 Primary vs. Secondary Sources 148
Craig Martin

32 Professionalization 153
Richard Newton

33 Public Humanities 158
Richard Newton

34 Readings 163
Craig Martin

35 Recruiting Majors 168
Richard Newton

36 Seminars 173
Steffen Führding

37 Senior Seminars 178
Rita Lester

38 Student Evaluations of Instruction 183
Russell T. McCutcheon

39 Syllabi 188
Richard Newton

40 Teaching Assistants 193
Steven Ramey

41 Theory 199
K. Merinda Simmons

42 Transferable Skills 203
Steven Ramey

43 Undergraduate Research 209
Suzanne Owen

44 Writing 213
K. Merinda Simmons

Afterword—The Introductory Course: Less is Better 217
Jonathan Z. Smith

Extended Glossary 225
Russell T. McCutcheon

References 294
Notes on Contributors 295
Index 298

Acknowledgments

I would like to thank Elaine Smith, for her kind permission to reprint her late husband's brief essay on teaching the introductory course (as the Afterword to the volume) and to acknowledge the fundamental influence that his approach to teaching has had on both my own career and the careers of many included in this volume. With these contributors in mind, I wish to thank each of them for so generously agreeing to include on each of their already busy "to do" lists writing a short chapter or two on aspects of college teaching that the experienced among us might take for granted—entries that newcomers to the exercise will undoubtedly find useful. I must also thank Bloomsbury and the members of its production team, for an interest in publishing this volume. Finally, I should mention the thousands of students whom I have taught since beginning work in a U.S. college as a full-time instructor back in 1993 (after having been a Teaching Assistant for quite a few years back in Toronto). We did not talk about assessment and high-impact practices, let alone the so-called scholarship of teaching, back then but the challenge of engaging students, planning a course to be something more than a list of facts conveyed to them across a semester, all of which were in need of memorization and reproduction on a test, and using whatever was at hand to illustrate a point or to apply a finding was all just as relevant then as it is now. And if we multiply the students whom I've taught by all of the contributors in this volume, then there's quite a few people out there who, at some point in the past few decades, tolerated (and hopefully benefitted from) our experiments in classrooms and lecture halls, patiently waiting for us to gain just a little more experience and familiarity with the material and our role as a teacher, and who therefore helped to make us better at this really very important part of our jobs and our careers.

About This Book

This volume provides a practical orientation to over forty topics of direct relevance to instructors currently teaching undergraduate students (many of which are relevant for graduate/post-graduate classes as well). Although written by scholars of religion, the essays will each be of use to anyone working in the liberal arts; for, regardless the academic discipline, we must all address issues from assessment, class participation, and learning management systems to grading, creating a syllabus, and promoting undergraduate research. An essay on pedagogy and an extensive glossary conclude the book, with the latter providing succinct comments on each of the main chapters' topics while also adding many others that are all related to navigating one's place in colleges and universities today. The volume will therefore be of wide use—not just to graduate students and novice teachers but also to seasoned faculty aiming to remain relevant and engaged with recent innovations and requirements on their campuses.

Introduction

Russell T. McCutcheon

Oh, and can you also teach a course on myths and rituals. . .?

I was asked that very question later in the spring of 1993 during a phone call with the late Charlie Reynolds, then the longtime Chair of the Department of Religious Studies into which I was being hired as a full-time Instructor, for the 1993–1994 academic year. I was a doctoral student at what was then known as the University of Toronto's Centre for Religious Studies, about two thirds through writing my dissertation and now in the process of acquiring my first passport, since the short-term position that I was moving to was at the University of Tennessee in Knoxville, in the southern United States. I was being hired to teach sections of the Department's lower-level world religions course along with another class that was also for first-year students but that was more of a thematic introduction to the field. (A faculty member, the late Ralph Norman, had recently moved into the senior administration, now working as Vice Chancellor, as I recall, and the Department had funds to replace him, temporarily, in the classroom; that first year they hired two of us and, although I didn't know at the time, I would be lucky enough to continue alone in that full-time Instructor role for two additional years.) But, as I learned on that phone call, another faculty member on their staff, who had long taught a course entitled Myth, Symbol, Ritual—the late Stan Lusby—was retiring and, given that this upper-level undergraduate class had been quite popular among their students (i.e., it recruited majors and generated dependable credit hour production for the unit), finding someone able to teach that class come fall was now also among the Chair's priorities. Presumably that course was already on the books and had enrolled students (what with registration for the fall having taken place the March before).

And so, to his question, I remember replying, "Yes I can"—knowing that now was hardly the time to say that, apart from being a graduate teaching assistant for a variety of courses on world religions, religion and science, and even the New Testament, I had never been involved with, much less taught on my own, a course devoted to myths and rituals.

To be fair, or so I must have reasoned during that call, I *was* writing a dissertation that was, at least in part, on the work of the once influential historian of religions Mircea Eliade (just a few years later a revised version became my first book), and so understanding his approach to such narratives and practices—an approach that was still quite popular at the time, but one with which I disagreed—would at least be a starting point for such a class. (For all I knew at the time, such an approach already informed the class, at least as it had been taught.) But where to go from there—classes are 16 weeks or so where I've worked, after all...? And so, between that conversation and arriving in Knoxville in early August, I had some work to do, not just to get a couple of brand new 100-level intro courses planned and ready to teach but to figure out just what I would be doing in an upper-level seminar on, of all things, myths and rituals.

I open with this anecdote, from what is now thirty years ago, to indicate that every person teaching in a university is, at one time or another, in well over their head—whether because of their unfamiliarity with the subject matter when asked to teach a new course or perhaps because of the sheer volume of choices and new duties that come with teaching a course. But more than this: it's not that we've all just been there—as if hard-won experience eventually inserts a distance between us now and the past tense of our once novice teaching selves; no, even the most experienced among us are continually revising their courses, changing the readings, tackling new topics, devising new assignments, learning new software, or even sometimes something as mundane, but consequential, as trying to identify more current pop culture references than the now dated examples that so easily come to the mind of a faculty member while teaching a class. Being a good teacher—or maybe we should complicate that value judgment from the outset and instead say engaging, effective, and even resilient—is a constant process of reinvention, learning, and experimentation (something that the abrupt, worldwide switch to remote teaching, during the time of COVID-19, made so plain to absolutely everyone back in the spring of 2020). This means that, when it comes to walking into a classroom on the first day of the semester, there's less distance than you might imagine between me now and that inexperienced doctoral student in Toronto. Sure, I've got far more today tucked inside my back pocket, as they say, that I can quickly draw on when trying to persuade students of something or illustrations that I can rely upon to press a point during class, and, yes, I don't write out my lectures in full anymore, the night before each class, as I quite literally did that first time teaching Myth, Symbol, and Ritual, back when I would actually read those lecture notes during class so that I didn't get lost or forget to say something that, at least ahead of class, I thought was important. But the classroom is filled with new students every time that you teach a topic that may seem old and familiar to you, making it a place with many variables and unexpected moments—or should I call those pedagogical opportunities, maybe? And so, veteran teachers know that their experience will carry them only so far. Continual hard work and an always contagious enthusiasm for their subject matter is likely what will get them, and their students, to the end of each semester.

For me, some of that early hard work when asked to teach something unexpected involved reading and taking detailed notes from a variety of books, such as Brian Morris's still important *Anthropological Studies of Religion: An Introductory Text* (1987)—notes that, when mixed with my own expertise, experience, and goals for the class, then became the basis for many of my lectures. My now tattered copy of that book, with the broken spine, which I purchased in Toronto back in 1989 (at the insistence of my then classmate and good friend Bruce McKay, according to a notation that I made inside the front cover), is still on my office shelf, filled with underlining and scribbled comments, such as the NB (*Nota Bene*, Latin: note well—which I adopted from an earlier professor of mine who wrote this in his own book's margins) or the exclamation marks that pepper the margins. It wasn't the only work that assisted me that first year of full-time teaching but, with the steep learning curve presented to me by having to tackle that myth and ritual course in mind, it played a key role in giving me the content that I needed—content to fill a class's 150 minutes of lectures each week and content on which students could be tested occasionally or on which they could draw in writing their essays.

But when I look back on that first year I realize that I was so inexperienced that I failed to see that teaching undergraduate students is about so much more than the content of a class—that is, the names of all of those rivers crossed by all of those ancient but supposedly important people on which students are routinely tested; sure, the content is crucial, but during a lecture or a seminar there's so much more going on in the head of a good (and yes, please recall my earlier qualification of that word) teacher than anticipating the next tidbit or factoid in a string of facts that makes up the usual lecture. For such instructors are also monitoring the room continually, judging the level of their students' comprehension from a variety of cues, trying to see if there's a question emerging from that person over there or maybe possible evidence of a puzzle forming in the mind of the one on the other side of the room. Something that they heard on the radio this morning while driving to work, or maybe on the news last night, suddenly strikes the teacher as unexpectedly relevant to the class, maybe as a quick illustration of what is often a tough point to convey and maybe grasp—so, you quickly wonder to yourself how to work that into the discussion, and then, if you do, how to get back to the main point after spending some time on the aside. Wait, can I easily find the audio of that radio story online, using the classroom's multimedia system, or will searching for it take so long that it'll sidetrack the entire class and lose the momentum we'd already built up? Oh, and precisely what was the main point that I was trying to illustrate...? And how much time is left in the class today—should I end it here or can we start down the road of that new topic which we'll focus on the next day? (For a syllabus, at least in many Humanities classes, is much like an essay—outlining a persuasive argument on some topic that unfolds during the course of a semester.) And don't forget to announce that film the Department is showing tomorrow night or the list of new courses being taught next semester... This and so much more is happening during any given moment in a class—like the many browser windows that are often all open on a desktop, which, during a good class, are all in synch and talking to one another as the teacher works through the class. And *that's* what I didn't know back then, wedded, as I was, to the content contained in the controlled text of my pre-written lecture, and thus only able to handle one or two variables in any given lecture. But with more experience comes the knowledge that far more than one or two other things are happening during any lecture, during any seminar. The content of the class is among them, indeed, but it is hardly alone—and sometimes it is far from the most important thing happening in the classroom. It took me time to realize this and so I certainly didn't know it when talking to Charlie on the phone about my upcoming job.

Which brings me to the volume that you now have before you; as its editor and one of its contributors, my hope is that its readers will indeed be underlining things and making some marginal comments of their own, even though the specific content of their teaching may rarely be mentioned in its pages, if at all—and surely that content will vary widely from one reader to another. (Aside: the contributors were not selected for their content expertise, as if we needed to check boxes for all of the world religions, but, instead, for their hard-won experience and style in the classroom.) Success for this book, judging by my copy of Morris's volume, is that it'll be used so much that, sooner or later, the spine will crack in a few places and the pages will become loose and dog-eared. For if that happens then it will indicate a reader who understands that the content and thus the specialty that they've worked so hard to acquire is only part of the story of a good class, a good assignment, or a good semester. (And don't forget my earlier complication of that misleadingly simple moralistic judgment.) There's so much more going on, from knowing the difference between a survey and an introductory course or understanding how assorted material can be tested in different ways to learning how to accommodate for different students' needs and learning styles, not to mention how to rely on more than just an expensive textbook for a class. To help readers think through this and so much more we've assembled an international group of contributors, all with much teaching experience at the undergraduate level, and all experts in their own field—but, as already suggested, all equally committed to seeing successful teaching as being about far more than merely conveying and then memorizing the facts. So I venture to guess that all who have joined this project would agree with me when I say that many of our students will likely forget much of our content but other, often unexpected elements of the class will probably hang on with them for decades to come, and be applied in innumerable and sometimes quite curious places. A good class, led by a good teacher, always keeps this in mind.

A final word or two on the structure of the book: although all of the contributors are scholars of religion—something that will likely be evident from the historical or ethnographic examples that they may use to illustrate the points that they're making in each of the following entries—this volume addresses what, despite the field or discipline in which you happen to work, are common topics or challenges of the contemporary undergraduate classroom all across what we used to refer to as the liberal arts. Accordingly, there's no chapter on "Defining Religion," "Theology vs. Religious Studies," or "The Insider/Outsider Problem"—there's plenty of other discipline specific resources already out there for that. Instead, readers from almost any field, and with almost any sense of what the study of religion ought to be, will benefit from the following chapters, devoted to such topics as assessment and rubrics or the sometimes unexpected things that are entailed in making a syllabus. (And this wide applicability of the book illustrates a larger theoretical point also important to the contributors: the study of religion is *not* a unique academic field of deeply important meaning; it is, instead, but one more site where we get to study people by means of what they do and what they leave behind when all of their doings are done.) Each of the entries, arranged alphabetically, examines a discrete moment or item (maybe even buzzword) in the current university classroom, allowing readers who are either novice themselves or experienced but new to some topic to benefit from the experience of someone who has thought a bit about how a specific course fits into a larger curriculum or what an instructor is to make of the sometimes unexpected comments they receive on the anonymous course evaluations that their students often submit at the end of the semester. (Yes indeed, speaking as a longtime Chair who read these each semester, I've quite often seen only the female faculty have students comment on their clothing— something I make note of in that entry in the volume. And by the way, I have never used the scores on such assessments to rank or evaluate the faculty with whom I've worked over the years.) The entries are hardly exhaustive, to be sure, but the volume covers much of the sometimes unspoken and often unnoticed elements to a good class, offering some assistance for busy instructors either early in their career or those who may themselves be outside the tenure-track system, as I was for the first three years of what turned out to be my own career, let alone those who may have been teaching for years but who are stumped by an administrator talking about some recent pedagogical initiative that seems designed to do anything but innovate in the classroom. To speak honestly: in my experience, "initiatives" on university campuses are often make-work programs thought up by would-be professional administrators who are looking for a competitive edge on the job market, i.e., a new C.V. line to help them land a better job at another university, such as instituting a mid-career faculty mentoring program or forming a committee to write college bylaws. And so, many of the innovations that impact the classroom are top-down initiatives—something one must simply get used to when working in the modern university, whether the initiative comes from governments, credentialing bodies, or the administration itself. How to adapt to them, manage (with) them, and sometimes even succeed despite them are all challenges facing faculty. With that last comment in mind, I should add that the entries are all constructive but that does not mean that our contributors are naïve to how the modern university works or the pressures on instructors today; so they were all asked to be frank in their approach to each topic but, in doing so, always to offer readers a leg up on even the most challenging classroom issues or trends. Each entry ends with suggested entries in the volume that may also be of interest to readers.

Referencing yet again that complicated notion of a "good class," at this point I should say explicitly that this volume is well aware that success in the undergraduate classroom can often be defined by students let alone faculty rather differently than, let's say, by university administrations, with the latter often focusing (at least where many of us work) on the dictates of credentialing agencies and the initiatives of government offices. How a university professor can manage in such a situation, when they can be pulled in what they may see as competing or even contradictory directions, often depends upon them learning how to address the larger needs of their employers and profession while also being able to tailor a class or even an assignment to meet the specific needs of their students and the overall logic of their course and their own aims for it. They need to be nimble and strategic—something that I hope they might acquire in greater depth after reading the following entries.

Apart from a substantial glossary, containing a variety of professional and technical terms used throughout the book (whether or not it is included as a main entry), the volume ends with an afterword from the late Jonathan Z. Smith (included here with the kind permission of his widow, Elaine)—a person many of us judge as being among the most influential scholars of religion over the past several decades—which was first published in 1991. His entire teaching career focused, often exclusively, on undergraduate education, and Smith's specific approach, nicely illustrated in this brief essay on teaching, has been influential of many of this volume's authors, including myself. That he produced some of the field's most influential scholarship while also mainly teaching undergraduates at the University of Chicago should encourage those who, like many of us here, are rather suspicious of all the rhetoric in modern universities around specialization and the apparent priority of graduate education—sadly, too many of us in the field think that our legacy is determined by how many doctoral students we supervise. For although we were ourselves all graduate students at one time, and while some of us also now work with graduate students, teaching students who are earning a Bachelor's degree is, in many of our cases, our career's main work—students who, though sometimes taking few courses in our field, may remember certain things from these classes for a lifetime. If the following entries can assist such faculty in further engaging these and other students, by thinking through a few issues and demands on their time as teachers, then we will have done our job in helping to support some engaging, effective, and even resilient teachers at a time when working in universities, especially within the Humanities, can present us all with some real challenges.

And so, as I've been told Smith would often say to start one of his classes, let's get to work.

1

Academic Misconduct

Leslie Dorrough Smith

I teach at a small private liberal arts university. As one aspect of my university service, I have held a position on the academic dishonesty review committee for several years. Academic dishonesty (also known as academic misconduct) involves a student misrepresenting their academic capacities, products, and/or skills. This happens most commonly through cheating (i.e., the use of unauthorized sources or prohibited collaboration with others) and plagiarism (i.e., the misrepresentation of another's work as one's own, usually through a failure to adequately cite one's sources). Our committee decides on the penalty students will incur after a pattern of academic dishonesty arises; in a typical hearing, this deliberation occurs after the student in question appears and provides their own explanation of what happened.

While many people may assume that students engage in any number of forms of academic misconduct because they are lazy and want the easy way out, I can say with great confidence that the majority of students do not enter college intending to break the rules. Rather, in these hearings, students express a wide number of reasons for their behavior, which often include: struggles with time management; poor preparation for college-level writing and research; and a series of other cultural/social factors that make dishonesty appear to be the best in a series of bad options.

An instructor's ability to identify these factors is not meant to imply that students are not responsible for their behaviors, but we can set them up for success while saving ourselves from the considerable labor that a misconduct charge involves, particularly in the areas of detection and reporting. While some professors opt to do all assignments in-person to circumvent some of the conditions that cause academic misconduct, that approach shuts down a number of important academic experiences (such as paper writing and drafting), and so is not appropriate for all courses. Nor is it even possible in some settings, particularly in a time when many of us do not control whether we teach online or on campus.

With these things in mind, what follows are some of my own thoughts and practices regarding why misconduct happens and some ideas on how to prevent it. These ideas offer a template rather than a one-size-fits-all approach, but as with all things related to teaching, experimentation is a necessity.

A lot of academic misconduct happens because of a simple cause—desperation—which itself is usually fueled by a number of other problems or issues with which many students struggle. One of the most common is time management. As most of us know, college is one of the first places where students are often solely in charge of managing their own schedules. While it is a skill that can be learned, acquiring those basics can also feel completely overwhelming. Misconduct often happens, then, because of a time crunch.

Fear of asking for help is another factor. This often has to do with students' feelings of inadequacy (they are often afraid to look stupid or to reveal that they weren't paying attention when an assignment was being discussed, for instance) or a more generalized sense of intimidation about meeting with faculty. The latter can be compounded for first generation students who may see professors less as fellow humans who want them to succeed and more as intimidating authority figures. For students in this position, admitting that they're unsure about how to handle college and its expectations can seem like the ultimate badge of failure even though those feelings are completely normal, shared by many, and thus part of the learning process.

Ignorance also plays a role here, particularly in the case of plagiarism. For newer students, whatever educational practices preceded college will often set the tone for what is normal. While many have been told at some point in the past that they must "cite their sources," whether they know what this means or have practiced it enough so that it doesn't feel clunky is a different matter. As time goes on, this problem may be aggravated for students in majors where they may not frequently engage in writing assignments, making writing-intensive classes feel laborious. Ignorance may also be a particularly tall barrier for some international students, who may have learned different expectations regarding citation practices.

Finally, there are students who will participate in academic misconduct simply because it feels like their best option. Taking the path of least resistance may seem a reasonably good bet for those juggling a million other things in life, particularly if there is a poor campus reporting system for dishonesty and thus they feel like they are unlikely to get caught. A very small silver lining for those of us on the grading and assessment end of these assignments is that most students are unaware of how obvious their deception or collaboration often is. With the advent of AI paper generators, though, that advantage may be increasingly diminishing.

The cultural landscape that enables academic misconduct involves many points of rocky terrain, but there are approaches that we can take to bypass those paths. I'm taking for granted that most professors already know about the many websites and other forms of technology that can check for plagiarism as well as for AI-generated text, all of which can be very useful for detecting academic misconduct after it has happened. I am also assuming that most of us recognize the importance of giving different exam questions and essay prompts each semester to avoid students passing along old exams and papers to each other. Beyond those considerations, the following are tips and techniques that have proven successful in my teaching, mainly because these strategies address head-on the factors that stoke desperation. But again, experimentation is key.

To combat student ignorance of proper citation practices, perhaps the most important thing that I do to prevent academic misconduct is to talk about it with my students frequently, complete with providing examples that show what misconduct is and what better alternatives look like. Ideally, this is not just a lecture given by the professor, but is accompanied by an actual written exercise where students are taught (and must, in turn, show) proper paraphrasing, citation, and any other related skills pertinent to the course. This may seem like it's an exercise geared only toward students with weak writing or research backgrounds, but we should presume that all students come to us with gaps in their knowledge of academic integrity. For example, I was an excellent student who loved writing when I entered college, but there I learned for the first time what constituted proper paraphrasing, as my experience with citation in high school mainly involved direct quotes. It is thus helpful to remember that there is not a single curriculum on academic integrity that all college-bound students have heard and understood.

Explaining to our students why academic honesty is important is also helpful, although I spend less time focusing on the "academic theft" conversation (which is not motivating to many) and more on their own possible future pitfalls if they don't learn and practice these skills now. For those who believe that they'll never have to know how to do this again, I often provide examples of high-profile plagiarism or cheating cases outside of the academic or literary worlds so that students can understand that these are concerns that will endure across their professional careers. I also remind them that, in my course, making a low grade on an assignment completed honestly is worth more points than the zero they will receive if I catch them plagiarizing or cheating. Even if they are not sensitive to the ethical argument, they are often open to the mathematical one.

Finally, it's important to have reasonable expectations of your undergraduate students' citation abilities and writing skills. Earlier in my career I expected more grammatical perfection from students. I later learned that the more I expected a caliber of prose that they could not deliver, the more likely they were to resort to outside sources to do their work for them—and to some degree, who could blame them? I was expecting them to write as if they had the skills of amateur copyeditors. Now I teach students to write in different ways, using a different set of supports (some of which I discuss below). The result is that I spend much more time with them drafting written assignments, partnering with our campus writing center more intentionally, and structuring those assignments in different ways. What I've learned is that students don't practice a different way of writing and citation simply because I tell them that their papers are lacking. They get better when they know what to improve, how to improve, and then are given the time to practice it with feedback.

It's also important for instructors to think a few steps ahead about the aspects of their courses that may more readily open the door to academic misconduct. In my classes, one of the most common reasons students give when I confront them about academic misconduct is that they shared their lecture notes with each other. While sharing notes alone usually doesn't yield the types of duplication that I sometimes see, the fact that it's common practice for students to get notes from someone else in order to catch up from an absence or other missed material means that we have to consider the possible implications of this practice.

What typically transpires in a case where students share notes is that they copy portions of those notes verbatim into their own papers or assignments. They may be working independently but from a common pool of information, in other words, thus making it impossible to tell if the duplication was intentional. In other cases, however, the degree of similarity between students' assignments may make the unauthorized collaboration quite clear, and for this reason I give students the following advice about notetaking: 1) they should take their own notes; 2) they should treat my lectures as a source that needs to be cited; and 3) they should work on paraphrasing their notes rather than just regurgitating verbatim a PowerPoint slide from the lecture. If they follow these pieces of advice then sharing their class notes should not lead to misconduct. This is but one reason why I think it's helpful to repetitively practice paraphrasing as a skill.

Another example of an area that deserves attention involves the types of questions professors ask on exams and other assignments. In general, if you are asking a question that students can successfully search online (e.g., "How can we apply Foucault's ideas to the study of religion?") then you should instead consider how to individualize and nuance your prompts (and if you're not sure, search for it yourself before assigning it!). In my introductory classes, for instance, I often use a major theoretical or methodological concept to help structure the course, and then in the course assignments, I ask students to draw on specifics or case studies from their readings to address these concepts. Because my requirements are very specific, it's harder to plagiarize that material. This could mean that the earlier, more generic question about

Foucault could become something like: "How do Foucault's ideas about Q relate to readings X, Y, and Z from this course?" In short, we can make it more difficult for students to commit academic misconduct when we create more nuanced assessments that can't be easily searched online.

In addition to making sure that we avoid creating questions and prompts that are too generic or open-ended, we can also re-think how we structure assignments to build better writing (and with it, academic integrity). One popular technique for helping students achieve success and avoid misconduct is scaffolding assignments. Scaffolding involves breaking up an assignment into its smaller, constitutive parts. This makes the task more palatable to students who may get easily overwhelmed (thus reducing the aforementioned desperation), but it also builds in time management and drafting skills, all of which normalize sustained work on a single project. Assignments can also be structured so that students work on multiple drafts of the same assignment, or they can address a larger assignment that has been broken down into smaller components or questions that are completed across time. In the latter case, those individual questions together can serve as the final product or portfolio for the course rather than assigning a wholly new paper or writing assignment in those last desperate days of the semester. In terms of tracking growth and development, there are also many opportunities for making a visit to the writing or tutoring center an actual step in a scaffolded assignment.

Another method to make students less likely to commit academic misconduct is to incorporate introspective or other meta-level observations into the assignment itself. I often ask students to provide specific, well-explained examples about how their critical thinking has changed about a topic pertinent to the course. Both the students and I find this a really fulfilling type of exercise. Alternatively, consider making a point-earning assignment out of a well-timed meeting with you. Some professors use oral assignments or discussions to keep students accountable for their learning. I spend the week before finals meeting one on one with my students just to check in, discuss their progress, help them plan for the final paper or project, and talk through any types of loose ends as we move into finals week. This assignment strategy is effective at reducing desperation because it requires that the student engage in pre-planning and asking for help. I find that those last-minute meetings are also a great time to discuss any extenuating circumstances (and the possible need for deadline extensions) that may otherwise lull students into the types of misconduct that are often so tempting at the end of the semester, when fatigue and desperation are both high.

Academic misconduct is likely a perennial part of the teaching experience, but with some well-placed strategies, it doesn't have to become a dominating force. If we can acknowledge that students are responsible for their own academic integrity at the same time that we can point to predictive factors that make misconduct seem appealing (particularly for those students who come to us with a number of missing skills or difficult life situations), then we are much better situated to create assignments that work well for everyone and that promote more productive forms of learning.

See also: Assessment; Grading; Professionalization; Writing

2

Accessibility

Russell T. McCutcheon

Although there was a time when accessibility on a campus was a key word exclusively associated with addressing the needs of students with physical disabilities—and thereby often used in conjunction with such architectural features as elevators installed in older buildings or ramps to facilitate access to a building from the street for those in wheelchairs as well as so-called handicapped accessible hallways and bathrooms—today the term is used rather more broadly to name a variety of sites where colleges (let alone virtually any employers) are generally required by law to ensure that all of their resources, and not just their spaces, are available to the wider public. With this broadening comes implications for instructors and teaching; for although an individual instructor certainly has no direct role to play in complying with building code concerning the width of doorways (to allow a wheelchair to pass through unobstructed), such instructors do have a responsibility to enable all of their students to acquire course materials and have unimpeded access to course content. Although this by now well-established initiative still includes ways of eliminating possible physical barriers to students, employees or guests and the general public alike—one might be surprised by the number of older, multi-story buildings on some campuses that yet lack elevators or lifts—discussions on accessibility now also routinely involve such things as so-called technological or web accessibility, since so much of a university's services are now offered online. Thus, providing ways for hearing or visually impaired students to use sites associated with a course and its lectures or to access online readings now regularly falls under this far broader sense of accessibility.

In some cases colleges now offer training for all employees, given the legal ramifications of being found in non-compliance with what are often legal requirements; this training may focus on such things as the correct way to create or manage a webpage or the proper way to create a portable document (PDF)—if by correct and proper one means a format compatible with programs used to turn computer text into spoken language (so-called screen readers) or translate word processing or HTML text by means of a Braille display. From using styles feature in programs such as Word (to distinguish various levels of headings from the main text of a document, to signal to a screen reader how to navigate a document) to ways of inserting images, whether a so-called functional image (i.e., an icon that initiatives a program or process) versus images whose content is relevant to the text with which they are associated on a website (whether they are merely decorative or informational), many aspects of the documents an instructor shares with class can rather easily be modified so that they are useful to those students who are using assistive devises. In the case of images, alternative text (what is commonly known as alt-text), written in a way that is helpfully descriptive but succinct, must be associated with images so as to be read by a screen reading program, to allow a visually impaired user to understand the content of the page or document. Such programs work with the various digital tags inserted into the document—something that is preserved, for instance, in a Word document when converted to a PDF via the "save as PDF" feature but which is completely lost when "print to PDF" is employed (the latter process basically results in a text file being converted to an image file).

In many cases accessibility procedures are already built into the software or LMSs commonly used by an instructor (some will allow users to review a document to determine the extent to which it is accessible, such as the accessibility checker built into Word, which also recommends fixes for problems encountered), requiring them to learn it in order to use it properly. In most cases this is relatively easily done but complexities can arise, such as a PDF working with a screen reader to read the document not in the order of the text on the page but, instead, in the order in which the text was added or edited in the document. Thus, to maximize the effect of accessibility initiatives, instructors would be wise to take care in the presentation of items for class use and to take full advantage of any resources offered by their campus. But more than this: in many cases it has been determined that anything public-facing on a university's website, such as a faculty member's page, a page listing past award winners, or one announcing upcoming student association events, must also be accessible should the general public visit the site. To say this another way, password protected sites or sites accessible only to students (e.g., via a learning management system) may not face the same expectations as a public website—though, the potential variety of students who will need access to even these protected materials means that accessibility always remains a key consideration.

On some campuses a separate Office Accessibility Services or what others might term a Student Accessibility Office may manage training, implementation, and compliance reporting for this campus-wide initiative though, in yet other places, it may fall under the responsibilities of an Office of Disability Services (with accessibility not to be confused with accommodations, of course); in all such cases, accessibility is more than likely understood as but one component in a university's diversity, equity, and inclusions initiatives. Often so-called Centers for Teaching and Learning, which are often established by the university itself as opposed to any of its colleges, faculties, or departments, may also play a central role in guaranteeing an accessible classroom, from devising campus-wide guidelines (often based on the Web Content Accessibility Guidelines [WCAG], developed by the World Wide Web's Web Accessibility Initiative [with 2018's version currently being their most recent—see https://www.w3.org/TR/WCAG21/]) to offering training to, in the words of the WCAG: "make content more accessible to a wider range of people with disabilities, including accommodations for blindness and low vision, deafness and hearing loss, limited movement, speech disabilities, photosensitivity, and combinations of these, and some accommodation for learning disabilities and cognitive limitations."

Inevitably though, when it comes to the classroom, regardless the support provided by either a campus or the various software packages used in teaching, the responsibility will come down to the individual faculty member to determine whether all of their course materials are available to students regardless their needs or circumstances (i.e., taking students' sometimes very different levels of financial accessibility into account may motivate some faculty to move away from expensive textbooks). Given that students who will benefit from such initiatives are not necessarily registered with disability services, and are therefore not already identified as being in need of specific accommodations under the law, proactive faculty addressing these issues early on, during their course planning, will most definitely prevent problems from arising later in the semester.

See also: Accommodations; Diversity, Equity, and Inclusion (DEI); Learning Management System (LMS)

3

Accommodations

Rita Lester

Although I regularly consult our campus's Americans with Disabilities Act (ADA) coordinator, I write as an Arts and Humanities professor at a small U.S. liberal arts university who came to the job without a professional commitment to accessibility. In religious studies, I invite undergraduate students, most of whom are not specializing in my discipline, into thinking with "religion," that is, to critically self-reflect and reconceptualize assumptions in order to identify and critique socio-political power dynamics. Critical consciousness about learning in and with religion have motivated me to rethink a deficit-minded approach to accommodations. Accommodations are not just mitigation of functional limitations, but involve identifying and critiquing stereotypes and privilege in learning in order to take steps to increase access and equity.

ADA staff at U.S. universities keep faculty up to date with current practices and terms, consider student experiences across both the curriculum and co-curriculum, and know the legal implications and liabilities. ADA staff communicate reasonable accommodations for undergraduate students with diagnosed disabilities to their faculty on a case-by-case basis. After students provide their documentation of relevant diagnoses to the ADA office, the ADA office at my university contacts faculty with a letter listing the legally required "reasonable accommodations" needed by the student, to help them to succeed in the class. Accommodation letters may arrive anytime during a semester because the process is initiated by the student. Students may postpone taking the steps to initiate ADA protections for various reasons: because they want to try without accommodations, they have not yet pursued diagnoses, or they assume (incorrectly) that college ADA protections are automatically applied or renewed, much as their high school 504 (school-level customized learning environment plan, named for Section 504 of the Rehabilitation Act of 1973 guaranteeing certain rights for people with disabilities) or IEPs (K-12 individual, special education and related services plan) might have been. Talking with a professor about difficulties, obstacles, or challenges may be the student's first time hearing from a college representative that ADA accommodations are available and how to pursue them.

After reviewing the ADA accommodation letters they receive, faculty should talk (privately) with the student. If the reasonable accommodations required include note-taking for lectures but my course does not have any lectures, I might assume that arranging for a note-taker is unnecessary. But when I talk with the student, I may find out that the notes are not just for traditional lectures but for all class-time verbal communication such as assignment clarification, online environment explanations, or changes in scheduling. Having a conversation with the student also prevents me from assuming that apparent similarities in diagnoses (professors will not be informed of diagnoses only accommodations, but some diagnoses are more easily visible such as when the student uses a guide-dog or a safety walking cane). When other sources for accommodating visual impairment were not available, one student liked the sound of my voice recording readings but another student was loathe to listen to my voice any more than they already had to! I didn't know either of these until I spoke with the students involved individually. I have worked with the ADA office months in advance for a student anticipating their upcoming schedule but there is also the student who lets me know the night before the assignment that the website or data interface for the class is not accessible to them. The (at least to my mind) last-minute student with accommodations should not be held to a higher standard than any other (non-ADA aligned) student. After all, I suspect more than a few of my students start preparing, if they do at all, for a class session right up until the start of class most days.

Reasonable accommodations might be different than (even) a flexible, understanding, or empathetic professor might think. Case in point, for students with a late assignment accommodation, I allowed two weeks without penalty for late work until my ADA officer recommended two days. In this case, I was the one with the apparently less rigorous standards, not the student with said accommodations and certainly not the ADA coordinator. As my ADA coordinator says, faculty serve access, not success.

If your ADA office knows your class's required books, they can request braille from the publisher (this it better done far in advance if for math, music or a charts). If you have readable PDFs (i.e., able to be read out loud by various computer programs), students with visual impairments can access them. For writing or typing accommodations (which could be temporary, like a broken arm), your ADA office can recommend dictation software. Ensure podcasts for your class have transcripts and videos have captioning. At my college, the Registrar moves assigned classrooms for wheelchair or service-dog accessibility. Also at my college, the ADA office arranges for American Sign Language translators to attend class time. Your campus may also have testing or proctoring spaces with staffed hours. When interviewing for faculty positions, consider inquiring about the school's current commitment to and plan for accessibility.

We teach criticality in our disciplinary field of study. By criticality, or critical socio-political consciousness, I mean we identify, critique, and challenge existing power structures and dynamics. We support students rethinking their assumptions, agency, and how to enact change. This culturally relevant pedagogy teaches students the language to name privilege and debunk clichés, making the space and time to interrogate the status quo and implicit bias. Extend this critical consciousness to teaching and learning.

Universities also serve students who do not, for cultural, personal, or financial reasons, have access to ADA protection and, for this reason, consider accommodations as resources for universal design. As Roman Mars of the *99% Invisible* podcast points out, although curb cuts were designed with one accessibility challenge in mind, i.e., people in wheelchairs, curb cuts also benefit a wide variety of people crossing roads. Designed as a specific accommodation, curbed ramps at intersections make sidewalks and crosswalks easier for a range of walkers and riders. Instead of requiring the walkers, riders, and pushers of strollers to ask for special assistance or go in search of a different way to their destination (or not to go at all), curb cuts address access right in the design of the built environment, benefiting a larger number of people.

In much the same way, and when possible, go for universal design in your classroom and assessments. Screencasts, videos, readable copies, accessible websites, course software with accessibility checks are all things institutional design instructional staff can help with. Specific strategies for accommodation with a specific student in mind can be opened up to benefit all students. Here are two of my own examples where building accommodations into the course, that is, making them universal, benefited a wider range of students.

For fall of 2022, I anticipated hearing impaired students' accommodations in my course design by assigning *Religious Studies Project* podcasts because most have transcripts (RSP is currently working on transcripts for their entire episode library). Although I did not end up receiving accommodation notifications for hearing-impaired students in that course, an apparent hearing student came up to me after class following the first listening assignment to express gratitude for the transcripts. The transcripts for the assigned podcast enabled this student to prepare for class when their baby had fallen asleep on them.

Reasonable accommodations for anxiety may include being late (check with your ADA coordinator what they consider reasonably late) with assignments, but one of my students with this accommodation for anxiety found that a later due date only postponed their anxiety of facing a blank page. Their struggle to get started was not mitigated by a later due date alone. In consultation, we decided to try a warm-up/placeholder for the assignment (e.g., outline, quotes, notes, very rough drafted argument with some evidence), which would be due at the regularly scheduled time. The student with ADA accommodations was grateful for the step of a warm-up draft with a due date because, they said, it helped them to start, to get over the blank page. They said this step made completing the assignment by the end of second day (the reasonable accommodation recommended) easier than just having two "extra" days.

However, I decided that the built environment of that course should be a so-called curb cut for everyone with this pre-assignment warm-up/placeholder, so I extended it to the whole class. Immediately upon offering this option to every student, I was worried that all the students in the class would take advantage of the offer, it would destroy my grading timetable, and perhaps more damaging, would make me feel like students were taking advantage of my flexibility. To my surprise, most students never used the placeholder-to-get-two-days offer, at most about one-quarter of the class ever took the opportunity, and they all submitted drafts to "hold their space" until they turned in the final version within two days.

There was a benefit to this placeholder universal design that I had not anticipated: one student (without ADA accommodations) turned in a placeholder draft, but neglected to submit a final version. They said that they just got too busy to revisit the assignment. But because they were required to submit a placeholder draft on time, I graded the placeholder draft. And, for my class, a placeholder draft never scored as low as a zero. Having something graded, in online gradebooks that can be constantly and instantly available to students, is better than ungraded/waiting. It allows the teacher to finalize the gradebook in the online course management software without empty spaces or dashes that mark an absence of a score which could present the student with an artificially high score because ungraded has no score impact (at least in a software like Canvas).

A placeholder submission, initially an experiment created in conversation with a student with ADA accommodations for lateness, helped the student overwhelmed with the blank page to get started, helped the students who utilized the placeholder assignment with ungraded drafts that lead to potentially better submissions in two days, helped the student for whom life got in the way turn something in on time, and helped me as the professor keep a timely and accurate online grade book for all students.

Turning accommodations into universal design also changed my own attendance policy (at my institution, attendance is a course specific, not a school-wide, policy). Accommodations for attendance, which includes anxiety, sleeplessness as a side-effect of medication, and COVID-19 which saw students out for 5–10 days at a time waiting for test results or quarantining, are now built into every session of every course with alternative work for students not present in class time for any reason. Alternative work is designed for access to the same material. As a professor, I do not want to be in the business of ruling on (or keeping a record of) what is legitimately excused or unexcused: theatre trips, sports, hospitalized relative, sick baby, choir tour, optional art department field trip, car trouble, bad weather/bad roads but school not cancelled, religious/ethnic/national holiday, depression, illness, etc. I also do not want an attendance policy that compels students to divulge family events or health experiences. Some students continue to contact me to update me as to why they were not in class, but generally, because I am not ruling on excused or unexcused, I am grateful for fewer emails describing personal situations. And because car crashes and other emergencies happen, alternative work is not due at the start of class, but at the end of the session, day, or before the next class meeting. Although this volume contains more on attendance in the chapter of that name, universal design initiated by accommodations is the foundation of my alternative work for every session policy and practice.

Last fall, during a syllabus review activity, I asked what students want from their professors. One student's response was memorable for, with what I would learn over the course of a semester was mature confidence with a side of adventurousness, they said "compassion." If we are focused on enhancing student *learning* and not *performing*, or at least recognize that some students perform well without learning much and other student may learn a great deal but do not perform so well, we can resist reproducing education as gaming the system and instead, model rethinking accommodations as professors' compassionate, active contribution to equity and love of learning.

So, to sum up, do this:

- Find out what your ADA staff want all faculty to know including a statement for your syllabus and ADA contact information on your campus.

- Inquire with faculty development about support or training available to ensure accessible design and delivery.

- If your school has an Instruction Designer, request to meet with them, individually or with department, to inventory accessibility with your course management software.

- Develop a plan to, on a rotating basis, inventory each of your courses and update with accessible materials and promising practices for accessibility.

- Consider recommended accommodations as resources for universal design, that is, accessibility built into the design and delivery of your course.

See also: Accessibility; Attendance; Diversity, Equity, and Inclusion; Learning Management Systems; Library Resources; Syllabi

4

Assessment

Steven Ramey

The term "assessment" can refer to many different aspects of teaching. We assess our students' learning (both knowledge and skills). That type of assessment is the focus of other entries in this volume (e.g., Assignments, Grading). Here the focus is on faculty self-assessment, specifically in relation to teaching. Is our teaching effective? Did the assignments help students develop the skills and knowledge that we intended them to develop? Yet, even in the realm of faculty assessment of teaching, "assessment" can signify at least two different practices. First is our constant evaluation of our own efforts, in an attempt to revise and improve our teaching, what I term self-assessment (reflecting both the process and the primary audience for this type of assessment). Second is the assessment regimes with required reports that our administrations and, ultimately, accreditation agencies have instituted, what I term "reported assessment."

It is important to distinguish these two types of assessment so that we can strategically identify ways that they differ and overlap. Self-assessment can be a very intuitive process. We recognize from the looks on our students' faces or their unwillingness to answer a question that something is not working. So, we make a change in the middle of a class session. We repeat information. We rephrase the question. We inquire about their unresponsiveness. All of these are generally intuitive forms of self-assessment that we seldom name as such and often do not reflect on in any real detail.

Faculty self-assessment can also be more empirical and deliberate. Students do poorly on a quiz or other assignment, and we know that something did not work. Perhaps the question that three-quarters of the students missed was poorly written or classroom activities did not fully prepare students for the tasks that we intended them to master. In these situations, the empirical data requires a certain amount of reflection to determine where the disconnect is and how to improve their learning. Faculty regularly make changes based on such information, such as revising an assignment, reframing a lecture, rewriting questions, in an effort to help the current class, or a future class, learn even more.

Both on the individual and department levels, self-assessment also can be more systematic. Reflecting on what students need to learn in specific classes and across the curriculum is useful. It is not necessary to continue to teach the same information, in the same way and with the same goals, as before. It is important, especially in a period of declining support for the humanities, to be intentional about what students learn in our classes and how they learn it. In my experience, the transferrable skills of critical analysis and communication of ideas are often more important than data for a religious literacy test. In an age when Google puts so much data right at their fingertips, training students to find and assess information critically is more imperative than memorizing terms. Spending time reflecting on what we teach well and what our students benefit from the most, and then aligning course objectives, assignments, and class sessions along those lines, is highly beneficial, both as an individual and potentially in larger conversations with department colleagues. Listening to students and alumni talk about what they gained from the religious studies classes has been especially illuminating to me, helping me to reflect on course design and specific assignments. Then, assessing how well those assignments and class sessions educate students in relation to those skills and the relevant information becomes part of a feedback loop, ideally, whether happening intuitively or systematically.

This standard self-assessment has now become institutionalized, however, through a variety of endeavors, including a need to document that we are doing these important self-assessments, since some fear that faculty do not assess themselves as deliberately and rigorously as they should. At the University of Alabama, where I have spent most of my career, the administration promoted these efforts of self-assessment through particular campus-wide initiatives, namely the Learner-Centered Initiative (which later became the current Active Learning Initiative). New, tenure-track faculty had to attend workshops that promoted self-assessment and related reports that document such assessment, which became required in their retention and tenure dossiers. The stated objective was to create a culture in which professors did not simply repeat the same classroom material that has been presented for decades (with an aim toward increasing student learning, yes, but also engaging and thereby retaining more students in our degree programs and, ultimately, enhancing our graduation rate). Of course, my colleagues (and admittedly my primary contact was with humanities colleagues) already did most of this, at least informally (and often intuitively). We collectively and individually focused on what our students were learning and constantly worked to strengthen their learning since, in my experience, most faculty are committed to their students and the self-assessment that can enhance student learning.

The stated objectives of such initiatives, as readers probably recognize, were not the only objectives. Much of the workshop assignments focused on defining measurable outcomes and reporting those outcomes (and a related action plan) in a standardized form. This formatting provided a means of enforcement, as already suggested, inasmuch as faculty reports of the self-assessment had to be documented in retention and tenure dossiers (already tenured and promoted faculty were thus not quite as subject to this enforcement). The notion of measurable outcomes, for example, required framing the intended outcomes for a course in such a way that numerical results could be reported for each course taught—a result more fine-grained than just an overall grade for a course. A course outcome, for example, that students recognize and understand specific foreign terms might involve the measurement and recording of what percentage of students correctly identified those terms on a certain quiz. If a class met the instructor's target, great. If a class falls short of the target, then faculty need to provide an action plan to attempt to improve it the next time the course is taught. We were repeatedly assured that failure to meet our own goals was fine, as experiments sometimes do not work as anticipated. Notably, the expectation that a professor will not meet every objective as hoped has become a required component of the process. If a professor meets every objective fully, then the assumption becomes that their measures or objectives are not ambitious enough (maybe 90% of students should recognize those terms, not just 80%) or that they were not taking the assessment practice seriously enough.

This dynamic of the reporting regime now means that reported assessment, both for an entire degree programs and an individual faculty member, must always have strategies for improvement. Plans for perpetual improvement (often labeled "continuous quality improvement" or something similar) are necessary, even if the action prescribed involves altering the measurable outcome by raising or lowering expectations. This reporting process, however, ultimately results in a focus primarily on the reporting of the results—the proper formatting and inclusion of improvement plans. Less significant is the actual content, not to mention the vital (in my opinion) intuitive and deliberate self-assessments that most faculty automatically conduct. A primary driver of this formal reporting process is that the administration has to demonstrate ongoing self-assessment to accreditation agencies and even governments. These agencies, like the Southern Association of Colleges and Schools (SACS), which accredits universities in our region, require some form of documented assessment (though it might have a different name depending on where you are).

Here is where it is important to distinguish self-assessment from reported assessment. Continual self-assessment often comes naturally to faculty who are invested in educating students (as I presume you are by your choice to spend your time reading this volume). The reporting process becomes an administrative task to convince someone else that faculty are doing this. In my experience, separating the two forms of assessment provides a certain freedom to consider what needs to be accomplished in the classroom and in our degrees. The reporting mechanism does not have to drive the self-assessment process, which is indeed often more intuitive and sometimes much more complicated (if a department wants to reconsider their curricular goals, for example). We therefore do ourselves and our students a disservice if we allow the reporting requirements to drive the actual self-assessment.

If we flip this to emphasize self-assessment, then the reporting process can become easier. Many times, in chatting with a colleague, they will mention a time in class that week when something did not go as planned. They recognized that students were not getting something, or in the first session of a repeated class prep an exercise failed so they revised it before the second session of that same prep. Occasionally I encourage them—especially tenure-track and contingent colleagues—to make note of that revision, which can become a narrative example for a future report of a measurable outcome with subsequent action taken. In other words, forefronting our ongoing, informal self-assessment and making it more explicit so that we can later fit it in the required reporting format allows us to satisfy some of the requirements with what we are doing anyway.

Departmental assessment reports (concerning entire degree programs) can function similarly: begin with what outcomes the department faculty already values, aims to accomplish, and perhaps even measures, and then report on those, shaping them to fit whatever the required formatting is. In that sense reported departmental outcomes should begin with what its courses are already doing and report assessments accordingly—building program-wide goals rather organically from the goals toward which its faculty and classes are already working. Assessment reporting can provide an occasion for the faculty to discuss as a group what is most important for students to gain in each of their classes, but that discussion may not be feasible in a divided department. Even in a collegial department, that discussion can take enormous time and energy. Finding ways to satisfy the reporting requirements efficiently, with results that faculty are already generating (perhaps massaged slightly to fit the format requirements), is a sensible approach, until the time that a department wants to revamp a portion or all of their outcomes. Even then, the conversation about what students should learn and develop through the curriculum should drive the conversation more than the requirements of an assessment report.

Different institutional contexts will have different types of expectations, of course. It is possible that administrators will closely monitor all assessment reports and reflect on whether the department or faculty member has performed their assessment adequately. But administrators and review committees from accreditation agencies have a lot of demands on their time, too. In many cases, it seems as if the assessment report is adequate as long as it exists and has the required elements, such as a set number of outcomes, measurable results for each outcome (with some being quantifiable), and at least one action plan. If that is the case at your institution, then use the assessment reporting efficiently, generating needed conversation when that is desired and reporting quickly what is expected when the larger conversation is not warranted. The outcomes listed in the assessment report may not be the ones that are most important; they might happen to be the ones that are easily measured and reported on to satisfy the reporting requirements. In fact, they can only be representative of an instructor's many goals for any given course rather than encyclopedic of an entire course or even program. Those outcomes that faculty consider most important, hopefully, are already being assessed intuitively and regularly, even if they do not fit in the assessment report format easily.

When faculty are doing regular self-assessment, considering what students are learning and how to help them succeed even more, then we should all celebrate that faculty are meeting the spirit of the assessment requirements. If ever asked about it or need to defend an assessment report, faculty who continually self-assess can talk about different things that they automatically do, because they are going above and beyond what reporting regimes require. If any reporting is deemed to be lacking at some point, that is usually easy to fix. Perhaps even the reported assessment action plan includes revising the reporting mechanism based on other self-assessments.

In other words, we should not let the assessment reporting requirements of the modern university determine the content of our own assessment of our teaching. Figuring out the simplest way to report what we already do and attending to the report in terms that match the expected form is what is essential from the reporting side of the process. What is even more important, however, is the constant self-assessment, the concern for our students, and the commitment to enhance their learning. To the extent that the required assessment report can be submitted efficiently so that we can spend our valuable time on our self-assessment and reflection on teaching, that provides the most benefit for students, departments, and institutions.

See also: Assignments; Curriculum; Experiential Learning; Final Examinations; Grading; Large Lectures

5

Assignments

Teemu Taira

When I started my studies at university in the 1990s, staff members told stories about older professors who used to have oral exam as the main assignment in their courses. During my studies, the typical assignment was a written exam after a series of lectures. The preparation for the exam was based on memorizing the lecture notes, if one was still able to figure out what the notes meant—notes were typically written in pencil and sometimes copied from a friend who had attended the lecture, as there were no PowerPoints back then. In addition to lecture notes, there were some additional materials to study such as book chapters, articles, or monographs. The typical exam contained two to five questions and one was supposed to answer them in two or maybe up to four hours, by writing up to several pages by pencil on paper. Sometimes the instructor was not able to decipher the handwriting, which may have worked in favor of the student.

There were also essays of different kinds. They were anything between four to twenty-five pages, depending on the credits, usually based on assigned class material. Essays would often summarize the main content of the course, rather than developing an original argument or analyzing unique data, but at least students familiarized themselves with the topic. Pedagogy experts demonstrated that when students were later asked to talk about the topic, they had learned more deeply in writing an essay than in having an exam. My personal experience confirms this: I have forgotten most of the content of the exams, but I can still talk about some of the essays that I wrote as a student, even from a few decades ago. However, writing essays was clearly a new thing back then, an option supported by some study programs more than others. Essays were exceptional; the exam was the norm. Other types of assignments were rare.

In the current situation, however—at least in the institution where I work—the written exam is about to go extinct. There are still scholars who prefer them, mainly because it can be the most convenient assignment in large lectures. Essays are still doing well, but the new norm is a combination of learning diary and a short essay. Other types of assignments are also in use, but what is the point of assignments in the first place?

Although some experts find it useful not to grade students in some courses, most agree that there has to be something by which the workload of courses are measured and the learning goals tested. Various tasks we call assignments are a way to do those things.

The exam-driven thinking many teachers were socialized in by their own studies often locate assignments to the end of the course. This is by no means an obligation in most cases. Some or even most assignments can be delivered earlier, such as small tasks that are due every week or more laborious ones required a couple of times during the course to ensure an evenly spread workload. If your institution allows this kind of flexibility, then it is best to think about what types of assignments can be finished before the end of the course (keeping in mind your own eventual workload as a grader). In my institution students typically have between two and four courses in one period; one course is five ECTS (i.e., European Credit Transfer and Accumulation System— or about 140 hours) and one period lasts eight weeks. If the assignments are all at the end, students will have a very busy week or two at the end of each teaching period. In addition to a more balanced workload for students, it is also more effective for learning if students get some feedback on their writing (or other tasks) during the course and not simply at its conclusion, so that they can see that they are on the right track or to improve, if their performance is not meeting the required standards.

The most important things in assignments, from the students' point of view, can be condensed into two terms: *alignment* and *variety*. In this context, alignment means, first, that the assignments measure the learning objectives of the course, and second, that the assignments are relevant for the overall goals of the study program. It is important to get the first right, whereas the objectives of the study program can be achieved even if some courses do not contribute to them in a meaningful way. Moreover, individual instructors may have little power to control the whole program. However, the place of the course in the study program or curriculum should be considered, because that is how one can make sure that the course, including its assignments, builds on students' previously acquired skills and expertise.

Variety is another significant term when it comes to assignments. Variety is what students want; variety is also what they need. Therefore, in this context it means, first, that a single course can have internal variety in assignments as long as they are all aligned with the learning objectives, and second, that the variety of assignments is visible in the study program, preferably within every academic year. For example, in my institution, members of the program board evaluate whether the following academic year has multiple types of assignments in the teaching program. If most courses offered to the BA students propose, for example, a learning diary as the main assignment, then the board may intervene and suggest to some instructors that they change the tasks. Sometimes the suggestions provided by the board are based on student feedback. Students complain, sometimes, if too many courses contain group work, for instance, mainly because they consider it to be time-consuming. This is tricky as pedagogy experts tell us that group work is often a very effective learning method. Again, variety is the key: students should do group work in some courses, but if they have that required in (almost) every course, the good intentions by the instructors turn against students.

Variety is a value, but variety cannot be random. It should be aligned with learning goals in a course. Group work is great for learning how to cooperate with others, as most students will use that skill in their later work-life, and sometimes tasks can imitate collaborative research, but the skills to analyze material from the academic point of view—by applying methods, using theories, and theoretical concepts—may be even more crucial to learn if the aim is to educate future generation of scholars. One can also include more practical tasks among the assignments, for example, writing a book review with the intention of getting it published. Even if it is not published in the end, the student has had to get to know the content of the book well, evaluate its strengths and weaknesses, learn how to draft a review, and learn about potential publication venues.

In case some of these guidelines feel like they are filled with pedagogical jargon, here is more condensed advice: whatever the form of the assignment, figuring out how the assignment challenges students' everyday understanding and invites them to think, is a significant step toward successful assignment.

If one wishes to develop assignments that are always perfect from the students' point of view, then one may end up spending a lot of time preparing the course. The one thing pedagogy experts do not talk about is how to invent assignments that are appropriate for students and also beneficial for you—either for your research or development as a teacher.

As a teacher, reading learning diaries by students is, arguably, an even better way of receiving feedback than the standard feedback forms. For in the learning diaries the instructor sees *whether* or not the students have understood the main substance of the course, and *how* they have understood it. In reflecting their own learning, the instructor also gets to know whether the content has been appropriate for the level and whether students find the content of the course to be making a useful contribution to their overall learning (with regard to their previously acquired skills and substance and also in relation to their everyday life and future prospects). This type of information is valuable to an instructor, especially when teaching a new course for the first time. Having an exam or essay as the sole assignment does not provide any of this information for the instructor, although they may well offer enough tools to evaluate whether the students have achieved the course's learning goals. Of course, it is sometimes boring to read a big pile of learning diaries, and it may be frustrating for students to write them course after course, but because of the feedback they offer, I tend to favor them: I'd like to believe that reading learning diaries have made my courses better, improving my teaching more than standardized feedback forms.

In addition to considering how to improve one's courses and teaching skills on the basis of assignments, there are multiple ways to integrate classroom assignments into one's own research. Imagination is the limit but let me offer a couple of recent examples. I have been teaching a course on atheism in news media and media culture, and the topic is part of what I have been researching recently. One assignment consisted of analyzing almost any kind of media data (e.g., news item, a film, internet or social media page, discussion forum, popular music, etc.) dealing with atheism or atheists. The main point of the short essay was to introduce the data and reflect on it in relation to the material discussed in the classroom and previous research. (We dedicated at least one week to atheism and/in news media, internet and social media, films, and popular music; we read articles during the course and other recommended readings were provided.) This way I was able to find new material for my own research—one student analyzed a film I had not thought relevant for my research; another student wrote an insightful essay about God on Twitter and it inspired me to examine that topic more closely in my writings on atheism and social media.

In another recently taught course on religion in the history of Western popular music, two assignments contributed to my own research. As I had been writing a book-length manuscript on the topic, the students had to provide feedback for one of my draft chapters. If students were not experts in any popular music genres covered in the manuscript, they were still able to write meaningfully, by pointing out the gaps in my prose and inconsistencies in my examples. Some, however, were specialists in particular genres (e.g., extreme metal, hip hop) and thus capable of correcting me in the details that I got wrong, supplementing my views with additional examples, confirming my interpretation on the basis of their experience, and, in some cases even offering alternative views that challenged my argument. This was not the only assignment that benefitted my work—another was a short essay in which students analyzed the construction of religion in artists' music (mainly lyrics) or in their self-representations (in interviews and biographies, for example). Again, this provided me valuable information about some artists I had not covered substantially in my manuscript.

If one chooses to design at least some of the assignments according to one's research interests, then one should be cautious in not exploiting students' work. In case I utilize directly the analysis a student has made, I refer to it accordingly and do not claim it as my own. Sometimes a footnote acknowledging the student's insight will do. In most cases, the research value of assignments is to check that my analysis is understandable and to test whether other types of material—other examples—introduced by students might force me to refine my own analysis. However, as said, all of this must always presume that the assignments serve the student and learning goals first, but I cannot see why this more instructor-driven point of view could not also be explicitly included when developing assignments for a class.

In addition to these reflections, it is recommended to browse various websites and read pedagogy textbooks dealing with assignments. Both offer standard practical guidelines and checklists that one should consider, from thinking about the correct workload for assignments to deciding how much each assignment (or its part) should be worth, and, further, to reflecting on whether class time could be used to help students complete the assignment and to preparing for possible problems that one may encounter (e.g., late return, plagiarism and so on). In the end, one should find reasonable compromise between the ideal learning experience and the available practical resources and time, which are both always limited.

See also: Assessment; Curriculum; Group Work; Student Evaluations of Instruction

6

Attendance

Leslie Dorrough Smith

For the more than twenty-five years that I have been teaching, I've had a lot of mixed feelings about taking attendance, and I've done it many different ways. I can sympathize with the reasons why some faculty don't wish to do it at all: it can be a pain to track; it's hard to remember conversations with students about their various reasons for missing class; and sometimes it's nearly impossible to decide what constitutes a legitimate excused absence (let alone handle the documentation that may accompany this). While I teach at a small university, I can only imagine how these issues could quickly compound with larger classes at larger colleges, particularly if TAs are not available to assist.

There are also students who see rigid attendance policies as inherently problematic. Some argue that if they can succeed on assessments without being in class everyday then they shouldn't be expected to attend consistently. Others feel that attendance policies make their lives stressful and harried in ways that are counterproductive, such as when they experience pressure to come to class when sick (a particularly important issue in light of the COVID-19 pandemic). Further, some fear that harsh penalties will unfairly disadvantage those who are genuinely committed to the course and yet are prevented from excellent attendance by issues that are beyond anyone's reasonable control (such as a sick child).

I am sensitive to the concerns expressed in these arguments. However, my current thinking is that a clear-cut and yet compassionate attendance policy often resolves many problems before they arise. I'll admit that I wasn't entirely comfortable with creating such a policy until some of my attendance-related interactions with students began to generate enough labor for me that I felt I had no choice. Wanting something that worked for everyone, I made the effort to speak with my students about their attendance concerns, pondered what attendance requirements actually achieved in my classroom, and changed my policies to make things both clearer and easier for everyone. What follows are some of my conclusions, but it's important to recognize that there is not a one-size-fits-all approach to this. Everything from institutional policy to a student's individual circumstances, as well as the instructor's workload and class size, will require consideration.

First, regarding the importance of attendance, I'm not generally sympathetic to the notion that students should be able to attend class only to the degree that they are successful in exams; by that logic, a comprehensive book could easily replace me and the classroom experience altogether. While we're all aware of certain culture critics who like this idea, this seems reasonable only if one thinks that what happens in college is the mechanistic transfer of facts from one entity (the professor) to another (the students). Rather, those of us trying to create rigorous and stimulating learning environments recognize that "the facts" are often far less important than the building of critical thinking and social skills, which involves discussions with others, hearing alternative viewpoints, and engaging with the type of nuance that it's difficult to communicate in isolation.

Second, we model good professionalization skills when we consistently expect and hold students accountable for being present. College is a time when students are building independence and maturity, and in the absence of extenuating circumstances, failure to show up to places where and when one is expected to is a sign of moving backwards, not forwards. While I'm not one to argue that the university experience is solely about career preparation, there's also no doubt that reliability is an important element of all areas of life (career included). Students know this, too, and particularly our traditionally aged populations. Many have shared with me that they like the idea of fewer attendance rules and yet they also do poorly without them because they are learning to navigate their independence. Like any other skill, accountability has to be developed and practiced.

Third, and perhaps most important, having a clear attendance policy generally sets everyone up for success. It's common sense that when students miss class or are consistently late that they not only miss course content but also important announcements, assignment explanations, and in-class exercises. Having to repeat this information or schedule make-up activities creates labor for me, as well. Critically, poor attendance is also frequently a harbinger of other problems where instructors can provide support. For instance, when a student has a pattern of missed classes, this can often be a sign of a mental health issue or a problem with juggling work and school (leaving them to decide between whether they attend class or pay tuition). Many institutions are prepared to provide help to students in these circumstances, and yet we might never know to reach out if we aren't aware of their attendance patterns in the first place.

With these considerations in mind, I have created an attendance policy that I believe is manageable for both me and my students and that also holds students accountable for their consistent and engaged presence in class. Again, there is no such thing as a one-size-fits-all policy, so what I do may be quite impractical in larger, face-to-face classes, where many instructors might choose to encourage physical attendance by building in a series of interactive experiences that must be completed in-person rather than track each student's daily presence in the classroom. This can be really successful (and can avoid creating a mountain of grading) by using clickers, websites, or phone apps where students engage with an ungraded quiz or other type of interaction that simply records that they participated. These technological methods also work well for online courses, as many of us learned during the height of the COVID-19 pandemic.

Where I work we have a large number of student athletes. The institution's policy is that they cannot be penalized for missing class due to games or university activities. As such, I find it more straightforward to simply take daily attendance. Each sports team provides me with their game or activity schedule in advance so I know when they will be gone. Taking daily attendance allows me to see at a more detailed level the attendance habits of each person in the class and, as a huge bonus, helps me learn their names much more quickly. This is an attendance motivator since they know they are not anonymous.

My general attendance policy involves giving all students four excused or "free" absences; after that they may incur grade penalties. (Student athletes have these four absences on top of the days they miss due to their sport.) I chose the number four because that seems to account for the length of a typical illness (two or so days) plus two more classes that may be missed because of normal life events, like a car that won't start, or a doctor's appointment, etc. Since most of my classes happen twice a week, four missed classes is the equivalent of missing two entire weeks of the course. This may seem like a lot—and it is—but I would prefer to err on the side of a little more leeway to avoid having to handle too many exceptions. Most students also find this to be a very generous standard. I keep attendance on Canvas (our learning management system) so that each student can see where they stand.

Other instructors do something similar by awarding points to students for attending class. This is not my philosophical preference, but I fully recognize that my system of providing a set of excused absences works in a very similar way. I prefer the free absences approach, though, because it encourages students to stay home when they're truly sick and it also saves me from extra work in email management, which is an area where I get quickly overwhelmed. Giving students points for coming to class tends to generate many emails from those very students who wish to explain their absence in the hopes that

I will make an exception. I tell students that giving them four free absences means they do not need to contact me about why they are absent unless there is a larger or more serious concern they wish to share. Barring those circumstances, this approach substantially cuts down on the amount of individual cases I have to manage (one of my major concerns) while also making students feel that they won't be penalized when they legitimately need to miss class (one of their major concerns).

What happens after four missed classes? Missing beyond those four free absences will cause students to incur certain grading penalties, although I do make certain exceptions part of the policy. In the absence of one of the conditions that would trigger an exception, I reserve the right to take off a certain percent from the student's final grade for every absence between five to seven, building up to eight absences, at which point they may be awarded an automatic "F" in the course (which seems appropriate since that is the equivalent of missing a full month of class). I often do not have to enforce the automatic "F" policy since students with that many absences are often failing anyway. But the role of that policy is more than just symbolic. At least annually I have a student begin the course, attend only sporadically for a period, and then reappear with the expectation that they can satisfactorily finish, even when I explain that it is mathematically impossible for them to pass the class. Having this policy at hand seems like a more compassionate option since I can simply award the "F" rather than allow them to put in large amounts of work for a goal that they simply cannot achieve when their energies would be far better spent on their other classes.

I am always happy to make exceptions for students who are in situations outside of their control (e.g., extended illnesses, hospitalizations, family emergencies, etc.) if it is clear that they can still competently finish the course and if I am in a position to manage the additional labor. There are also certain circumstances where I make exceptions that are automatic, like suspected or confirmed COVID-19, the aforementioned athletics policy, or accommodations approved by our Student Access/Disability Services office. Once an exception has been made, I often discuss with the student how we can adjust assignment deadlines and I follow that with an email confirming that conversation so we all have a written record. The discussion itself is important because I find that students are often a little too optimistic about how quickly they can complete makeup work or return to class.

When students are absent, I encourage them to meet with me if they have any questions about missed material, I keep my lecture slides on Canvas for easy access, and I have begun the habit of starting every class period with a five to ten-minute overview of what we discussed last time so that we can all begin the new session on a more level footing. When I have them available, I will send absent students a link to the online lectures I recorded during the

COVID-19 pandemic so that they can at least have something to watch. On that note, I occasionally record an in-class lecture when I know that I will have many students absent and then post that link on Canvas. I never polish or edit them to save myself the time, and I've found that it does the job quite well.

Having described these exceptions, it's important to note that I still do some in-class activities that cannot be made up by those who are absent. These assignments are never worth enough points that missing one or two will substantially alter a student's grade; since we often do these at the beginning of the class period, I find that they help discourage serially tardy students—who are not permitted to make them up unless they're there on time—from coming in late. For students who are concerned about missing one of these assignments due to a legitimate absence, I always attempt to create at least two extra credit options so that they may recover some points, but I don't believe that it has to directly mirror what they lost due to their absence. It's perfectly acceptable, in other words, to communicate to students through the assignment structure that what happens in the classroom matters and is different from other types of experiences.

On that note, there are times when I won't approve certain exceptions, or when a student's reasons for being gone are very valid but their absences make it impossible for them to successfully finish the course. In those cases, an honest conversation about whether it's the right time to take this course is often in order. It's always their choice on how to next proceed, but I find that the conditions that contribute to students' repeated absences can often coincide with a lack of awareness of how they're performing in the course, and sitting down to talk about this frankly can be very clarifying for everyone involved.

In sum, what I've found is that taking attendance—and taking it consistently makes everyone's role easier in the long run, but a good policy will require taking multiple vantage points and experiences into account. It's important for instructors to identify the aspects of their teaching that they find particularly challenging and think about whether overhauling their attendance policy can help alleviate some of that pressure. I also strongly recommend having the same conversation about attendance with students and then looking for overlapping areas of strain. The policy that I employ may be a little more work up front, but in the end, both my students and I end up with less stress in the areas where it matters most.

See also: Accommodation; Extra Credit; Grading; Participation; Professionalization

7

Class Participation

Khurram Hussain

What is the purpose and value of class participation? Theories abound. Old school lecturers often find the unruly and uninformed musings of students to be an unnecessary distraction from the august task of educating them to be, well, less unruly and less uninformed. I too have found myself, at times, sliding unknowingly from class discussion to lecture mode as my frustration quietly grows with the quality of student participation and finally presents as me talking at them. The struggle is real. . . But recent research has clearly shown the enormous pedagogical value of engaged participation by students in conversations with their peers and with their professors, no matter the class size. In almost all cases, an orchestrated mix of lecture and class discussion is far more effective as a teaching framework than lectures alone. There are many reasons for this. With their short attention spans, keeping students engaged during any given class session can in and of itself be a heavy lift. Encouraging (and perhaps even demanding) participation invites students to collaborate in the process of their own education and eases the burden on the instructor. This is especially true if by class participation we mean not only class discussion but also at least some student investment in the construction of the syllabus and their regular input into how any given course unfolds over time. Also, this collaborative and ongoing back and forth either in-class discussion or in-course development has the added benefit of keeping the professor well-informed about what the students are or are not learning and to adjust accordingly. Additionally, in an age where the distinctions between fact and opinion, between argument and preference, and between critical engagement and summary judgment have become increasingly blurred with the advent of the internet and especially of social media, our students urgently need training in how to argue effectively in public and to sublimate disagreements with others into constructive and instructive conversations. The classroom provides an ideal setting to hone these skills under the careful guidance of a seasoned instructor. For these and also many other unlisted reasons, I have made it a point to incorporate student participation at all levels of my teaching.

This is all well and good, of course. But my charge in this chapter is more specific—not class participation per se but rather class participation as it applies to the particular case of teaching the study of religion. Here we find additional benefits but also many pitfalls. Many years ago, Russell McCutcheon of the University of Alabama headlined a multi-day workshop on the study of religion at my university; it was intellectually one of the most productive few days I had early in my professional career as a scholar and a teacher. As it concerns my pedagogy, the most important lesson I took from McCutcheon's contributions to the workshop was a charge to introduce our students to the complexities of the study of religion on the front rather than the back end of their engagement with the field. Which is to say not to build up to these complexities but start with them. The study of religion occupies an odd place in the modern Western academy. For many of us who have grown up in this academy and almost regardless of field, the rejection of superstition associated with clerical and other religious institutions and the concomitant triumph of reason is a fervent foundation myth of how we came to be. So the study of religion is both an academic discipline within the university but also in some important sense a generalized reiteration of the modern university's fabled beginnings. To study religion, then, is to study something special, gently set aside from other disciplines in its own eccentric corner, and a constant source of confusion for administrators and students alike. Even some faculty have a hard time with what to make of it. Do we study religion to debunk it? Or are we training priests of the future? Are scholars of religion spiritual advisers? Representatives of their own faiths? Or our first line of defense against the resurgence of an old, vanquished enemy? Now, none of these questions are particularly good ones vis-à-vis the actual study of religion, yet they do circulate widely in the academic ecosystem and students often arrive at their first religion class with some version of these either/ors firmly ensconced in their minds; and with little real facility with what it means for something called "religion" to be an object of academic inquiry and not another "just so" story.

Many of our students have also been socialized to be deeply uncomfortable talking about religion in anything but the most vacuous of liberal-tolerance-speak, if they are to speak about it at all. And those who themselves come from religious backgrounds (if they even take our classes) tend to also be quiet but for different reasons; few topics in the American public square are more fraught and less understood. The first order of business then is to disabuse students of whatever assumptions they bring to our classes and to begin again from the ground up with ease and confidence. I have found lectures alone to be largely ineffective via-à-vis this task. Students can conceivably learn to question their assumptions merely by being passive recipients of this or that theory of religion but that is about it. Any critical self-reflection, to say nothing of critical engagement with the concept of religion itself, requires forging new conceptual synapses through ongoing conversations that actively interrupt the students' preconceived notions about the study of religion and that challenge them to articulate coherent and convincing arguments rooted in scholarly knowledge. Cognizant of the peculiar place the study of religion has in our academy, and attendant to the fact that our students arrive with much baggage, *all* religion classes (no matter where they go whence forth) must therefore begin with the most basic and also the most difficult questions about "religion" in general: What is religion? What does it mean to say that religion is a social phenomenon? What is the study of religion? What is the relationship between study of religion and religion as an object of scholarly investigation? Does studying religion enhance or illuminate our understanding of the human condition as such? And if so, in what ways? These are the right kind of questions to ask in order to set our students on a path to possible discovery! I often use J. Z. Smith's "The Necessary Lie: Duplicity in the Disciplines" to get this conversation going. Selections from Tomoko Masuzawa's *In Search of Dreamtime: The Quest for the Origin of Religion*, Talal Asad's *Genealogies of Religion*, or Russell McCutcheon's *Manufacturing Religion* also provide much rich terrain for debate. Different instructors can, of course, have different preferences and use different texts. But the idea is to get the students comfortable with the historical and discursive terrain of the discipline itself before we proceed to the specifics of this or that course.

It is for this reason that my religion courses all have two basic structural similarities. First, each class session is organized around specific questions that guide our engagement with the assigned reading and the answer(s) to which are sought in class discussion. This allows students to process the course material from the beginning less as an amorphous mass of information that they need to internalize and more as a series of discrete yet interconnected inquiries into the subject matter in search of insights about the world they inhabit. By the end of each semester, then, these students would have inquired into and sought answers to between five and ten basic questions about the field and between forty and fifty questions about the specific course itself. All these questions put together constitute a kind of critical scaffolding for their newly constructed understanding of the course and the study of religion. I am also a huge proponent of group-based work not just for doing research projects but also in the classroom itself. Each class session begins with about a fifteen-minute in-group discussion where each group grapples with the aforementioned questions among themselves as I walk around the classroom clarifying the meaning and intent behind the inquiry and facilitating conversation as much as I can. This loosens them up to have a more robust general conversation with their other classmates for the rest of the session and also gives them ownership over the various answers they come up with in their in-group discussion. I have noticed that different kinds of answers emerge from different groups because they bring different life experiences, educational backgrounds and unique gifts to the table. Disagreement and debate across these different groups only become more intense as their own particular intellectual identities congeal over time throughout the course. As a general principle then, instead of peeling an onion, layer by layer, down to the core, I try to grow the onion layer by layer out from the core together with my students so they can witness its construction from the inside out in conversation with me and their fellow classmates. It is for this reason that in my classes there tend to be no grand reveals, or some unexpected twists at the end of the course. I trust students with complex, fundamental ideas upfront which we then explore together in constructive dialogue.

After all this it is still inevitable that a sizeable number of your students, maybe even the majority, will not participate in class discussion in any meaningful way. That is just the lay of the land these days. Students are sometimes deeply insecure and afraid of how others may react to what they say, and especially when it comes to religion—perhaps rightly so. But there are ways around this. I like using the questions posed before and during each class session as a framework to elicit responses from the quiet ones after the session is over through a shared Google document or blog post. And I begin each class with a summary, review, and discussion of these comments so they are constantly being incorporated into ongoing class discussion, even if I am the one sounding out the argument and not the student.

The important thing to remember about class participation, especially in the early days of a class on religion, is that student discomfort with the topic is real, and their presumptive baggage is heavy. Class participation will not occur organically (whatever that means) and even when carefully orchestrated will be prone to slide back into the vacuous inanities or deep suspicions that they have been socialized into. Do not lose heart. It gets better. For there are plural voices inside the classroom, plural voices outside of it, here in the U.S. and out there in the world. Managing plurality is no easy task, whether it is in the classroom or in societies. But the classroom has one advantage: it is a controlled space. Students participate, yes, they take ownership of parts of their education as well, certainly, and you can involve them in the ongoing construction of the syllabus. Still, in the end, you have to lead them somewhere guided by your own personal teaching dicta. For me, the most important dictum has always been to contribute toward creating a critically informed citizenry that is essential for the continued well-being of a pluralistic and democratic society. Nothing ventured, nothing gained!

See also: Assessment; Assignments; Experiential Learning; Grading; High-Impact Practices; Peer Tutors; Seminars

8

Core Curriculum/ General Education

Craig Martin

General Education (GE) curriculums are fundamental to undergraduate education (at least in the U.S., given the particular role played by broad-based undergraduate education there). GE programs require that students take a number of courses, outside their major, in the arts and sciences. In New York, where I work, the state requires students in liberal arts schools—no matter their major—to take at least half of their 120 credits required for graduation in the arts and sciences. At my college—a small liberal arts college (SLAC)—this means that students must fulfill certain so-called breadth and depth requirements. There are three levels to our GE program. For the first, students must complete basic 100-level writing, math, and science courses. At the second level, the focus is on breadth of content: students must therefore complete 100- or 200-level courses on things like foreign languages, "global cultures," literature, creative arts, history, social science, and either philosophy or religion. At the third level, students must take three 300-level "Gateway" courses that, theoretically, build off of their prior GE courses and connect them to contemporary social issues and global problems.

No GE programs are identical: they vary from college to college. In addition, one of the main reasons why they vary so much is that their creation is always contingent upon many factors: locally specific faculty, institutional constraints, and the social and political investments of those creating the programs. For example, when we revised our GE program several years ago, there was a great deal of controversy over whether to keep or discard the two-semester foreign language requirement. Several things affected the discussion. First, some faculty thought that one cannot gain much practical proficiency in a language in only two semesters, so what is the point? Second, New York *requires* all education majors to take two semesters of a foreign language, so we couldn't eliminate foreign language altogether. Third, none of us wanted the new GE program to result in the layoffs of our colleagues whose services might no longer be required. The resulting GE curriculum that we approved was fundamentally conditioned by these particular, local constraints; faculty in institutions elsewhere (with different staffing, different philosophies on the importance of language, or different state requirements or different political investments) might have come to rather different conclusions.

All of this is to say: the shape of GE programs is fundamentally contested and negotiated, often subject to periodic reorganization, and, even when it cannot be overhauled, there are lots of ways to slip and slide under the existing requirements, which are always, at least to some extent, vague and therefore can be interpreted in novel ways. (I'll say more on this last point below.)

What does all this have to do with teaching religion? Frankly, for many of us at SLACs—perhaps a majority—our jobs would not exist were we not serving our campus's GE program. Student interest in programs like English, history, philosophy, and religion has plummeted over the last two decades. In particular, after the worldwide economic crisis of 2008, parents and students everywhere increasingly were looking at college as a vocational school that ought or must lead directly to a career. Why pay hundreds of thousands of dollars for something like a history degree when, given the dried-up job market, it might result in no significant increase in one's job opportunities? It would be better, many parents thought, to major in something that offered more of a job guarantee: major in education to become a teacher, major in criminal justice to become a cop, or major in finance to get a job on Wall Street (and thus the recent successes of many campuses's so-called professional schools). Under these social and economic conditions, the number of students willing to major in something more esoteric, as they might characterize it, dwindled. If I still have my job today, it is not because we have students majoring in religion—we don't—but because I have made myself indispensable to the GE program.

How did I accomplish that? Not by increasing the number of religion requirements. Under the former GE requirements, every student was required to take at least one religion course *and* one philosophy course (a requirement that, on some campuses, more than likely indicates the denominational identity of the college, either still to this day or at least at its founding). Under the new GE guidelines, the requirement was diluted: every student is now required to take *either* one philosophy course *or* one religion course. That rule change potentially cuts in half the number of students in our religion courses—something that directly impacts the annual credit hour production of the unit and thus, at least in the eyes of some administrators, the unit's possible status and viability.

Increasing the number of religion requirements would have been impossible, given the competition for those sacred GE spots from other programs similarly faced with declining enrollment (GE revisions can often pit units against each other, all vying for enrollment from the same students). Instead, what I have done is to leverage those parts of my training in philosophy and method and theory to teach courses outside religious studies narrowly defined. In addition, my college has an honors program, which requires students to take a minimum of six dedicated honors courses in order to graduate. Many of my colleagues cannot teach for the honors program because, for instance, our psychology program is understaffed—my friends in psychology have all of their time taken up just teaching the required courses for their own major. However, *I* can, since I don't have any religion majors. For the same reason, I can therefore also teach GE Gateway courses that other faculty simply don't have room in their schedule to teach. Consequently, while I do teach typical religion courses such as "Religion & Society," "Islam & Western Imperialism," "Hinduism & Buddhism," or "Evolution of Jesus" for the GE religion requirement, I also teach a course required for computer science majors called "Ethics in a Technological Society," along with Gateway courses like "Philosophy of Social Science" and "Politics, Religion, and Political Philosophy," as well as honors sections of any of the above, when possible.

In addition, my dean has encouraged faculty within the School of Arts & Social Sciences to develop an interdisciplinary major, rooted in sociology, focused on social policy and civic engagement. I've agreed to contribute a theory course to the program that's now under construction, putting to use my knowledge of Marxist theories of hegemony and social domination, my knowledge of poststructuralist theories of power, identity, and desire, and my knowledge of social scientific research on unconscious bias. I learned about all of these things when earning my PhD in religion, but it turns out that they are relevant across many fields of social scientific inquiry, not just religion.

One reason why this is so easy for me, intellectually speaking, is that I don't view "religion" as a completely distinct from the rest of culture. For me, there's nothing that makes so-called "religious" institutions all that different from seemingly "non-religious" institutions. Consequently, my approach to studying religion is useful for studying a wide range of social formations, not just "religious" ones. My primary teaching goals are, first, to show my students that societies are never set up in ways that benefit everyone equally and, second, to show them by what social mechanisms—habitus, naturalization, discourse, or ideology—inequities are maintained. I can do that sort of work whether I am talking about religion, social science more generally, first amendment jurisprudence, or the ethical challenges raised by evolving technologies.

To be clear, this strategy of making myself indispensable to the GE program is made possible in part, first, by the fact that I work at a very small SLAC (with approximately sixty full-time faculty members and only a thousand full-time undergraduates) and, second, by the fact that my colleagues are not particularly territorial. At a larger institution with a more territorial faculty, it might be impossible for a professor of religion to branch out into philosophy, computer science, or social policy and civic engagement. However, that does not leave religion professors in such settings without any strategies.

As I hinted above, there are lots of ways to slip and slide under the existing requirements, which are always to some extent vague and therefore can be interpreted in novel ways. This is possible because the definitions of words are never fixed or self-evident. When we updated our GE program, we ended up cutting the language requirement, but—in order to save the jobs of faculty who taught languages at the college for decades—we created a "Global Culture and Languages" category, where students could take a language course *or* something a little bit different. To ensure that all of their courses would be enrolled (since GE requirements also implicitly function as an enrollment management system, sending students to specific disciplines for reasons specified by the GE rules), some of our language instructors created courses under the new guidelines that focused on, e.g., Italian history and culture, rather than the Italian language. As soon as the new guidelines were in place, I went through the process of getting my Hinduism & Buddhism course cleared as a "Global Culture" option; because there are so few GE courses at my college focused on what we might broadly (and crudely) refer to as "non-Western" cultures, it was easy for me to make the case that the cultures of South Asia and Asia fit under the new category. Although the category was primarily created for the language professors, others were able to get a toe-hold in it. While most of my students in that course take it to get their religion credits, there are always a few added to the roster who needed it because, e.g., they weren't interested in Italy.

Similarly, our third-level Gateway courses must address a contemporary social issue that is in some way globally relevant. But what counts as globally relevant? My course on "Religion & Capitalism"—originally just a religion course—focuses on the lineage of scholarship rooted in the works of Marx, Durkheim, and Weber, but I also discuss how South Asian and Asian traditions have been appropriated, adapted, or commodified for American consumers. Obviously, in this course I refer to matters outside North America or Western Europe, but my focus is on how they've been appropriated *within* an American or European context. Is that sufficient to count as "global"? It turns out that the answer to that question appears to depend on two factors: 1) whomever in particular is on the General Education Curriculum Committee this year, and 2) whether or not they are in need of more Gateway classes for students to graduate on time. If there is a surplus of Gateway courses available next year, then the committee is free to define "global" rather narrowly. If there are fewer Gateway courses available in the near future, they may be required to define "global" more broadly so that their students graduate on time. (And, once a course is approved, the approval applies in perpetuity, no matter the future enrollment requirements.)

If, as is often the case in our field, you work at an institution where you serve the GE program more than you serve religion majors—and if you desire job stability—I would encourage you to read through the fine print of your college's GE curriculum. What work are you already doing that can be slotted in elsewhere? How might your existing "religion" courses be tweaked so that they could arguably fit into other categories? How might you, or your entire unit, if this is a priority for the department, cleverly interpret—or stretch—the vague terms in the fine print to cover what you are teaching? And, if your colleagues on campus are not too territorial, what courses outside of "religion" proper might you be able to teach, given your academic training? Perhaps something in anthropology, sociology, history, philosophy, etc.?

Along the way, even if your colleagues are not particularly territorial, be certain to remain attentive to how changing the GE program or expanding the courses that fall under the existing categories might affect other faculty and departments positively or negatively. My overworked colleagues in psychology might be relieved to no longer have to teach GE courses so they can focus on the classes required for their major; my colleagues in Spanish and Italian might be offended by my attempt to add Hinduism & Buddhism to a category that formerly belonged to them alone—for moving into their space arguably introduces some level of instability to their job security. Whenever I propose a new philosophy class, I always make sure to check with our one philosopher to make sure I'm not treading on his toes, so to speak.

In sum: *Use your ability to analyze social formations and those critical thinking skills you are teaching your students to analyze your own institutional conditions*. No social structure is natural, and as such social formations are perpetually subject to modification. Pay attention to who benefits and who does not by the existing distribution of rights and responsibilities within the GE program and attend to how you might intervene in ways that benefit you without disadvantaging others.

See also: Honors; Prerequisites; Writing

9

Critical Thinking

Emily D. Crews

In his foundational 1975 treatise on the rights of animals, philosopher and bioethicist Peter Singer argued the following: "Philosophy ought to question the basic assumptions of the age. Thinking through, critically and carefully, what most of us take for granted is, I believe, the chief task of philosophy, and the task that makes philosophy a worthwhile activity."

Singer puts thinking critically and carefully—and the power of such thought to shake us out of unexamined assumptions—at the center of the task of philosophy, an entire intellectual and academic enterprise that spans millennia. Noted scholar of religion Jonathan Z. Smith makes a similar, though more modest, claim (in the Afterword to this volume) about the significance of the skills of critical thinking and analysis for the introductory Religious Studies classroom. "An introductory course is concerned primarily with developing the student's capacities for reading, writing, and speaking—put another way, for interpreting and arguing," Smith writes. Thus, as Kathryn Lofton notes (albeit in an article criticizing what she saw as Smith's failure to live up to his own pedagogical standards), "Smith encourages teachers not to worry about subject mastery as much as they should be teaching practical communication and interpretive skills." Teaching students *how* and not *what* to think, then, is the task of the instructor.

Like Singer and Smith, in my time in the classroom I have given pride of place to critical thinking, as I know many other instructors of Religious Studies courses have done and will continue to do. It took me several years of teaching, however, to develop that nascent priority into a pedagogical framework with a set of strategies that actually engaged and engendered critical thinking in my students. In this essay I want to walk readers through that shift in my teaching by showing how we might define critical thinking, what sorts of difficulties or drawbacks there might be in making it a central goal in our teaching, and share some practical suggestions for instructors who want to make the shift to more actively focusing on analytical skills.

One of the first formal definitions of critical thinking comes from American psychologist and educational theorist Edward M. Glaser. In 1941, he wrote:

Critical thinking calls for a persistent effort to examine any belief or supposed form of knowledge in the light of the evidence that supports it and the further conclusions to which it tends. It also generally requires ability to recognize problems, to find workable means for meeting those problems, to gather and marshal pertinent information, to recognize unstated assumptions and values, to comprehend and use language with accuracy, clarity, and discrimination, to interpret data, to appraise evidence and evaluate arguments, to recognize the existence (or non-existence) of logical relationships between propositions, to draw warranted conclusions and generalizations, to put to test the conclusions and generalizations at which one arrives, to reconstruct one's patterns of beliefs on the basis of wider experience, and to render accurate judgments about specific things and qualities in everyday life.

Glaser's definition of critical thinking is centered on the idea of the problem—a cognitive conundrum or conflict a thinker is able to identity, analyze, and solve (or answer) through appraisal of and interaction between pieces of evidence. Such problem-solving ultimately allows the thinker to examine their own assumptions about not only the topic at hand, but other ideas or issues that might be connected to it in a larger web of taken-for-granted thought and belief.

Glaser and others set critical thinking in opposition to something we might call memorization, rote memorization, or rote learning. That is, critical thinking is understood to be a higher (and more important) level of thinking than memorizing facts without reflecting on them or incorporating them into our broader thought processes and intellectual schema. It may seem obvious to us as twenty-first-century teachers, but the idea that learning does not begin and end with memorization is still a relatively new phenomenon.

Later scholars have distilled Glaser's framework into a definition associated with clear stages of cognitive action. Michael Scriven and Richard Paul, for instance, argued in 1987 that "[c]ritical thinking is the intellectually disciplined process of actively and skillfully conceptualizing, applying, analyzing, synthesizing, and/or evaluating information gathered from, or generated by, observation, experience, reflection, reasoning, or communication, as a guide to belief and action. In its exemplary form, it is based on universal intellectual values that transcend subject matter divisions: clarity, accuracy, precision, consistency, relevance, sound evidence, good reasons, depth, breadth, and fairness." Leaving aside a critique of the problematic notion of transcendent, universal values (ever a challenge for this scholar of religion), Scriven and Paul offer a useful clarification of Glaser by focusing on the five stages of: conceptualization, application, analysis, synthesis, and evaluation. Those stages continue to be the ones recognized by scholars of education and psychology.

Since the 1980s, at least, scholars have sought to enrich the concept of critical thinking by, appropriately, thinking critically about it. Some have noted that the student implicit in most scholarly reflections on the topic is white, male, and middle class, and thus may be predisposed to reject certain kinds of academic orientations and behaviors, like thinking contextually, with emotion, or in embodied or ritualistic fashion. Even so, critical thinking remains a major focus in pedagogical theory and practice, including at the college level.

Now that we know how critical thinking has been defined, how do we decide if we want to teach it? And even if we do, how do we balance it against the demands of universities' often reductionist metrics for a successful classroom experience? In the increasingly corporatized world of higher education, where students' learning is so often packaged as a product that we must sell them on consuming, choosing to focus on seemingly blurry "soft skills" or ambiguous learning goals might be a risk. There are certainly some institutional contexts in which instructors may not feel comfortable articulating that teaching students how to think critically is a primary aim of a course, particularly those settings in which debates about similarly named Critical Race Theory currently rage.

And what about content? Most of us teaching college students how to study religion have spent years studying it ourselves. We've likely earned (or will earn) PhDs in the subject, having successfully convinced a committee of leaders in the field that we are experts on some material or another. Doesn't all that time learning Hebrew or formal logic or ethnographic methods entitle us to focus on the content that we know and love?

Never fear; content can and shall remain important to your classes. The choice to privilege critical thinking and other interpretative and analytical skills over content does not mean that we cannot or should not teach students facts about things that we identify as "religion." Indeed, one cannot think *with* conceptual frameworks if one has nothing to think *about*. Nor does a thinking-based approach necessarily dismiss the idea of literacy about a given topic. Instead, like Singer and Smith, it insists that the most important task of the classroom is to teach the skills used to analyze some data. It is the skills that come first and that are ultimately the most portable and useful.

The choice to center critical thinking as a pedagogical priority requires the same kind of risk and values assessment any instructor must make when deciding what to teach and how to teach it. It also requires the choice to engage in work that is often more time consuming, more tiring, and less obviously effective than lecturing and having students take exams that measure whether or not they have memorized certain dates or terms. Whether or not one has the time, energy, or incentive is, of course, an individual decision.

Let us say that your institutional context or personal values (or some other preference or another) has inspired you to commit to critical thinking as a central component of your teaching. What comes next? Below are a few suggestions for where one might begin.

1. *Be explicit.* Studies have shown that telling students that you are teaching them how to think critically is a key component of them incorporating such lessons into their intellectual schema. Rather than simply imagining that students will pick up on what we are teaching and naturally incorporate it into their ways of understanding the world, we must have them actively reflect on what they have been taught and connect those reflections to the goals of the exercise. We can do this by walking students through the major stages of critical thinking and assigning assessments or experiences that are directly connected to that stage.

2. *Focus on definition and classification.* An important aspect of teaching critical thinking is helping students to create categories into which they can successfully sort relevant data. Even more importantly, it is welcoming students into the enterprise of discerning and then critiquing the very categories that organize their lives, and giving them the space to debate the common-sense classifications of your topic of discussion. There is a strong and compelling history of precisely this task in the academic study of religion, particularly in the work of scholars who might be associated with something like the "critical" study of religion (including the aforementioned Jonathan Z. Smith and this book's editor, Russell McCutcheon). For instance, one of the central goals of any course that I teach is to have my students take ownership of their own definitions of religion. I want each student to know what their definition is, where they learned the definition, and what its consequences are (who and what it allows in and leaves out, for instance). I often begin my classes, especially Introduction to the Study of Religion, by asking students to reflect quietly on the questions, "What is religion? What is not religion? And, importantly, how do I know?" I then have them engage in the same exercise throughout the term, revising or refining their definitions and sources of authority as they take in new information and engage in new modes of analysis.

3. *Focus on dispositions.* Teaching critical thinking goes beyond simply offering analytical exercises or structures to students. It also requires

the inculcation of a disposition of critique, which in turn requires a degree of patience and a tolerance for ambiguity. These dispositions can be encouraged through repeated exercises like close reading.

4   *Encourage translation*. One of the key components of critical thinking is the ability to translate complex ideas or statements into simplified language and, conversely, to nuance or complicate simplistic ideas or statements. In a Religious Studies class, this might look something like putting a definition of religion on the board—say, Durkheim's or Otto's—and asking students to re-write it in colloquial language or slang. It might be asking them to interpret the definition in movement or drawing or a TikTok. Or it may be asking students to find real-world expressions of religion that they can describe in scholarly language they have read during the term.

5   *Aim for transferability*. Critical thinking is not the product of any one field. Instead, it should be transferrable across the disciplines in which it is taught and, more importantly, outside the classroom. A major goal of my teaching is that students are able to leave my courses with a conceptual framework that they are able to apply to topics that might be (or at least seem to be) entirely distinct from or unrelated to religion. It is my hope that when students graduate and become engineers or nurses or the presidents of non-profits, they are able to draw on the big-picture thinking skills they learned in the class, even if they have no recollection whatsoever of Zora Neale Hurston's ethnographic method or what exactly Mary Douglas said about Leviticus. My hope is that by engaging critically with religion, through idioms of naming, defining, and classification, they are building an apparatus for thought that they can take with them into their futures out in the world.

See also: Assessment; Class Participation; Curriculum; Experiential Learning; High-Impact Practices; Professionalization; Theory; Transferable Skills; Undergraduate Research

10

Curriculum

Rita Lester

When you select a university as a student or as a professor, you agree to its curriculum. Sometimes called the General Education or Core Curriculum and likely branded (such as the Archway Curriculum), the curriculum is the list of courses and experiences that faculty as a whole designated as important enough to be required to graduate from that institution. The curriculum, more than a sport team, president, location, new science building or old humanities building, is what makes the university distinctive. It is a shame if it is an afterthought or worse, a surprise, for prospective students or faculty. If you are interviewing to join the faculty, the job description may not help you accurately assess the role that position serves in the larger and sometimes sequential program of study but knowing that larger picture, especially at a teaching institution, clarifies what you will spend most of your time and skills doing, the student feedback that will comprise most of your evaluations for continued employment, promotion or tenure, and why students will enroll in your courses in the first place. Depending on how your university manages advising students on progress through their degrees, you may also be the primary source of input for some students regarding the content, intent, and outcomes of the curriculum.

When thinking about how the study of religion can serve the curriculum, take stock of the transferable skills from your discipline to public, career, and social life. Any small major in the Arts and Humanities in the U.S. is familiar with the "bread and butter" practically of offering courses to the general undergraduate students that focus on skills the curriculum-to-career initiatives value, summarized by Dawn Whitehead at the American Association of Colleges and Universities as: ability to work with others, critical thinking, ability to analyze and interpret data, application of knowledge in "real world" settings, and digital literacy. These are not the skills my own education overtly stressed nor are these the skills employers were ranking as most important even a few years ago, but that is less the fault of high schools and colleges than the weaknesses of my own graduate education, which assumed that my primary job was training my replacement or teaching graduate school. About once a decade, I work with an undergraduate student who seems to me to have a better-than-equal chance of replacing me or moving up the academic pecking order to, say, a Middlebury College. Instead, the overwhelming number of students, even in my major, are not going on to religious studies graduate school. They go into law, medicine, politics, business, art, non-profits, even politics but the skills our courses can teach, practice, and self-critically reflect on serve those careers as well. As a Dean at my school says: "we are not training students for their next job but for the jobs they will be doing three jobs from now!"

Religious Studies, or in my case Philosophy and Religion, gets called a service department, meaning most courses serve the general undergraduate population, even if the courses are also required in the major. A curriculum with required religion courses may present as attractive for ensuring faculty employment but schools that require a religion course as part of a Core Curriculum tend to be schools with stronger contemporary ties, financially or administratively, to a religious organization (in the U.S., usually a Christian denomination). Schools with a religious expectation in the graduation requirements are more likely to prioritize or require membership or orthodoxy in religious studies (or theology), as well as other areas of the curriculum or co-curriculum like Student Affairs. Many more private colleges have a historic or founding relationship to a Christian denomination whose control or influence may not continue in the religion department. More often this influence continues in the campus ministry office.

This bring us to the added complexity of how department colleagues (let alone non-departmental colleagues) approach religion as a subject, the relationship between religion and theology, or whether Christianity (or even just a certain form of it) is implied or implicit in the course offerings, particularly if required courses for general education. Both implicit and explicit Christian theological assumptions thrive in public and independent as well as private colleges, shaping many of the course offerings, not surprising given that many religion departments are comprised of faculty who attended a Protestant seminary for some part of their higher education. The chaplain or university minister may teach in the religion department (or other departments), local religious leaders without PhDs may be hired for contingent, visiting or sabbatical replacements, and Bible courses (e.g., Introduction to the Old Testament or Introduction to the New Testament) may be the assumed core or the most regularly offered of the religion courses. These assumptions are not limited to campus, but extend to the public and prospective students and their parents. If you are in Religious Studies, the role of devotional, theological or religious organizational history and funding (and assessment for accreditation) are specifics to navigate that shape what may be unspoken expectations about your approach and your role in the department and curriculum.

As faculty president during the most recent overhaul of the general education curriculum at my small university, I witnessed the time, work, arguments, and strategizing that go into building or updating a curriculum. Jobs depend on those decisions, particularly in departments with a smaller number of majors or whose major students are recruited not as prospective students but as current students who discover an interest when they happen to enroll in a course taken for Core credit. (As one of my colleagues said, in a twist on Simone de Beauvoir's argument against essentializing gender, religion majors aren't born, they are made, in college!) Here are some investigative questions I would ask or mentor junior faculty to ask when on the market to ascertain the role the department does, can or should play in the curriculum.

Does the discipline or department deliver required courses in the curriculum and is that curriculum distributive (i.e., requiring a sampling of courses from across a variety of what were once known as liberal arts fields, such as two math courses, two English classes, one history course, one science course, etc.) or integrative (in which broad themes, like sustainability or creativity, are explored via a variety of courses across a degree)? If the curriculum requires a content area course that your department serves, such as history, scriptures or cultural diversity, the faculty for that content will have the most regularly offered and enrolled courses. The more prescriptive (i.e., this specific course is required) then the less excited students may be to enroll. If there is flexibility in the content area requirement, negotiate a balance in your regular teaching load between repeating courses and other courses you might also teach on occasion. This can preserve both your interest and appeal to the enrolling student demographic and ability to periodically teach closer to your research interests. If the courses fulfill integrative curricular requirements, such as writing, speaking, internships, service-learning, undergraduate research, project-based learning or other skills and practices, rethink your schedule to best scaffold skills in assignments and plan for the expected outcome, whether community engagement in a project, poster, policy statement, or other public deliverable. With the rising influence of so-called high-impact practices as pedagogically relevant, be ready to teach in ways that you were not yourself taught! Initially, you may be suspicious of integrative and high-impact approaches, seeing them as diluting content, requiring significant upfront design work, or being a challenge to manage because a new way of teaching for you; but, realistically, integrative and high-impact courses achieve more memorable learning than individual research writing alone for most students and this impact (and service) strengthens the case for faculty development, funding, promotion, and tenure.

What are the required skills (writing, speaking, research) or experiences (internships, performing arts) included in the curriculum? If there are skills and experiences required to graduate, such as writing, internships or community service-learning, then start with the assumption that you want in on that service to the curriculum and find the places where your skills and risk-tolerance are needed and will be rewarded. Maybe there is a glut of first-year writing courses, but nothing writing-intensive in the sophomore offerings or maybe a global diversity requirement is bottlenecked because another department has reduced offerings or personnel. No course or requirement is an island. Knowing larger patterns in enrollment, hiring, and revised criteria (for, say, diversity) will allow you to strategize the most effective ways to get students to consider your course even if they never thought they would take a religion course. To paraphrase Jonathan Z. Smith, they may only take the one course, so that one (lower-level) course is the most important one you teach! Undergraduate students are more likely to cross your course's threshold when the course is highlighted in registration and advising as offering curricular skills or experiences that fulfill graduation requirements.

Also inquire as to how conducive the curriculum is to double majoring and double minoring? The number of credit hours required for graduation divided by the ideal of four years (minus Advanced Placement, International Baccalaureate or other transferred credits) leaves a limited amount of credit hours for majors, double majors, minors, and more than one minor. Some other majors require a high number of credit hours, making it difficult for students to double major or even minor. If, for example, designing a new Religious Diversity minor aimed at Education majors, anticipate how difficult it will be for those majors to be able to complete courses if the offered times conflict with their required courses for certification in education. At my institution (and I suspect this has something to do with participating in everything in small, rural high schools), many Religious Studies or Philosophy and Religion majors are double majors (Biology, History, Psychology, etc.), and many minors are double (or triple minors). For this reason, it is smart for our courses, requirements, and schedule of courses to work well with other programs, accepting courses for the major and minor, such as Psychology of Religion, Sociology of Religion, Reformation History, and Art of Asia. Moreover, at my school, the integrative curriculum is organized by themes, so my department tries to make sure every theme (democracy, health, environment, chaos, justice, sex and gender, innovation, etc.) contains the option of a religion course. This way, we reach possible new majors/minors and ensure a path to completing the major/minor, no matter what theme a student pursues in the curriculum.

If your college curriculum requires diversity or what is now more than likely known as "diversity, equity, and inclusion" (DEI) courses, do courses on religious diversity fulfill those DEI requirements? The American Association of Colleges and Universities recent initiative with the IFYC to increase awareness and experiences of religious diversity on campuses (Interfaith Youth Core) encourages campuses to classify religious diversity as a required curricular or co-curricular (non-academic) diversity. Faculty in religious studies might initially find this identification of religious diversity content as curricular diversity appealing. But be careful what you wish for! This may also mean that other areas of study (such as International Business, Intercultural Communication, World Literature, for example), well outside our field, can also apply for their courses to be accepted and coded as fulfilling a DEI requirement. Faculty not trained in religious studies, in this way, can propose to teach what they consider religious diversity in an integrative curriculum in a way they might not in a distributive curriculum where students are required to take a course from the religion department. Who decides if a course counts as fulfilling a diversity or DEI requirement in the curriculum?

The shared governance or faculty body that manages curricular decisions, such as whether courses outside of religious studies including what they propose as religious diversity in their contents earn curricular credit for graduation requirements, is in the hands of a faculty curriculum committee which likely has academic divisional representation (but which may merely make recommendations to the administration). When you propose a curricular change, at the department or general curriculum level, this is the committee reviewing and evaluating your proposal. Usually, any faculty can attend and the minutes are available for samples of proposals, revised majors, and general education learning outcomes for courses marked with certain skills or content like writing, speaking, or project-based learning.

The curriculum is and remains at most schools, I hope, the business of the faculty, albeit only the voting faculty which may or may not include contingent faculty—check with your faculty president because contingent faculty may need to request voting rights. If you are in a position to be or become voting faculty, get to know the current undergraduate curriculum and rising trends like your position and relevance depend on it.

See also: Diversity, Equity, and Inclusion; Experiential Learning; High-Impact Practices; Transferable Skills

11

Digital Humanities

Michael J. Altman

A senior colleague will sometimes remind me that there was a time when academics listed "word processing" as a skill on their CVs. I have never listed word processing as an important skill worth noting alongside my publication and teaching record because my scholarly generation takes the use of word processing software for granted. I'm using it right now to write this. In the wake of COVID-19 teaching in the Humanities has gotten even more digital. In my most recent undergraduate course, students never turned in a single sheet of paper. Everything went through the institutions learning management system. But there is a difference, I argue, between teaching a Humanities general education course with digital tools and something else called "digital humanities" (DH).

The website "What is Digital Humanities?" will allow one to cycle through over 800 answers to its question from scholars participating in the Day of DH from 2009–2014. Broadly, one can divide definitions of DH into those that construct it as a *method* for doing humanities with digital tools that can be found across disciplines and fields and those that argue for DH as a *field in itself*, with its own research questions and forms of scholarly production. Across these two broad differences there are also those who include bringing the questions and methods of the Humanities to born-digital sources as part of DH. All of this is to say, what exactly "counts" as DH, both in research and teaching, is up for grabs. The boundaries of DH are currently contextual, disputed, elastic, and often driven by particular interests, academic or otherwise. A simple answer to "what is DH?" might be "whatever the grant funder says it is." Yet, when it comes to DH and teaching, there are three main intersections to consider, regardless of what definition of DH one adopts: DH content in courses, DH assignments and assessments, and DH courses.

One place digital humanities shows up in the classroom is through pieces of course content. For example, an instructor might use a digital exhibit or digital archive as an instructional resource, an assigned reading for students, or an example in class. In my own courses, I have used digital projects such as Uncivil Religion, American Religious Sounds Project, and the Database of Religious History as resources for course readings and as examples in class. The American Religious Sounds Project even has a page of sample class activities on its website. In these cases, DH intersects with teaching by making use of the DH work of other scholars in the classroom. Some of these DH projects might also be described as "public humanities" (though the overlap or relationship between "digital" and "public" humanities is a conversation for a different essay).

DH can also show up in course content as an instructional method. For example, on the first day of my recent "Introduction to Religious Studies" course, I had the 200 students in the class each write a definition for the term "religion" on a shared document. I then, in front of them, copied and pasted their definitions into the text analysis web application Voyant Tools and used the various analytical tools in the application to reveal different patterns in their definitions. We noticed, for example, that "belief," "higher," and "power" were the most frequently used terms in the corpus of their definitions and that they were also frequently collocated together. Without taking the time to read all 200 definitions, Voyant Tools allowed us to discover that "belief in a higher power" was the dominant definition of religion among the 200 students in the class. Rather than using existing DH scholarly products, Voyant Tools allowed us to quickly use the DH method of text analysis as an instructional method.

By far the most common way DH intersects with teaching today is through the use of digital assignments and assessments. Two of the three resources mentioned above, Uncivil Religion and American Religious Sounds Project, have relied on students in courses to produce or curate the content in the projects. I was a co-director of Uncivil Religion and I organized my entire "Religious Studies and Public Humanities" course in the fall of 2021 around the curation and construction of the project by the graduate students in the class. Similarly, many of the sounds on the American Religious Sounds Project were recorded by students as part of various course assignments. Digital projects such as podcasts, portfolios, websites, curated collections, or annotations offer students a chance to experiment with digital humanities methods and digital scholarly production. While utilizing whatever content is important to the course, these projects are also skills-driven. They teach certain digital skills necessary for completion but also more traditional humanities skills such as communication, teamwork, and problem solving. All of these are skills that students can use beyond the specific topic or discipline of the course.

These digital humanities assignments present a few challenges, however. First, they require a certain level of technical expertise on the part of the instructor that they might not already have. If you want to assign a podcast as a final project instead of an essay, you must know how to record, edit, and produce a podcast yourself and be able to troubleshoot whatever issues might come up for students. Also, even if you have the necessary skills for the assignment, these digital projects might require platforms, software, or hardware not supported by your institution's IT department or unavailable to you or students. If you want to include a digital assignment in a course, it is best to begin by surveying the relevant and available resources on your campus. Is there some sort of digital humanities center on campus (often they're affiliated with a campus library)? Are their librarians or instructional technologists who might be of help? Who else can help support these projects so you don't have to do all of it on your own? Does your institution have site licenses for the software that you need? How much can you rely on commercial or open-source software and platforms? These are all questions worth asking as one plans out a DH assignment.

Additionally, do not assume that students are so-called "digital natives" (as common as it is now, that's a terrible term on so many levels) and that they will take to a digital project more easily than a traditional essay or presentation. Students have had years of schooling pushing them toward traditional academic products like essays, tests, quizzes, and presentations. Rarely have students in the United Sates encountered DH in high school. So, a digital project will require another level of instruction about the technologies needed for the project. A colleague in my department gave me a very useful rule of thumb: only introduce one new piece of software or technology in a course. New students have to learn the learning management system (LMS) for your campus and they also have to learn the student email system. Those sorts of things don't count. But if you decide to use a different platform for class discussions instead of the usual LMS discussion board, and then if you also ask students to post video responses to the readings on this other website that you found, and then you also want them to make a podcast as a final assignment—well, you are doing too much. Give students one novel piece of technology and only one.

A better strategy, especially if the goal is a particular DH assignment at the end of the semester, is to keep the class logistics as familiar as possible for students except for that final assignment. It also helps to slowly build to that final assignment by creating smaller assignments that teach a few of the basic technology skills along the way. So, if your goal is a five-minute group podcast as a final assignment, have an assignment early in the semester where students have to record ten seconds of audio. Then another a few weeks later where they have to interview a friend by asking them three questions, record it, and edit it. Next have them draft a script for their podcast as a group. Much like one might stagger out the steps of researching and writing an essay and scaffold it into course assignments (e.g. topic, thesis, bibliography, rough draft, etc.), the same is especially useful for DH assignments.

Finally, DH intersects with teaching through entire courses and even curriculum and degrees dedicated to digital humanities. There are PhD programs that offer doctorates in various forms of digital humanities, including "digital history" and there are more and more courses and curriculum on DH at the undergraduate level. For an instructor looking to build a new DH course the questions that face the DH assignment are even more important. On top of these, however, anyone interested in adding a DH course to their department's curriculum has another set of institutional questions to think about: How does a DH course in your discipline fit within the overall curriculum of the department? How would a DH course align with departmental-, college-, and university-wide goals? Who else on your campus is doing DH and with whom would your DH course compete or, even, collaborate? And if you are the only instructor who has the technical expertise to teach this DH course, does your department have the luxury of keeping courses on the books that only one faculty member can ever teach? Does upper administration see value in the digital humanities across campus? Do colleagues who sit on reappointment committees even know how to judge and then value the work involved in DH projects?

So, while a "Digital Humanities in Religious Studies" course sounds like a cutting-edge addition to the curriculum, it takes a lot of thought about whether the infrastructure exists on campus to support such a course, whether such a course will help the department reach the metrics used by upper administration to evaluate it, and how to pitch such a course to students so that they will register for it. Remember, most undergraduate students do not know what "digital humanities" even is nor do they know why they might be interested in it at all. The same is true for many deans and provosts—not to mention some chairs and colleagues.

We need more DH in our teaching, regardless of these very real challenges. Instructors interested in DH or doing DH research should find ways to bring it into their classes. Because there is already a broad pedagogical literature from DH scholars about teaching and DH, I have kept my focus here on the more practical issues and questions. As more scholars learn from DH and more research and teaching find their way into digital forms, we might find that "digital humanities" becomes more like "word processing"—something that scholars do on a regular basis without thinking it worth labeling and singling out on the CV. At some point, digital humanities might just be "humanities."

See also: Core Curriculum/General Education Examples; Learning Management Systems; Online/Remote Courses; Public Humanities; Transferrable Skills

12

Directed Readings/ Independent Studies

Khurram Hussain

Curricula have holes. Scarcity is an inevitable reality. There are only so many teachers, only so many classes, only so much time. Many possible topics of relevance and interest to professors and students alike can either not be offered as classes or seminars on a regular and timely basis or, for whatever reason, cannot be offered at all. The study of religion is a vast cornucopia, and its many tangents and links to the various other disciplines on offer at a modern university make any kind of comprehensive coverage at the undergraduate level nearly impossible. Luckily, there is a way around this problem. Not a cure-all by any means but certainly a mitigation. I am talking, of course, about directed readings or independent study courses. In my ten odd years being a professional scholar and teacher, I have directed over a dozen of these independent studies and the experience has been both rewarding and challenging. Here's my short take on the matter; hopefully it will be of some use to other instructors in our field.

In my experience, directed readings come about in one of three ways: 1) A student may have interest in a topic that is not being offered as a class; 2) a professor could want to explore a subject matter in depth with one or more students; or 3) a student may want to catch up on required credits and prefer an independent study to a regular class. I almost always say no to this last option, but the other two are mainstays in my teaching schedule. Especially when it comes to the study of religion, well-planned and well-orchestrated directed readings can be a real opportunity for both professors and students to extend out of their comfort zones and discover avenues of exploration that otherwise may not be available. Let me explain.

Student-initiated independent studies are rarely well thought through in the initial stages of their development. Since I usually announce at the beginning of each course that I am available for running directed readings for students who may be interested in special topics not being offered in the course catalogue, I tend to get at least a few inquiries every semester, though most of these don't go anywhere. This is because I require students to do a single-spaced, 1–2-page write-up, prepare a tentative bibliography and have a clear question or set of questions to guide our studies going forward. This weeds out those who may be interested in some topics but are not willing or able to put in this effort on the front end. Those few who do make this effort then spend at least a few sessions during office hours with me in anticipation of the directed reading the following semester, honing the topic and questions, editing the reading list and generally getting ready for a semester-long slog. Like I said: rewarding but also challenging.

Over the years, these kinds of directed readings have run the gamut from a study of Mayan and Aztec religion and its impact on American Catholicism, the particularly fraught religious and political history of Pennsylvania (the home state of my university), and a comparative analysis of Islamic banking and modern, to Western forms of finance (with a business school student) and a deep dive into the religious aspects of extreme sports fandom cultures (with a special emphasis on English soccer hooligans—check out Bill Buford's excellent book *Among the Thugs*, for example), among many others. Students come to these topics through a variety of reasons, sometimes personal, sometimes incidental. But the key is not how they got there but to get them prepared for the scholarly study of their chosen subject of inquiry. Getting them from interested in a topic in an informal sense to the formal trappings of a university-level "class" and all that this entails requires professors to be transparent about their expectations from the very beginning and clear about their required assignments (written or otherwise) and/or any other evaluative criteria they will be using to grade the student. This last part about grades is unfortunate but sadly an intractable reality; at least at my university, students care a lot about grades, and I suspect that such is the case in most colleges and universities across the country. Setting clear standards early on (as one would do in a regular class with a syllabus and list of assignments/requirements) helps a lot on the back end.

But these kinds of student-initiated directed readings are only part of the story. Especially for the study of religion, I have found professor-initiated directed readings as the gold standard for both teacher and student getting the most out of the semester (or year). The process I use for developing and executing these is a little more complicated and requires more work on the part of the instructor. It all started with a student I'll call "Abe" (not his real name), a computer science major who took some classes with me and was interested in working professionally on therapeutic Virtual Reality apps and platforms with a healthcare firm in his native Boston. In long conversations with him during office hours and in more informal settings, I realized that the study of religion could provide an excellent complement to his technical training by adding a more holistic and humanistic understanding of the nature and meaning of VR and other emerging technologies, and of therapeutic interventions into human suffering. We did a whole semester on how Buddhist mind science, ontology and ethics could allow us to better appreciate how human beings can and do operate in "virtual" spaces and how the psychology of suffering as enunciated in Buddhist philosophy could provide incredibly useful insights for the work Abe wanted to do in his professional life. This directed reading also allowed me to delve deeper into the topic of emerging technologies (e.g., VR, AI, biogenetic sciences, nanotech, etc.) from the standpoint of being a religion scholar. Having gone through this incredibly rewarding experience, I have continued to recruit students especially in the technical disciplines and applied sciences to work with me on how insights from the study of religion(s) can be usefully deployed to make sense of the contemporary human condition, and its many opportunities and challenges. The added benefit for me of course is that I end up learning as much from them about their fields as they do from me about mine!

The key insight guiding my efforts in this regard is that other academic units on a modern university campus rarely if ever look to the study of religion as having anything useful to add to their scholarship and teaching. Some of this has to do with the peculiar place the study of religion occupies in Western academia. There is also the increasing over-professionalization of academic disciplines at the undergraduate level that leads to an unnecessarily narrow and focused education. Regardless, as scholars and teachers of religion we should do all we can to identify and recruit students that can benefit from our own scholarly expertise and through whom we ourselves can begin engaging effectively with major issues affecting the world we live in.

Consider the following examples (this is not an exhaustive list by any means): a psychology and material sciences student deeply interested in Sci-Fi literature whom I recruited to explore how "religion" may operate in non-terrestrial environments; a pre-Law student who worked with me for a year on the multiple, layered, and sometimes countervailing legal systems within which ultra-orthodox Hasidic lifeworlds of communities in Brooklyn are embedded; a finance student specializing in algorithmic AIs used in making financial trades much faster than a human being ever could who spent a semester with me on the ethics of automated systems that mimic human decision making but without an attendant human agent to hold accountable. These kinds of projects may appear to be examples of providing "service" to other, non-humanistic units on campus but to my mind that is a deeply cynical way of approaching the "fall" of the humanities in the modern university. We have a lot to teach our students, no matter where they are located or what they currently intend to do with their lives. By engaging with them where they are at, but also stretching their interests and capabilities out from under the rubble of specialization and an overly instrumentalized notion of education, professor-initiated directed readings offer a tremendously consequential learning opportunity for our students. It is service, yes, but not in the pejorative sense we often associate with the term.

To conclude, my approach to directed readings requires much preparatory work on the front end, whether they are initiated by the student or the professor. Early transparency about expectations, assignments and schedule is key to a successful semester (or year). In terms of research questions, topics or areas of interest, and reading lists, these must be embedded carefully within a formal scholarly research program designed by the professor in consultation with the student. My primary concern when leading these kinds of independent studies is to bring insights and approaches from the study of religion to bear on intellectual, technological, political, social, economic or cultural issues and concerns that we face today. Others might take a different approach, rooted in different interests and different concerns. But directed readings directed in whatever manner and in whatever direction can quickly go off the rails without clear, formal parameters of what is to be studied and why, and in what order and to what end. Humanistic inquiry, undertaken for its own sake, is a good in and of itself. But we must begin to think more broadly about what we mean by "humanistic inquiry." The very condition of being human is constantly undergoing adjustments and amendments parallel to, and in light of, the changing socio-cultural and technological environment in which human beings exist. These changes have only intensified and accelerated into our contemporary times. It is our scholarly charge as humanists to engage with these developments. But formal mechanisms for doing so in an overly specialized, STEMified, and professionalized academy are few and far between. Directed readings that are intentionally initiated, carefully planned and well-orchestrated can provide an effective way out of this predicament.

See also: Class Participation; Critical Thinking; High-Impact Practices; Professionalization

13

Diversity, Equity, and Inclusion (DEI)

K. Merinda Simmons

Diversity, Equity, and Inclusion (or DEI) are a trio of words that have come to represent a single initiative on many college campuses, one that takes many different shapes, depending on what kinds of resources and priorities an institution has. The U.S. context from which I'm speaking extends a specific perspective as well. Despite the particularities, however, DEI is worth considering as an operational phenomenon in higher education. In that vein, we can examine how DEI came to exist as an institutional category, as well as how it functions in unique ways for administrators, faculty, and students. Especially in recent years as critical race theory (dubiously defined by politicians to suit their own purposes) has come under fire and as "identity politics" has become a fraught rhetorical vessel for competing ideologies, the structural presence and various roles of DEI deserve attention.

Long available exclusively to white men, U.S. colleges, and universities—many of which were built with slave labor—granted access to women and people of color only in fits and starts until the 1960s, when student activism galvanized and inaugurated an institutional sea change. Over that pivotal decade, new voices demanded to be heard with the rise of a number of organized social movements that saw young people protesting the war in Vietnam and calling for the civil rights of African Americans, women, and gays and lesbians. These uprisings played out academically in higher education as well. In the late 1960s, colleges and universities began forming departments and programs in black studies, and the first women's studies program arrived at San Diego State University (then College) in 1970. These distinct curriculums and programs spoke more directly to a more diverse student body and inaugurated academia's slow trajectory toward the contemporary landscape of DEI.

Colleges and universities in the U.S. then scrambled to come into compliance with a spate of new pieces of non-discrimination legislation and federal orders throughout the 1960s and 1970s. In the '60s, Presidents Kennedy and Johnson both issued Executive Orders requiring that government contractors take affirmative action to create more job opportunities and ensure ethical treatment of minority groups. The Civil Rights Act of 1964, of course, forbade employment discrimination regardless of government contracts, and 1972's Title IX prohibited sex-based discrimination at schools receiving federal funding. Today, just about every academic job ad (for public colleges and universities, at least) has a statement affirming the institution as an equal opportunity employer and encouraging women and minorities to apply for the position in question. On the campuses themselves, DEI offices and programs play a significant part in institutional attempts to demonstrate inclusive practices and initiatives that recruit and support a diverse student population. At many schools, you can find an office devoted to DEI with its own full-time staff and programming. Unsurprisingly, these initiatives evolve over time and take on new dimensions. Over the last decade or so at the public university where I work, for example, what began as a patchwork committee of faculty on a diversity committee has become a university-wide Division overseen by the Vice President and Associate Provost for Diversity, Equity, and Inclusion. That division houses the Intercultural Diversity Center and Safe Zone Resource Center. Meanwhile, within the College of Arts and Sciences itself, there is an Associate Dean of Diversity, Equity, and Inclusion. Part of a College's initiative may be to ask that each department have its own DEI committee so as to address matters of equity and inclusion at multiple levels. But just what do these DEI offices and committees *do*, and how do they describe that work?

As one example, here's the language from my university's DEI site:

The Division of Diversity, Equity and Inclusion provides leadership for the University to build on its core principles of inclusiveness in learning environments, programs, workforce and strategic partnerships. To that purpose, the Division seeks to do the following:

- Recruit, retain and graduate more diverse students.
- Recruit, retain and promote more diverse faculty and staff.
- Build a more inclusive and welcoming campus environment.
- Develop a more culturally competent campus community.

In affirming UA's commitment to equal employment opportunity and affirmative action, the Division will establish a holistic and integrated vision that fosters a welcoming and supportive environment for students, faculty, staff, visitors and the community at large—regardless of cultural differences, beliefs, values, ethnicity, race, age, gender, sexual orientation, disabilities, gender identity, or religion.

These goals—concerted and consistent efforts to recruit and retain diverse student and faculty populations, to educate and train allies in supporting those students and faculty, to create and maintain curriculum and events reflecting those efforts—are important ones, to be sure. But, while certain pragmatic steps can be taken, there inevitably appears the difficulty of definition. Central terms and concepts in the description above invite a variety of connotations: "diverse," "inclusive," "culturally competent," "holistic and integrated," "welcoming and supportive." The different meanings that might be applied to any of these adjectives are very much reflective of the power dynamics framing their usage. In this context, exactly who or what groups does an administration have in mind in formulating a plan for DEI? Who decides? And who determines what kinds of steps should be taken to execute a plan once formulated? What kinds of resources are devoted to that plan? What kind of accountability measures are in place? How is the success or failure of institutional efforts determined?

No bureaucratic or administrative group instantly or easily coheres around (let alone creates) a clear and thoroughgoing vision, especially across multiple domains of institutional reach. Thus, the answers to such questions too often remain vague and nebulous. This is especially the case for colleges and universities whose presidents and Boards of Trustees remain predominately white men (i.e., most of them). It is not uncommon to see the language of diversity put to use for the purposes of touting a self-congratulatory narrative of institutional progress. Even if administrators have the very best of intentions, their perspectives (situated in power) necessarily contain myriad blind spots. What's more, consulting other perspectives outside their own should not come at the cost of outsourcing hard work and putting the onus on BIPOC and women faculty/staff, who are often already responsible for a disproportionate amount of university service. The challenge for a new faculty member is therefore in determining just what an administration means by DEI and what kinds of resources there are in its name. Doing so can productively shift one's focus from abstract notions of identity to specific axes of inequality.

As already reflected in this brief discussion, DEI tends to extend primary focus to matters of race and gender. This delineation still begs certain questions about presumed referents, however. For example, a Latinx student once talked with me about their own feelings of invisibility on a campus where diversity was framed in terms of both a black/white binary and a gender binary. They were right. I have heard similar sentiments from trans students, students with disabilities, and first-generation students about the cis-bodiedness, able-bodiedness, and economic presumptions at work in certain definitions of diversity, equity, and inclusion. That is not to take anything away from the efforts that had been made to begin with, of course—the student mentioned above had made an appointment to talk to me because of the Safe Zone sticker on my office door, after all. It is only to state what is perhaps the obvious: even in needfully addressing particular demographics, institutional editing is at work. In this way, DEI can simultaneously be super vague or broad, referring to an amorphous nebula held beneath the umbrella of diversity, and also quite myopic, referring only to particular categories or identifications without fully accounting for their intersectional reach.

One certainly hopes these matters of definition and scope are taken seriously at all institutional levels. The lip service is not always mirrored at the level of policy and resources, however. Indeed, following through with robust resources and programming is sometimes a very different matter. There can often be a disconnect between the rhetoric—even the best intentions—of administrators and the energy, time, and money they commit to those issues. Often mirroring this disconnect are well-meaning faculty who think big but act small. It can be tempting to define diversity politically or ideologically with lofty ideation about universality. We forget in those instances that so much about political investment and change is about the quotidian work at a policy level. Social movements have always included both inspirational speeches *and* the less rousing but vital efforts of people behind the scenes who make phone calls, knock on doors, etc., within their local communities. Too often, we romanticize the former at the expense of the latter. When thinking about DEI in an institutional setting, then, there important programmatic and procedural elements that faculty should not overlook.

Administrative aims at legal base-covering and compliance with federal law offer an opportunity for savvy faculty who want to foster assistance and advocacy for a school's minority populations. There is money invested in DEI initiatives, and, for better or worse, those initiatives necessarily have the eyes and ears of college administrators close by. As such, they are spaces where involved faculty can advance particular investments and advocacies for their students and colleagues in strategic ways. In other words, rather than seeing DEI only as a static piece of administrative compliance, savvy and engaged faculty might instead see it as an ever-evolving set of possibilities—not simply an idea, but even more so a tool.

See also: Accessibility; Accommodations; High-Impact Practices; Professionalization

14

Examples

Michael J. Altman

Near the end of a recent semester, I asked my "Honors Introduction to Religion" class what they thought worked well in the class. "The wrestling match!" one student replied. Others nodded their heads in agreement. The wrestling match in question was the WWF Championship match between Hulk Hogan and The Iron Sheik on January 23, 1984, in Madison Square Garden. The match is easily found on YouTube, but why it showed up in an introductory course on religious studies and why the students thought it "worked" is less obvious.

I got the idea to use the video of the match from my friend and colleague Alexander Rocklin, who I think might have gotten it from his graduate school professor, Bruce Lincoln. Lincoln was, after all, a wrestling fan. Either way, Alex convinced me that the match was an excellent example of "myth." In the match the tall, blond, Hulk Hogan runs to the ring wearing an "AMERICAN MADE" tank-top while the song "Eye of the Tiger," made famous in the movie *Rocky II*, plays. The Iron Sheik, on the other hand, speaks Persian during his pre-match interview, wears a robe, a keffiyeh headdress, and boots with curly toes. The Iron Sheik is the champion, the villain, and the Iranian foreigner. Hulk Hogan is the American hero and upstart challenger. In pro wrestling terms, Hogan and the USA are the babyfaces and Iran and the Iron Sheik are the heels. I won't spoil the match. It's worth your time to go watch it. But the fact that a professional wrestling match from decades before these students were born (and a few months before even I was born) worked well enough to stick with students all semester long reveals the importance and effectiveness of examples in the classroom.

By "example," I mean a specific sort of class content instructors use in their courses. I don't mean something like an example problem in a math textbook that shows the step-by-step process of solving a particular problem (though that isn't unrelated). Nor am I describing an example essay or example assignment where the instructor gives students a model for what their response should be. Rather, for my purposes an example is always an example *of something*. Hulk Hogan vs. The Iron Sheik is an *example of* myth (to be sure, an unconventional one for many students—but that's the point). So, an example is always two things at once. It's the thing itself, the wrestling match, and the concept/term/idea that I am trying to teach to my students, in this case myth. The example bridges between the abstract (myth) and the particular (a wrestling match) to help students understand the abstract concept. An instructor can give students a definition for a concept, narrate its intellectual history, and deconstruct its intellectual genealogy, but it is the example that allows the student to better grasp exactly how they might one day encounter that concept in yet other places. These examples can take a variety of forms: films, television shows, YouTube clips, court cases, poems. The list is really endless. The important thing is that the example helps students to recognize and apply the concept.

In my experience four things make something a good example in the classroom and I think Hulk Hogan vs. Iron Sheik has all four. First, as hinted at just above, the example should be unexpected. One expects to discuss Christian rituals or the Bhagavad Gita in a religion course. And, of course, eventually an instructor wants to work their way to the particular content relevant to the course topic and discipline. But as an introduction into a new concept the unexpected example is invaluable because it provokes curiosity. It makes students lean forward a bit in their chair because, for a moment, they aren't exactly sure what is going on. This is one reason Hulk Hogan vs. Iron Sheik works. They don't see it coming but, yet, here it is and now they have to figure out what to do with it. But the key is to make sure that the unexpected example prompts curiosity and not confusion.

That's why the second trait of a good example is familiarity, but not too much. If the example is unexpected and unfamiliar then it can lead to confusion and, instead of leaning forward, students will likely just tune out. An example should therefore be recognizable but just feel a bit out of place (that's the unexpected part). I want the student to think, "I know what that is, but why is it here?" To that end, lots of people know who Hulk Hogan is, even if he hasn't wrestled in decades. He might be the only professional wrestler some people know. And even if they've never watched it, most American college students are aware that professional wrestling exists. And if they have never watched professional wrestling and aren't even sure exactly what it is, this particular wrestling match is so over the top in its characters and so blunt in its presentation that it is quite easy to follow what's going on. I may think that myth is an interesting concept for analyzing the story arc of an obscure but critically acclaimed sixty-minute Japanese wrestling match but that does not make it a good example for class. So an example, at least initially, cannot be *too strange* to the student. On the other side, if something is *too familiar* then it can also be less effective as an example because it is harder to see the familiar thing as anything other than what it obviously is. Rather than curious the example now just seems silly. The sweet spot for a successful pedagogical example is something students are familiar with but do not know too much about.

Third, it should also be something that you, the instructor, do not know too much about. Put another way, the example should at least appear to shrink the expertise gap between the instructor and the students. I say appear because we all know that you *do* know a lot about this example because you chose it, but for the example to bring the student along, toward working with the concept that you are teaching, it must feel like you are all in this together. If I present students with a sermon from nineteenth-century evangelist preacher Charles Finney as an example of how "belief" works, they can immediately recognize that I am the expert on Charles Finney in the room. Instead, a good pedagogical example narrows that gap of expertise between students and instructor, so students feel confident that they have something to say about it. This also lowers the stakes. If you're wrong about Hulk Hogan who really cares?

Finally, a good example should have a lot of what I call "hand holds." If you are climbing a rock wall it is easier if there are more places you can grip with your hands and feet. When the hand holds are fewer and further between then the climbing is more difficult and you're more likely to fall. A good pedagogical example will have a lot of traits or aspects of the concept that you're teaching that are readily apparent to students. Hulk Hogan's "MADE IN AMERICA" shirt and Iron Sheikh's robes and headdress are good hand holds. The ways the play-by-play announcers talk about the two wrestlers are good hand holds. The red, white, and blue colors of the ropes around the ring, the dynamic, dramatic, and very different reactions of the crowd to each wrestler are good hand holds. These "hand holds" are all miniature examples in themselves, of aspects of the concept, in this case "myth," that I'm trying to teach. They make it easy for students to map the concept onto the example. And, if for some reason the class is having trouble seeing what I thought they'd see in the example, it's easy to ask questions that guide them: "What do you notice about the way the two wrestlers are dressed?"

A good pedagogical example can be used in different ways depending on the size of the class and your goals as an instructor. You can use an example at the very beginning of a class period as a kind of cold open. In this case you might ask students what they notice about the example or even give them some leading questions before you show it to them. I often do this and then after we discuss the example say, "Ok, now hold that in the back of your mind while we talk about. . ." I will then go on to present the abstract concept or idea that I want to teach. Then, you can circle back to the example again at the end of the class to conclude. "See, that's why we looked at that!" Or you can start with the concept and then move to the example to bring the idea home. In smaller classes you might discuss the example as a class while in bigger courses you might just include it in part of your lecture. You can also divide bigger classes into groups and have them discuss the example among themselves and then present their ideas to the whole class. In these ways, a pedagogy focused on examples can help you fulfill any requirements your institution may have for "active learning initiatives" or similar assessment-driven requirements.

You can also turn examples into assignments. As you use different examples again and again as an instructor, your students will get used to the idea that the concepts, terms, or ideas they are learning in class can be applied to all sorts of things in the world around them—your implicit message to the class: religion isn't special, it turns out; it's just people doing things, and so a scholar of religion might have something to say about all sorts of stuff that people do. So then you can ask them to go find examples of their own as an assignment. I have begun assigning "Show and Tell" assignments where students have to go find examples of the key concepts from our course and post them to a class discussion board along with a few sentences about why the thing is a good example. I'll then spend an entire class period showing the examples and we discuss them as a class. This can be an assignment to conclude a course module on its own or a form of review before a module test or quiz.

Most instructors use examples every time they teach, whether they are aware of it or not. The important thing is to be *intentional* about the examples that you choose so they are *effective* and help students to have a deeper understanding of the concepts, terms, and ideas that you are trying to teach. More than that, focusing on examples as an approach to teaching will help students see that what they are learning in the classroom is actually all around them. If anything can be an example in the classroom, then everything is an example outside of it.

See also: Class Participation; Critical Thinking; Films; Readings; Transferable Skills

15

Experiential Learning

Emily D. Crews

I remember the music a lot. It was kind of sad, like eerie. It made me reflect on losing my grandmother, which is maybe more of an important moment in my life and my ideas about religion than I realized.

One of the things I learned is that I don't like long services. It's hard to concentrate because there's a lot of stuff to focus on. I've been thinking a lot about how my life experiences are different when there's more sensory stimulation.

I think I understand de Certeau in a different way now. Walking around the city and examining architecture from that kind of perspective helped me see and feel the ideas he was laying out, instead of just reading them then moving on.

These reflections, offered over the years by students from a variety of courses I have taught, were inspired by assignments that asked them to engage in experiential (or experience-based) learning. In most of my courses, I make use of such assignments in order to vary my teaching styles and appeal to different modes of learning. But what *is* experiential learning? And should new instructors, already burdened by the steep learning curve that comes with managing a classroom, add it to the list of approaches they use?

Experiential (or experience-based) learning (EL or EBL) rests on the idea that the best way to acquire knowledge is through hands-on, real-world experience. It is most often associated with psychologist and educational theorist David A. Kolb, who in the 1970s and 1980s synthesized the work of a group of well-known scholars under the rubric of "experiential learning theory" (ELT). Kolb argued that rather than the passive learning involved in, for instance, reading or listening to a lecture, the most effective learning involves a productive interplay between action, experience, reflection, abstraction, and application. He prescribed a cyclical approach to learning in which a person performs a certain action; has a cognitive, sensory, or social experience as a result of that action; reflects on the experience with intention; and develops abstract knowledge out of that reflection. The person then engages in a practical application of that knowledge in "the real world," thereby beginning the cycle again.

Kolb argued that knowledge is produced when we interact with our natural, built, and/or social environments, leaving both the environment and the learner transformed. ELT posits learning to be a lifelong process that has no fixed end goal, but rather pausing or resting points on a continuous journey to an understanding that we constantly refine. Kolb and later modifiers of his theory have also argued that the value of the method is that we not only acquire knowledge about a given subject, but also about ourselves as learners. This meta-reflection on experience makes us more attentive, more developed thinkers.

There is evidence to suggest that experience-based learning can have a strong effect on memory, recall, analysis, and critical thinking, as well as empathy and ethical formation. It is becoming increasingly popular both in the college classroom and in higher education more generally. Institutions such as my own have embarked upon entire campaigns focused on "the engaged university," which insist that the best learning takes place when we metaphorically lower the walls of the classroom or campus in order to open up to exchange with community and civic partners. Programs for study abroad, internships, and volunteering are all part of larger strategies for engaged and experiential learning.

In a classroom setting, EBL need not be an all-encompassing approach. You can employ the ideas behind it in ways that make sense for your particular teaching style, student community, and (being realistic) time commitments and course load. You could try it once or make it some component of all your lessons. I use it as a companion to more conventional pedagogical approaches like: readings, films, and other media; writing or oral presentations; and class discussion and the rare lecture. A few of the types of EBL exercises or assignments you might try could include:

- site visits to religious congregations or "sacred" spaces
- hands-on exploration of material objects
- artistic or building projects
- acting out scenes/role playing
- board games or digital games

- moving/dancing or making music
- walking around a campus or city
- taking public transportation
- cooking or eating
- meditation
- group projects
- open-ended assignments.

A crucial component of all these activities is the reflection that follows. With any experience-based assignment, make sure to build in time for students to consider their reactions to what they saw, heard, felt, smelled, or tasted. Using guided questions or open-ended writing or discussion, allow students to ask themselves how a site visit or a sensory exercise might have expanded their thinking and how they might apply their knew knowledge out in the world. For instance, you might invite students to write or discuss the following:

- Where did you go?
- What did you do, see, touch, feel, or taste?
- Who or what did you encounter?
- What were your most/least favorite things about working on this activity?
- What emotions did you feel?
- What was easy or difficult?
- What surprised you?
- What questions resulted from this experience?
- What did you learn about the course subject?
- What did you learn about yourself?
- How does what you learned relate to other parts of your education or your life?
- How can you use what you learned?

For EBL to be effective, it requires time, planning, and investment from both the instructor and the students. As the instructor, you must research, design, and then test lessons or assignments that allow students to have new encounters with material you likely know very well (which may seem a waste of your already scarce time and energy). You must have a clear goal for and logic behind the assignment, otherwise it more closely resembles entertainment than education. And you must create a classroom environment of trust and collaboration. For EBL to be effective, students must feel comfortable trying new and potentially intimidating things and reflecting on experiences that are open-ended, are without clear right or wrong answers, and may ask them to learn through vulnerability or other affective responses. Creating such assignments and environments requires the expenditure of emotional resources that many instructors simply do not have, especially those who are contingent or have high teaching loads or service demands.

These personal costs say nothing of the broader structural issues that may obtain when it comes to EBL. There are, of course, issues around race, gender, class, and a host of other factors that affect whether and how one might engage in such modes of teaching. Not all students, for example, can expect the same kind of welcome to some congregations. Not all spaces are safe for exploration. And not all instructors will be granted the same credibility by students or community members. For the Religious Studies classroom, EBL that is not sufficiently prefaced (with readings, reflection, conversation) and guided by the teacher risks uncritically recapitulating insiders' perspectives or interpreting the effects of experience as the only form of viable knowledge.

Whether or not EBL is worth the potential payoff may be dependent upon any number of shifting factors, including the goals of the course. For me, it helps my classes to achieve one of the outcomes that matters most to me as an instructor, which is to fracture the naturalization of certain ways of thinking about religion as a concept. If I invite students to engage with the unfamiliar by listening to or telling a story, examining objects of material culture, or observing a service or ritual, or to engage with the familiar in modes that are new to them, I am potentially creating the opportunity for them to integrate novel ways of thinking and feeling into the frameworks they use to understand the world. Along the way, I hope to be a partner in a process by which they become more critical, self-aware, empathetic thinkers.

See also: High-Impact Practices; Public Humanities; Recruiting Major; Transferable Skills

16

Extra Credit

Vaia Touna

To give or not to give? This is a question most instructors will certainly have to consider, either as they prep their syllabi for the semester and most certainly at the end of it. That is, the question as to whether they should offer some extra-curricular assignment that will allow students to earn additional points to raise their final grade. It is very common, at least in North America: the request by students to be offered assignments above and beyond what the course requires (also known as extra-credits) in order to receive a better final grade. Although I'm not really sure when that trend began, by the late 1980s offering extra credit assignments both in high schools and colleges was certainly becoming a heated topic among professors debating either in favor or against it, so much so that it was included in pedagogical publications that tried to offer both the advantages and disadvantages of such a practice.

Having completed my undergrad and M.A. degrees in Greece, the idea of asking for extra assignments to earn a better grade, especially after one has received the grade, was not really a thing, at least at the time when I was an undergrad, some twenty years ago. Although it would not be unheard of for a professor to offer the possibility of an assignment if a student was unable to attend class (though attendance in most situations was not obligatory), that was to secure at the very least a passing grade. So, given my training and experience in Greece's higher education I'm not sure that I took the whole extra credit issue all that seriously when my colleagues, in North America, first mentioned it to me. I can even say that at first, I was dismissive, not to say contemptuous, of the whole idea on the grounds that this is not "real" higher education.

I might have offered an extra credit assignment or two the first semester that I taught a 100-level course in the U.S. but without giving much thought on it, yet I was shocked by the number of students who, at the end of the semester, were asking if there was a possibility to turn that B+ to A and that A into A+ (which is usually, in my experience, the range of students who ask for extra credits). I was shocked and frustrated because, on the one hand, I wanted to help, while on the other it seemed that it was too late to make up an assignment to accommodate those requests and, perhaps, a bit unfair to other students in the class who just accepted their grade. Also, my frustration certainly comes out of the false assumption one tends to have when first beginning to teach: that one's students would have a natural interest in the class in which they enrolled; of course they will care primarily about the content of the class and not the grade, one thinks, engage with the material, participate in class discussions, do the necessary readings, and assignments in order to succeed in the course. And thus, my role, as the instructor, is to help them do exactly that, and not offer them some extra-curricular activities to pump up their grade. Also, to a certain extent it seemed as if the students asking for extra credit were disregarding my judgement of what their grade should be, based, that is, on the grading standards that I had set for the course. Over the years, though, I have completely changed my view on extra credit, mainly because I realized that, as with any given topic that relates to teaching, things are not black and white; but certainly there are many variables that a professor needs to consider, weighing the benefits and drawbacks in order to make the final decision, while knowing that whatever the choice is if it doesn't work it can always change.

As I already mentioned, there are heated debates as to whether a professor should offer extra-credits opportunities; a simple search on the internet will reveal that. Surely, there are good arguments on both ends of the spectrum and they should be taken into consideration in order to make an informed decision in favor or against offering extra-credits. Some of the most common reasons that professors do *not* favor offering extra credits can be summarized in the following:

- It encourages students to care less about the class content and more about grades.
- It's unfair to those students who will not be able to take those opportunities due to time restrictions.
- It's unfair to those students who work hard throughout the semester to earn a good grade.
- Students who ask for extra credit are usually the ones who haven't put in enough effort.
- It creates more and unnecessary work for the professor.
- It lowers academic standards.

- It doesn't offer anything of substance in the learning process and, if it does, it should be integrated into the regular course material and assessments.

- Students may rely on extra-curricular activities to increase their grade instead of putting effort to study and do better all throughout the semester.

Some of those critiques against offering extra credit are certainly legitimate but for every one of them there is a counter argument. For example:

- It has an educational benefit because it encourages students to attend public lectures and events with an educational purpose, given that attending such lectures and events, outside class time, and writing a report, is usually the way some instructors create extra credit opportunities.

- It is an optional way for motivated students to reinforce learning outcomes and goals above and beyond quizzes and tests.

- It reduces student anxiety over grades, especially for students on the brink between two grades; opting to complete an extra credit assignment shows that they do want to do better and taking up extra work shows their commitment to learning.

While I was never completely against them, once I decided to incorporate extra credit assignments into my courses, I developed strategies that would try to address some of the drawbacks of this practice. In other words, I started thinking more seriously about how I can turn this into another pedagogical tool in my arsenal. Also, I have found that offering an extra credit was a great way to acquaint students with the life and student-related events of a small department such as mine, something that they otherwise wouldn't have done because, let's be honest, most students will not just naturally become interested in a department's events; sometimes they do need that *extra* motivation. Furthermore, over the years I came to realize that students in upper-level seminars will hardly ever ask for extra-credit. The requests for extra credit comes mostly from students enrolled in my introductory courses, primarily first years students or students aiming for a good GPA or those who enroll in the Intro to Religious Studies to fulfill a core requirement (that is, one of those Humanities [HU] designated courses that, in the U.S. system, may not relate to their major but that they need to take in order to fulfill the requirements for completing their BA degree). Hence, I mostly assign extra credit assignments to my introductory courses.

So, once I decided to offer extra credits it was important to include my policy on them in the syllabus. I make clear there that throughout the semester I will announce several extra credit opportunities and I stress that there will be no extra credit opportunity after the last week of classes. This is important because students know from the first day of classes that if they *do* care about their grade, then they have to monitor their standing and also take advantage of extra credits throughout the semester and not after their final grades are uploaded in the system. This, in my experience, makes students more responsible but also encourages them to do better because they have to pay attention to their progress.

It is very important for students to know exactly how extra credits will be graded and how much they will be worth in relation to their grade. So, in my courses each extra credit opportunity is worth 1 point, with the possibility of adding up to five extra credits in a 100-point system. I settled on that number for many reasons, primarily though because it gives the opportunity, to a student who is willing to do some extra work, to change their score by one plus or minus grading scale, which I think is fair for those students who are restricted from taking advantage of extra credits chances due to work, for example, or family commitments. Also, a *C* student will not become an *A* student just by getting extra credit points that would indeed be unfair to a student who is working much harder; those students, or any student for that matter, know that should they wish to do much better, then they have to contact me early on to help them with whatever it is that they are struggling with or to provide them with some studying tips, or when I teach large enrollments to attend the tutorials that are offered by my Teaching Assistant.

Although students can complete up to five extra credits, throughout the semester I offer more than five opportunities, doing so on a variety of times and days so that all students can have a chance to take advantage of them. Most of the extra credits are linked to my department's events, such as lectures, professional development workshops for students, brown bag lunches, undergrad research symposia, movie nights (which are followed by a discussion led by a professor), but also other university-wide events that I deem of relevance to our course. Although giving extra credit for attending those events may seem self-beneficial for a professor and their department, at the same time they can become an excellent opportunity for learning and reinforcing our course's learning goals.

Most of the extra credit that I offer to students requires them to write a short assignment related to the event and our class material. For example, if students are invited to attend a lecture, they are required to fill in their names in a spreadsheet making sure that they actually attended but also to submit a brief writing assignment which I make sure relates to the class. It is often quite nice to read in those assignments my students' efforts to use their knowledge from our class.

Not all of my extra credits are related with the class content, of course; at least one of them is not: completing the student evaluations for the course (known as SOI: Student Opinions of Instruction). Since those are now submitted online, instead of during class time, the number of students who will take the time to complete them is rather small, no matter how many emails and reminders professors send. Although it is certainly self-serving (though the administration does encourage faculty to find ways to increase the reporting for these surveys of instruction), it is an extra credit opportunity that all students can easily take and, actually, I am rewarding something that they are asked to do, so that makes everyone happy. For that one I ask that once they have submitted the SOI they take a screen shot that says they have completed the course evaluation and upload it on a designated assignment on our course's online site.

For sure, to be willing to offer extra credits creates an *extra* work for a professor but it can be beneficial for both the students and also for small departments. For they can motivate students to get involved by attending events, especially in a department that is not necessarily their major, that otherwise they wouldn't have attended—so these opportunities are a great way to introduce students to a discipline in more creative and fun ways, and perhaps attract potential majors. Attending those events (lectures, undergrad research symposia, professional development workshops, brownbag lunches, etc.) gives students an opportunity to think and apply what they have learned in the class, doing so in relation to broader discussions in the related field or discipline. In fact, in many situations, based on the extra credit writing assignments that I received over the years from students, attending those events helped many of them to think through some aspect of studying religion or reinforced something that I said in class. Also, not all students are the same—some have different needs than others, some are stressed about a good grade more so than others (for a variety of reasons, from securing their funding and scholarships to those for whom a good or bad grade may be a point of reference in determining their self-worth)—and this is why, in my experience, it is primarily students who are already doing well in the course that end up taking those extra credit opportunities. Overall, I think that any opportunity that students are willing to take, especially an opportunity to write and work through an idea relevant to class, above and beyond class assignments, should be encouraged and yes, rewarded!

See also: Attendance; Grading; Participation

17

Films

Khurram Hussain

At the most basic level, film is a medium for telling stories. Stories are neither fake nor real but rather meaningful. At least the good ones are. And meaning transmitted through narrative seldom presents as a series of facts or regulations and norms but rather far more often as an annotated meditation on the human condition. Religion is one such form of annotation. This is why the world's religions are so full of stories, based on stories, and sustained through stories. Storytelling in religious contexts allows complex theological, ontological, epistemological, historical, and soteriological ideas to be transmitted not just through explanatory exposition but also plot driven interplay between multifaceted characters inhabiting a world not of their own making and caught in circumstances not always entirely under their control; think, for example, Arjuna slumped over in anguish and besot with indecision on the battlefield of Kurukshetra or of Jesus on the Mount of Olives pleading for the cup to be taken from him and yet also willing to ultimately do God's will and not his own. And these are only the most sacred of stories—narratives abound in all interstices of the religious imagination and in all practices of religious exposition. They are literally everywhere. Inasmuch as film is a storytelling medium, its relationship to the study of religion is not hard to establish, if perhaps a little harder to explicate. But let us try.

I would say that there are at least three different ways film can be used in the study of religion at the undergraduate level. First, as its simplest possible treatment in the classroom, film can be used to tell the story of religion(s) through documentary movies or lightly fictionalized historical dramas. These run the gamut from great (e.g., *The Mission*, 1986) to terrible (e.g., *Kingdom of Heaven*, 2005)—scholarly and pedagogical selectivity is key to making these work either on their own or as substitutes for textbooks (this generation of students hates textbooks—as do I). Second, films with storylines and plot devices that linger on questions, concerns, or problems in the human condition that are also of intense interest to religionists can provide secure narrative hooks to climb up levels of discernment about the relevant subject matter with our students. For instance, sci-fi and fantasy movies that deal with the nature and meaning of reality itself (e.g., *The Matrix*, 1999), with manifest expositions of good and evil (e.g., *Star Wars*, 1977), with tropes like time travel (e.g., *Interstellar*, 2014) and end times (e.g., *Knock at the Cabin*, 2023), with what it means to be a human being (e.g., *Blade Runner*, 1982), hidden places and esoteric ideas (e.g., *Black Panther*, 2018), and of course with metaphoric treatments of contemporary issues, religious or otherwise (e.g., *The Children of Men*, 2006), etc., are particularly useful for this purpose, but certainly by no means the only genres that generate these kinds of films. Finally, a third and perhaps most challenging way of using film as a medium for the exploration and study of religion is to have students make films themselves in lieu of written assignments. But while the logistics of this kind of project are easier for our students to handle than they would have been for many of us at a similar age, and despite the fact that I have a long-standing relationship with our Department of Film Studies and Media Lab, which helps to a certain extent, these kinds of assignments demand serious time and energy from our students and some hand holding on the part of the instructor(s) is certainly appropriate.

Good, short documentaries on religion adequate for use in an undergraduate class are notoriously hard to find. Even when they may get the "facts" mostly right as far as we know them through the scholarly study of religion and history (although even good documentaries tend to be about twenty-odd years behind the scholarship at any given point in time), these facts are often arranged and orchestrated to fit some regnant, popular paradigm about what religion is and its proper place in modern society; so be on the lookout for tired tropes. The liberal imagination is especially prone to what Aaron W. Hughes calls normativity in the study and exposition of religion, and this often bleeds into popular treatments of the subject on film as well. "Good" versions of religion are progressive, private and peaceful, aligned with liberal modernity, while "bad" versions are the opposite. Description and evaluation comingle until it is difficult to tell where one ends and the other begins. The only question is whether any given religion belongs essentially in either the good or bad pile, whether the "authentic" version of it is said to be good or bad religion. These kinds of treatments may be morally tempting considering this or that political environment (claiming that Islam is a religion of peace and social justice, for example, in the regime of rampant Islamophobia in the West and elsewhere) or practically enticing toward mobilizing public opinion for this or that political project (Islam condones violence and is fundamentally incompatible with modernity, for example, during the ongoing War on Terror) but they are contrary to the academic mission. As scholars of religion we have a different charge than religionists and their detractors or supporters, and should avoid debates and discourses that are better suited to these latter interlocutors. But even otherwise solid films (e.g., *The Rockstar and the Mullahs*, 2003, or *Submission*, 2004) can be prone to walking at least part of the way down this unfortunate path. The problem becomes especially acute when one is dealing with historical dramas where heroes and villains are a narrative necessity. And even lightly fictionalized accounts are still more fiction than the "science" fiction that we call the study of history. In all these circumstances then, it is essential for instructors to pre-game any film, fiction or non-fiction, with students *before* they watch it, making them aware of the inevitable issues and priming them for a constructive, critical conversation about both the content of said film and the discursive framework within which it is embedded. This may make for less exciting viewing on the part of the students, having been exposed to spoilers perhaps, but it is necessary if any film is to serve a properly educational purpose and not distract from it.

No such priming is necessary when dealing with films from the second category, although perhaps some prior, rudimentary identification of the religious concept(s) that the instructor would like the students to focus on may be advisable. Here we are in the domain of pure fiction, with all its attendant opportunities and dangers. Movies that linger on emotional and epistemological registers that highlight otherwise hidden realities (both physical and psychological) are especially useful (e.g., *Contact*, 1997), as are films that problematize and explore the relationship between religion, science, and technology (e.g., *Ex Machina*, 2014). The key is to identify the particular concepts or ideas that one wants to explore with one's students and then find a film to match (perhaps with help from students themselves, although this can be tricky—our students are not film critics). Many of our students have been socialized into thinking of religion narrowly as a set of categorical beliefs securely ensconced in our conscience and a set of easily identifiable practices associated with this or that belief system. Stories in general, and films in particular, eschew lists for human drama. Perhaps the single most important overarching lesson that fiction films offer our students is that concerning human contingency—that our religion, our societies, our lives could always have been, and can always be, another way, a different way (i.e., that there is nothing "just so" about any human phenomena, including religious ones). In constructing worlds that proceed on natural and/or social assumptions that are different from our own, speculative sci-fi movies (e.g., *Dune*, 2021, and *Avatar*, 2009) are especially effective in demystifying our own worlds, revealing them to be both simpler and more complex than we could ever otherwise imagine. This allows our students to experience how particular understandings of the nature and meaning of the world, beliefs about right and wrong, and teleological accounts of the history and time are enmeshed within a human social context, and operationalized in human interactions. Especially considering the visual turn in our contemporary culture (TikTok, Instagram, Reelz, etc.), films are a resource in teaching the study of religion that we as instructors cannot afford to ignore.

The final frontier in the use of film in teaching the study of religion to undergraduates is to have our students actually make films as a class assignment. This is almost always a live option in all classes as an alternative to a written final group project. Most students who have chosen to go this route do so by making a documentary of some sort, with limited live action and mostly a presentation style interspersed with short videos. The quality varies from student to student, group to group, class to class. But the best use of this option in my classes was based on an original screenplay loosely inspired by the events at the Branch Davidian compound in Waco, Texas back in 1993. The student who wrote the short screenplay (25–30 minutes) also played "Khurram," the professor and leader of a cult of undergrad student devotees known as *The Khurramians* (2018), whose slow yet inexorable descent into a kind of social madness eventually leads to a terrible tragedy on the college campus. Identifying the propaganda potential of the classroom as a jumping off point, *The Khurramians* is a tour de force of religious concepts and tropes, ritual sacrifice, cult formation and its dynamics, and deep apocalypticism all on a modern university campus! Something this ambitious obviously cannot be an "every class, every group" kind of assignment. Still, encouraging students to think big is always a good idea.

Films are magic, their verisimilitude both exhilarating and unnerving. As a form of visual storytelling, cinematic renditions of the ins and outs of the human condition have great pedagogical potential if these are used with deliberate preparation and conscious intention. And now, especially with the proliferation of VR consoles and platforms, the capacity of films to create entirely new worlds for our students to explore and investigate is that much more effective. There is, of course, an old school tick in our profession that often makes us scholars uncomfortable with "newfangled" approaches and technologies in teaching the study of religion. Textual sources, material culture, and participant observation are the gold standard for doing this kind of work, but public story telling is at least as crucial to the salubrious persistence of religious traditions and hence also of their study, as anything else. Inasmuch as film is one such form of storytelling, its potential use in our pedagogy is not only advisable but, considering the world we live in today, absolutely necessary.

See also: Assignments; Digital Humanities; Experiential Learning; Group Work; High-Impact Practices; Library Resources; Presentations; Public Humanities

18

Final Examinations

Michael J. Altman

I stuck my head into my department colleague's office door at the end of one semester. "How's it going?" I asked them.

"Good. Almost done with all the grading! How about you, are you done yet?" they replied.

"Yep," I said smiling. "I was done last week."

"How are you already done?"

"I don't give finals."

Since my first semester as an instructor of record in the fall of 2013, I have never once given a final examination in a course. I have required students to turn in final essays or make final projects. I have even assigned students to make podcast episodes to cap off a course. But not once have I had them sit down in a classroom during a special exam week and take some sort of written assignment.

It's not because I'm lazy. I don't give traditional sit-down final exams because they don't accomplish what I want to accomplish. They don't assess what I want students to have learned by the end of a course. A multiple-choice, time-limited, in-class exam does a very good job of measuring how much course content a student has memorized. Such an exam can also do a great job of measuring whether a student can follow a specific process to find a singular correct answer. So, in a chemistry or geology course, where memorizing elements and rocks is a central goal of the course, these exams make sense. Similarly, in a math course they also make sense. But in my courses, the memorization and regurgitation of course material is a basic and foundational learning outcome. But it is only step one in the process. By the end of a course, my learning outcome is that students can demonstrate specific thinking and communication skills. I also want students to use course material to analyze, synthesize, and produce new ideas. The traditional sit-down in-class exam doesn't measure those outcomes well.

The final examination, or whatever final assessment an instructor may choose, should be designed in tandem with the overall course objectives or student learning outcomes of the course and the other assessments in the course. The final assessment (a better term than final exam) is the last chance to measure what students have learned and it should measure the things that are of greatest importance to the instructor and greatest value to the student. The other assessments (or assignments) in the course should build toward the final assessment, giving students opportunities to practice and receive feedback along the way.

In my courses, I tend to follow a loose structure as I design assessments across my syllabus that build toward the final assessment. First, the most simple and frequent assessments are meant to measure basic acquisition of class content. Did they do the reading? Did they understand the reading? Do they know the basic terms from class lectures? This is the "daily work" of the course and can take the form of daily reading questions, frequent quizzes of key terms, reading responses, or any number of other simple, quick, and content-driven assessments. The goal here is to measure the recall of the important course content. Next, another layer of assessment asks students to demonstrate that they can apply this content through analysis. For example, I may ask students to use terms and concepts from the readings to analyze a film or short piece of writing. This can take the form of a written assignment, an oral presentation, or even group work. The actual assignment itself can be tailored to the course and its context. It is the specific skill level I am assessing that is important. Here, I am giving them the example and asking them to demonstrate that they can use the content I assessed earlier to analyze it. Finally, the last layer of my assessment asks students to take the content from the course and use it to go find an example that they can investigate on their own. I am not giving them the example for analysis, but instead they are now charged with investigating the world around them. Again, the form of this assignment is wide open. It could be a traditional "research essay" or it could be something I call a "show and tell," where students post these examples that they find on a discussion board. The point is that, for me, student mastery of the course material is demonstrated when they can go out into the world around them and use the content of the course to produce new insights and make new arguments.

To circle back to where this chapter began, I have never given a traditional written multiple-choice in-class final exam because those exams do not measure what, for me, indicates final mastery of the course material. An instructor trying to decide what to do during the last week of class or finals week might figure it out by asking themselves what mastery of the material in the class looks like to them. Maybe they want students to know a lot of dates, names, events, and other stuff. If knowing all the stuff is mastery for your course, then maybe a traditional final examination makes sense. It will assess if students have memorized things. But if mastery of your course material is more skill-based or driven by curiosity and investigation, then what are those skills and what does that investigation look like? If students can demonstrate those skills and conduct that investigation, they will still have to know some stuff.

Practical concerns also affect what sort of end of the course assessment an instructor should design. Never forget: whatever you assign, you (or someone) will have to grade. If one is teaching a large lecture class of 100 or more students then grading writing assignments of any length is daunting, even with graduate teaching assistants. But perhaps there is a group assignment that will assess the outcomes of the course. Digital, or even physical, posters can be graded quickly and easily with a rubric. I know one colleague in my department who has assigned a "meme assignment" to end their large enrollment introduction to religious studies course. You can grade 100 memes pretty fast and they are more enjoyable as an instructor than writing a bank of multiple-choice questions. Smaller seminar courses offer the chance to design longer or more developed research and writing assignments. They can also be opportunities for other forms of final projects such as podcasts, posters, websites, videos, or works of art. Regardless of the size of the class, the more creative and less traditional the assessment and the more the assessment is tailored to the specific outcomes of the course then the harder it will be for students to cheat or plagiarize. Sometimes instructors spend energy trying to catch cheaters when they could just develop more creative assessments.

The important thing is to balance the assessment of course outcomes with the human limits of time, energy, and other professional responsibilities (one might have a dissertation project or book manuscript to get to, after all). Indeed, one's location as an instructor also limits what one might assign at the end of the semester. Departmental, college, or university requirements or unstated norms might require a more traditional final exam. What a tenured associate professor can get away with might get a contract instructor in hot water. A savvy instructor will talk with departmental colleagues and senior faculty members in the hallway or look at their syllabi to gauge these sometimes unspoken rules. Instructors should be creative in developing their final assessments, but meme at your own risk.

To conclude, I turn to an interview with historian of religion Jonathan Z. Smith where he mentioned the final exam in his "Introduction to Religion" course. On the first day of class, as he was going over the syllabus, he would give the students "two cigarettes" worth of time to write a definition of religion.

And I disappear and smoke my two cigarettes and come back in. And they've been told on the syllabus—because one of the things I always do with college students is tell them the final exam on the first day of class so they can prepare—they know that their final paper, their only paper for the course, will be to revise that definition with specific reference to the materials we've read together in the course.

SMITH 2018: 89

This is a final examination meant to assess the outcome of the class. Smith does not give an exam that measures how much the students can recall from the material they have read. Smith's course, as he explains in the interview, is not really about "religion" per se at but about definitions. And so, the final paper (the *only* paper) returns to the same definitional question that the course began with and allows the student to demonstrate what they have learned. That, in my view, is the point of a final exam: an opportunity for the student to demonstrate what they have learned.

See also Academic Misconduct; Assessment; Curriculum; Examples; Grading; Group Work; Teaching Assistants

19

Grading

Vaia Touna

"**G**rades," "marks," "scores," and "points" are some of the words used to signal student learning and progress. But grading, like all things related to teaching, is another complicated and much debated issue. We may all have heard the story about Albert Einstein and his lousy grades at school, yet we all also know that he represents the epitome of what a genius scientist is. In fact, occasionally, similar stories emerge, of so-and-so successful person whose grades in school or college were not that great. Stories like these, whether they are true or not, reveal the controversial topic of grading, wanting to make plain that success, or brilliance, or intelligence are not necessarily represented in the grades that one receives throughout their schooling years. Grades as a way of reporting student learning has not always been around but as schools and universities started to use them there was an immediate questioning regarding their value. So, questions like "what is the value of grades?", "what is the best way to grade and thus evaluate student learning?", "what is the best grading scale: numeric, alphabetic, percentile, or explanatory?", "are grades an adequate way to offer feedback to students?", "should we even assign grades to students?" are constantly discussed and debated among educators. And the fact that we have so many different grading scales and methods worldwide may actually speak to the fact that there is no consensus on how students' learning progress should be evaluated and reported.

We may all have some personal experience from our school years regarding the arbitrariness of grading, an experience that determined the kind of educators that we became. For example, I have many such stories but the one that played a significant role in what I now think of grading is from when I finished high school in Thessaloniki. In the Greek system, in order to go to university, during your last two years in high school you had to decide which of the four paths you wanted to follow—humanities, hard sciences, medical school, or social sciences—and then take standardized entrance exams specific to that path. I had chosen the humanities (in fact, the reason that I'd chosen the humanities was out of spite to my math teacher who, although I was doing very well, had decided one year to give me a low grade in order, as she said, to motivate me to try even harder!); so, when I finished high school, I had to take exams on Ancient Greek, Latin, History, and write an essay on a topic usually related to some social issue. Your score in all four test subjects would then determine what school you'd attend (whether History, Law, Education, Languages, Theology, etc.). For every subject there would be two examiners grading your exam in order to secure fair grading and, if I recall correctly, the average of their grades would determine the final score. I remember that my essay (which that year was on the importance of laughing) was graded with a big grade difference between the two examiners, so much so that the lower score would leave me outside university (a classic case of what some in academia now call reader number 2). In cases like this, though, a third examiner was asked to weigh in on the difference and it was due to their grading that I was successful—and the rest, as they say, is history. But this little anecdote says something important both about the arbitrariness of grading but also that despite the standards that I'm sure were there, and no matter how good a system is, it will also come down to personal judgement.

Why do we even need grades? It appears that, at least in the U.S., the need to systematically use grades to evaluate and report student learning started for very practical reasons. It was an easy way to process and evaluate the increasing number of students that started to attend colleges and it was an easy way to rank students. Although some form or another of grading has always existed, it seems that officially the first university in the U.S. to use a grading system was Yale, when, in 1785, its President, Ezra Stiles, used a four-grade ranking scale for the graduating students: Optimi, Second Optimi, Inferiores, and Perjores. Later this ranking scale was substituted with a 0–4 numeric scale with 2 marking a passing score, and it appears that this has also been the precursor of the modern 4.0 GPA (Grade Average Point) that is used in the U.S. today, but also by many colleges and universities worldwide. In 1897 Mount Holyoke College, a women's private liberal arts college in Massachusetts, employed a descriptive, letter and percentage grading system (A = Excellent [95–100%], B = Good [85–94%], etc.), a system that, with minor variations, has become the dominant grading system among universities, along with the 4.0 GPA scale to which these grades are often translated/normalized. Since then, of course, discussions on the purpose and value of grading have been constant. Among the criticisms to grading is that:

- Grades force students to avoid taking risks out of fear of a bad grade and as a result they may seek an easy A.

- Students aim for good grades without real interest in learning.
- Grades are not a sufficient way to give feedback to students.
- Grades may impact students' self-confidence and be a cause of extreme stress.

On the other hand, advocates of grading argue that:

- Grades can be motivational.
- Grades help communicate student achievement and status to third parties (i.e., to parents, to other universities, to employers, etc.).
- Grades provide students with information regarding their learning progress.

Over the years both schools and universities have experimented with several systems and methods of grading: from a variety of numeric scales (4-point, 6-point, 10-point, 20-point, 100-point scales), to alphabetic, to pass-fail, plus-minus, and even descriptive or narrative assessments of student performance.

Some of the grading methods that have been implemented among educators are the following:

- Grading based on mastery of specific goals and outcomes set by the instructor.
- Pass/fail grading, whereby the instructor merely offers a passing grading so long as the students are judged to have sufficient knowledge of the object of study.
- Grading on the highest score or what many call grading on the curve—in both cases grades are re-adjusted based on overall or collective students' performance. So, if most or all students scored low on a test their grades are re-adjusted based on a new standard or average.
- Qualitative feedback in narrative form, by which the instructor will give constructive criticism and advice on students' work, based on which students may be invited to revise and resubmit their work.
- Self-assessments and self-evaluation, by which students are invited to assess and evaluate their own work in light of the goals and learning objectives that were set by the instructor.
- Peer-grading, by which students assess each other's assignments or tests based on benchmarks, or rubrics set by the instructor.

- Penalty grades are sometimes given by the instructor if an assignment or test is late. The instructor will likely have some policy whereby if students miss the due date, they can still submit the assignment or test but a percentage will be deducted from their grade.

- Gamification whereby instructors will apply game concepts to mark student progress, like, for example, collecting points in order to get rewards and badges.

- Ungrading, which is the latest trend or at least a method some educators are currently discussing/debating. Ungrading as a method counts more on giving qualitative feedback, instead of grading various assignments and students are encouraged to revise their work based on the feedback that they receive. As part of the ungrading method students often use portfolios to collect their work, and, at the end of the semester those portfolios can present an opportunity for the students to self-reflect on their learning progress and, with their instructor's help, receive their final grade.

There's no system or method that is perfect or to be used indiscriminately; all of the above approaches to grading can have both positive and negative effects, and so, in the end, it is up to the professor to determine what works and what doesn't and in which specific context or for what sort of assignment. Grading and reporting certainly is not essential to the instructional process, that is, to teaching and learning, but it is a necessity in most class settings today and therefore requires our attention. And so, whether one opts for *grading* or *ungrading* in the end you will need to justify a final grade and therefore you will need to consider what the grade will be based on. I therefore do not approach grading as one fits all; I have certain standards, of course, but it is always a case by case or, better said, a class by class, and student by student approach that I follow (always aiming for equity and fairness, of course, along with transparency). I have never, though, used a penalty grading; I find it the least motivating for students. Also, I have stopped grading student attendance and participation to motivate students to speak in my classes; I have found that creating an environment in which students eventually feel comfortable to share their thoughts is better than simply forcing them to speak because they consider this part of grading, something which can make them worry about being right or wrong, and therefore less comfortable engaging in discussions.

Depending on the class that I teach I will consider the criteria that I will set for my grading method. Each class has different dynamics and different needs and should be approached accordingly, for example, large introductory courses cannot be approached the same as smaller size classes or upper-level seminars, for the simple reason that for each sort of course the instructor will set different goals and learning objectives which, in the end, will condition the criteria by which grading and assessment will happen. That is, whether there will be product criteria, whereby grading will depend on submitting final assignment, or process and progress criteria, whereby grading will depend upon several (possibly developmental or cumulative) assignments and tests. In the North American system, apart from the final grades, there are also often midterm grades (an early indication to students how they are performing in a course), a practice that was not present in the Greek universities that I was familiar with and, because of it, I've found it less appropriate for college students. Over the years, though, I have observed that it can be a useful tool. Personally, I avoid to whatever extent possible assigning low grades for midterms because, in my experience they can make students withdraw from studying and learning, as if their fate is already set in the course. Instead, a more generous grade during midterm grades can actually motivate students to maintain that grade and therefore get more interested in the class content. Midterm grades can also be used as an incentive to meet with students early in the semester and help them address any learning difficulties that they may have.

As I already said, depending on the class that I teach I will consider the criteria that I will set for my grading method. When I first taught my large enrollment intro course, I had two multiple choice tests and a final cumulative multiple-choice exam by which I graded my students; however, the last time that I taught the same intro class I had weekly multiple-choice quizzes, weekly discussion assignments, and three open book exams where students had to answer, in a critical manner, three questions. Each of the above requirements are doing different things and assessing different learning outcomes. Quizzes (or lower stake and brief tests) serve to assess particular concepts that I want my students to master while the short writing discussion assignments provide an opportunity for my students to write down their thoughts on a particular reading that I assigned, and then elaborate more in class; so long as students demonstrate in their writing assignment that they have done the reading they will earn the grade. The open book exams test my students' ability to critically synthesize the knowledge they acquired; I provide qualitative feedback and usually by the third exam there is significant progress in the grades that they will receive. Throughout the years I have experimented with a variation of the above, settling on the last one as a result of responding to the COVID-19 pandemic, something that fundamentally influenced my approach both to assessing students learning but also my grading practices. And I'm sure I will continue to change my assessment methods, based on future courses and future student needs.

As you might expect, in my smaller upper-level seminars I have a different approach to grading, which is mostly based on one-on-one meetings with students to discuss their work and give them feedback in order to revise it. For example, in some cases I give them the option to submit a draft of their final project a week before the end of classes and during the last week of classes I meet individually with the students to discuss their draft and how they can revise it. I do not grade their draft because I don't want students to stress over it and usually that helps, both for our meeting and certainly for their final work—although the draft is, in a way, optional given that no grade is attached to it, but students always take advantage of it.

Overall, I'm trying to be fair, meaning that I try to have clear and simple assessment and grading rubrics that will help students monitor their progress but also help them to self-assess their work. Generally, I'm trying to instill in my students that although I understand that grades are important for them, developing a studying method that is consistent, doing the readings, and paying attention to the lecture will easily give them a good grade, and in most cases this works. Yes, students do ask how they can "improve their grades," but I don't stay on the "grades" I focus on the verb, on them wanting to *improve*, and I do try to help them with that. I encourage them to reach out to me regarding their grades and I'm pleased when they do because it is an opportunity to discuss with them not just their grades but their studying practices, the class content and direct them toward the things to which I want them to pay attention, to retain, to apply. In other words, I don't see grades as necessarily bad or good, but I certainly see them as a pedagogical tool which I try to use in a way that is beneficial to my students.

See also: Assessment; Assignments; Attendance; Class Participation; Extra Credit; Final Examinations

20

Group Work

Teemu Taira

For a long time, the modeling of academic expertise—especially in Arts and Humanities—was based on the individual scholar. Traditional lectures were aligned with this type of thinking: an individual thinker was simulating the thought process they had when problematizing particular topics and solving scholarly questions. Cooperation in research has been primarily something the natural science people do in their laboratories, and the authors of publications in natural sciences often contain the names of the whole research group. In the Humanities, co-researching and coauthoring has been rare, though not non-existent.

Recently, it has become somewhat more common that scholars in Arts and Humanities, including the study of religion, write and research together—not always in large groups, but in twos or threes. This is also something that can be made visible in teaching, particularly in group work (and in group teaching as well).

Group work can mean almost any kind of task done by more than one person, but the nature of it varies significantly depending on the size of the group. Working in pairs is different from working in a group of three or four people, and they are all different from working in a group of twelve. There are also different ways to organize group work: it can be a small part of the syllabus or it can be a course's main working method.

Pedagogically speaking, one justification for the group work is based on the idea of cooperative learning (CL). This means that students cooperate in small groups to maximize their own and each other's learning. It can be, and often is, combined with problem-based learning (PBL)—student-centered learning based on solving a problem—or case-based learning (CBL)—also a student-centered learning approach in which students are introduced to hypothetical or real-life cases to solve, with the help of theoretical knowledge provided in the course.

Although the benefits of group work are constantly highlighted among the pedagogical experts, there are some problems or difficulties in it. From the point of view of students, group work may be time-consuming. It is often difficult to find the time to meet up with other members, unless the group work happens in class. Also, the workload can be heavy, no matter how much the instructor has tried to ensure that the workload is manageable. Moreover, the workload is rarely evenly spread within the group. There may be free-riders and sometimes this causes tension between group members. But this is how the group work often happens also outside the university classroom! Furthermore, the possibility of using peer evaluation is considered difficult by many students.

The instructor can anticipate these (and other) problems, and even prevent some of them, but it is likely that no group work exercise goes smoothly with every group, and the key is to talk about these issues in advance, so if it all goes wrong, students can see it as a learning process if nothing else. Of course, no one wants to design group work on this basis, so it is important to pay attention to the time management, to the roles individual group members have, and to make sure that the size of the group is appropriate for the task.

When keeping these factors in mind, group work has multiple gains. The group provides peer support: one is not left alone with the task. One can also test ideas and others can add elements to the ideas of others. This is how the students participate in active construction of knowledge (and thus learning is modeled according to so-called constructive teaching, that has been a big thing among pedagogy experts for years). Students also practice negotiation skills, project-leading skills, and they have to learn to get along with people who may not be their best friends. All of these transferable skills that students are supposed to learn, in addition to whatever the substance and discipline-specific content of the course happens to be, are best to make explicit for them. One of my students who was not initially comfortable with working with other people agreed to do it after I reminded him that in most workplaces you cannot choose your workmates. If this does not convince students, it is also possible to remind them that the development of humanity has been based on cooperation and so is its survival in the future.

Practicing group work is beneficial even for those who wish to stay in the academy. For even academia is slowly beginning to underline other than individually oriented working methods. My own example is useful here: although I have been funded individually for many years, one of the research teams in which I worked contained one professor whom I knew quite well and another scholar I had not met before. In such a situation it is best for all to learn quickly how to interact efficiently for the shared goal. More generally, there are still some in the Arts and Humanities who see little value in cooperation—one established professor even complained in a public report that I publish too much with others—but peers are increasingly seeing co-writing as an indicator of a strong research network and evidence of excellent cooperation skills. These may turn out to be crucial in recruitment. Therefore, it is not a bad idea to design at least some courses so that cooperative skills are practiced and the benefit of cooperation for knowledge production is made explicit to students. Group work is a great way to do it.

Because of its obvious pros and cons, too much group work may be "too much" for students. Some in my institution complain that they struggle with time management and even get frustrated in listening to other students if most courses contain group work, and they start yearning for traditional teaching methods where you sit back and, rather passively, listen to the professor deliver the lecture. But too little group work is another pitfall: when the balance is right, and the purpose of group work—both the pedagogical purpose and its utility in accomplishing the task—is clear, then students typically appreciate it even when the workload may be heavy.

Group work can also be integrated into a course that includes several learning methods. Many courses contain some kind of group work, even when the main part of the course builds on other learning methods. An example is when I taught an undergraduate course on religious diversity focusing on Finland. I included a small comparative task that contained group work in the classroom. Students had a couple of hours to prepare a presentation on religious diversity of a selected European country (excluding Finland). They were able to use the internet and I mentioned some databases that they were able to utilize. Then they made short ten- to fifteen-minute presentations in the class. This did not require any specific organization; it was very easy to do and yet students found it very useful. They learned to find information (including the use of a database), organize it in a group, figure out what is most relevant and reliable information to share with the class (given the insights they had regarding religious diversity in Finland), and practice their presentation skills. I trust that any instructor can think of similar exercises in their courses. This does not require anything special. And all the previously mentioned difficulties are not crucial if group work is only a small part of a class or the course.

The situation is slightly different and more demanding when the whole course is based on group work, especially research-based or problem-based cooperative learning in which the whole group attempts to solve one research problem as a group. There are several ways to teach such courses, but I'll share my personal example. Some years ago, I was doing a research project on media discourses on religion and the secular in Finland and my teaching was also focusing on those themes. At the same time, I did my studies in university pedagogy and I specialized in cooperative learning, so I decided to try that in my teaching more explicitly and self-consciously than I had done before. I organized two courses in successive academic years: the first focused on examining how the Finnish media covered the issues raised by one television program, mainly related to the attitudes of the Lutheran church (the main one in Finland) to same-sex relations; the second focused on examining how the Finnish media has covered the practice of the singing of the Summer Hymn in schools' spring term events since the early 1990s. In both cases there were approximately twelve students, which is a recommended maximum number for this type of teaching. They worked in pairs, meaning that each pair examined one type data (e.g., a newspaper or online news media) regarding the course topic and then the interaction between pairs started the comparative work and made the understanding of their particular data more substantial.

Most students were very satisfied with such courses. At least the experience differed from their typical courses. Even those who would have preferred to study religion in the media with other type of material and different focus, understood the value of such cooperation. As an instructor, I also utilized some of the data that the groups collected and the observations they made. I never published on the same-sex relation debate, but the material from the classes gave me more confidence to argue that even the most widely spread newspaper that Finns often see as relatively anti-religious is actually supportive of liberal, moderate Christianity and the Lutheran church. For the paper suggested that people who are supportive of same-sex relations should not resign from the church but change it from the inside, as members. Regarding the second example, I published an article on the case, and named all of the students in the publication (although I collected more recent data and the analysis did not resemble much the analyses made by students).

There are also other ways to make use of the group work. For example, my colleague Teemu Pauha decided in his undergraduate course, "Islam, Individual and the Community," to utilize group work and case-based learning method in order to write a Finnish-language guidebook for how to encounter Muslims in health care settings. The number of participants in this class was, admittedly, high for effective group work—almost thirty students—so they operated in smaller units of four or five students, to seek information about the conceptions of health among Finnish Muslims and about how religious diversity is (or is not) dealt with in the health sector education. The end product, a forty-six-page guidebook, was written by the participants (led by Pauha) and it contains practical advice regarding such issues as medication, blood transfusion, birth-giving, terminal care, and healthcare-related gender issues. In this example, it was pretty clear that all students were able to see how much effort it would require to produce such a guidebook without cooperating as a group. Some, or perhaps most, were also proud that their contribution is in use by at least some professionals in health care.

Overall, having students work in a group is often laborious but rewarding. Personally, by cooperating (and co-authoring) I have been able to accomplish tasks that would have been very difficult if not impossible to do on my own. The tricky part is to convey this to students in their group work, rather than ending up in a situation in which students weigh their workload over their achievements.

See also: Assessments; Assignments; Grading

21

High-Impact Practices

Rita Lester

Undergraduate faculty are regularly evaluated on something that many of us are not trained in: teaching. Evidence of teaching effectiveness is a significant part of a faculty member's file for review, especially at smaller, teaching institutions (whether for reappointment as a contingent or tenure-track faculty member or for tenure and promotion). Although I remember an optional training that included how to write a syllabus and manage a classroom when I was a Teaching Assistant in graduate school, I cannot say that I was prepared to teach, let alone be evaluated on my teaching effectiveness. My instinct, as a new professor, was to teach as I had myself been taught by my own faculty mentors. I was exactly the kind of student impacted by a well-crafted lecture, but this does not describe most of my students and likely not most of yours. Those of us who become or want to become faculty were probably not like other students, even when we were undergraduates—many of us were more than likely already highly motivated by the material that we now focus on in our own careers . So if we teach, as faculty today. as we were taught, we may not be reaching the students who are not like us, which means that we are not reaching most of our students, given how many, from a wide variety of majors, may take only one of our courses to satisfy a General Education requirement.

If you hear undergraduate faculty express frustration because they feel high schools have not prepared students for college, allow me to suggest a possible, productive reframing: our graduate programs did not prepare us to teach undergraduates. If you were trained as a replacement for your graduate faculty or if you were trained to approach undergraduate teaching as if training your replacement or only training students for graduate school in your field, I recommend rethinking this assumption. Instead, our teaching should engage the widest number of students.

What do we want undergraduate students to experience before they graduate, that is, what kinds of graduates do we want? Randall Bass captures this wish list when he says that we want graduates of our schools to be self-disciplined, critical thinkers who can solve problems, advance common good, conceptualize and engage difference in non-instrumental ways, and have the capacity to take on complex problems with creativity and resiliency. Consider your own discipline-specific wish list: I want learned, disciplined graduates with a critical consciousness about such things as implicit bias and social forces, who can persist and problem solve with humility and empathy. So, how does one teach for these outcomes?

The American Association of Colleges and Universities (AACU), a flagship organization for advancing democratic purposes of higher education by promoting equity, innovation, and excellence in liberal education, surveys what skills employers' desire in employees and makes the case that teaching and learning practices that shift to doing or critical action are more likely to achieve the desired skills (compared to the traditional lecture-test model). Doing leads to better thinking. This shift to critical thinking for the purposes of critical action with public outcomes, is now often highlighted as High-Impact Practices (HIPs). So what are HIPs and why should faculty be interested in what can be the significant workload to design and deliver the public-facing deliverables of HIPs?

Currently, AACU identifies eleven HIPs, but as Ashley Finlay said at a recent workshop at Nebraska Wesleyan University (May 2022), just because a practice is currently listed does not ensure that it is utilized in a memorable or impactful way, while yet other practices might be an as of yet unrecognized high-impact practices, such as advising. That said, here is a current list of HIPs:

- Capstone courses and projects
- Undergraduate research
- Digital or e-portfolios
- Writing instructive courses
- Diversity/global learning
- Internships
- Service learning/community-based learning
- Collaborative assignments and projects
- Common intellectual experiences
- Learning communities
- First-year seminars and experiences

AAC&U sees these undergraduate learning experiences as related to life-long career and social skills. Much of the list for desirable habits in our graduates is not directly teachable because such things as critical thinking, collaborating well with others, and writing better cannot be taught by fiat, let-it-be-so-style. Instead, and you already likely do this with speaking and writing, professors design courses' assignments to cultivate these experiences of writing and speaking in a structured, guided way, giving students choices for investment and motivation. I have not worked with all of the above HIPs but I do work on a campus that emphasizes most of these, many of which are codified in degree requirements for graduation.

Capstone Courses and Projects (i.e., Senior Seminars), Undergraduate Research, and Digital or E-Portfolios make the most sense in upper-division courses. As capstone implies, whether a research paper or project, it is significant, sometimes independent, and culminating research based on student-driven inquiry. The topic and research question can be discovered through critical self-investigation of themes in a student's previous course work and explored in new writing that connects intentionality and mean-making in previous course work in the major with vocational and career next steps or goals. Both the reconsideration of previous work and the articulation of through line themes or arguments utilize the university-supported space of digital or electronic portfolios (such as the portfolios available with Canvas or in separate software such as Digication). Housing or curating materials in a digital portfolio alone is not high-impact (though it may make sense in low-division courses), but making time, space, and credit in a capstone for rethinking previous work in light of more recent learning and experiences can be. It is the opportunity for intense, interventionist advising in the broadest sense, that is, advising about research projects and life-work opportunities, not just course registration or fulfilling graduate requirements.

Projects available at my college include working with undergraduate students as co-instructors in design, delivery and assessment of a course related to the subject of their senior research project. Faculty may be the content experts, but, as Peter Felton (Director of the Engaged Learning Center at Elon University) suggests, collaboration with students updates our assignments, helps us get to know the roles that our courses and the major plays in student interpretation and application of their education, as well as allowing students to focus their research on a problem that they want to solve. Consider a recent example of how student co-instructing complements and drives a research project: a junior in my major who posits an inconsistency between upper-division theory courses and the lowest level course, asks how can a gateway course on religions from around the world incorporate critique of the World Religions Paradigm (WRP) to be consistent with upper-level religious studies? The student's senior project examines the scholarly arguments for rejecting the WRP, investigates the national trends reflected in the syllabi collection at the Wabash Center for Teaching and Learning in Theology and Religion and, employing specific suggestions from Jonathan Z. Smith on undergraduate teaching, collaborates with the professor over the course of three semesters in their junior and senior year to (re)design, pilot, and collect assessment data regarding learning goals for the class.

Writing Instructive Courses and Diversity/Global Learning are ways to use your content to make an implicit learning goal explicit. Anything one teaches can engage writing instruction in my department (Philosophy and Religion) including writing practice, peer-review and collaboration, revision and a final, polished writing product. Diversity, perhaps implied in historical, comparative, or global issues courses, can be reframed as an explicit interrogation of power and critical investigation to de-center dominant assumptions, clichés, and stereotypes. The challenge for both writing and diversity is perhaps the scaffolding appropriate to your students and their context (i.e., what do they come with, what do you want them to leave with or having tried?). For religious diversity, my approach is more of what Khyati Y. Yoshi, co-founder of the Institute for Teaching Diversity and Social Justice, calls interfaith 2.0 (1.0 being a "we are here to work together") in that my courses are a slow burn exploration of Christian-privileged stereotypes, assumptions, and essentializing "operational acts of identification" (a term borrowed from Jean-François Bayart). To be high impact, the teacher needs to know the context of their students well enough to know where, when, and how to push to engage Diversity/Global Learning in the most meaningful and memorable ways, starting where your students start.

What Internships, Collaborative Assignments and Projects, Common Intellectual Experiences, and Learning Communities have in common is working with others to cultivate and motivate learning within communities, from smaller work groups for collaborative assignments, to campus-wide common intellectual experiences, to off-campus internships. Working with others is the point. Internships are a guided chance to find the intersection of one's interests, strengths, and needs in the world. Even an internship after which a student decides that is not a work option that they want to pursue is successful. Collaborative projects, like a productive meeting, means that everyone leaves with something that they didn't expect. Most of my work and life are collaborative, yet as an undergraduate I loathed what I considered to be group work! I think part of why some students dislike collaborative work is due to non-nuanced grading, that is, where one score is assigned to the whole group. Consider scaffolding team and individually submitted work that includes collaborator self-review/feedback of others' contributions to capture more dimensions for scoring collaborative assignments and projects. For example, for a collaborative project there can be team proposal, individual annotated research bibliography, individual research notebook/journal, team workplans, individual peer feedback, individual structured reflections and team project drafts.

The last two HIPs are community building on campus, such as a campus presentation all students attend and then discuss in smaller groups or a shared first-year (or summer before first-year) reading. My school, located in Lincoln, Nebraska, also has a first-year Lend-A-Hand-To-Lincoln initiative, taking place before regular classes start so that the first-year seminar students, student peer and co-instructors, and faculty can all work together on a non-academic project to help in the local community or on campus. Maybe the other thing these HIPs have in common is that they are ripe for what Susan Blum and Jesse Stommel call ungrading, self-grading in consultation with faculty/supervisor conversations, or the old-fashioned pass/fail, what medical schools call two-interval grading, where there is a defined threshold of achieving the established learning objectives. Most of the things that I do are more like pass/fail than traditional grading of A, B, C, D, F in that when I myself do not achieve a desired threshold of success, I am self-motivated to try again to keep learning until good enough (baking bread, riding a bike, training a dog, etc.).

First-year seminars and experiences anchor the in-coming students with direct contact with a faculty member, other first-year students, and at many universities, a fellow (upper-level) student peer-assistant or student co-instructor as a peer mentor. First-year seminars (or other campus-wide structured experiences for incoming students), along with benefiting student recruitment and retention, offer a kind of homeroom community in which students can have an on ramp to navigating college processes, resources, and habits at a point of need, practicing the skills that will help them succeed in a university setting. For the professor, the first-year seminar (for which some faculty can volunteer to teach, as part of their regular duties or in addition to them) is a rich teaching and learning lab as well as a valuable service to the institution. It is not for the faint-hearted or risk-adverse but it teaches the teacher that less is more, the best way to control is to control less, and that students will teach you a lot about students if you let them. What I have learned about teaching and learning in the first-year seminar directly informs and revitalizes my other courses.

As philosophy professor Geoff Pfeifer at Worcester Polytechnic Institute says about Project-Based Learning, professors might be better served to (re)imagine their role as less as teachers and more cognitive coaches, facilitators of learning, or project managers of learning experiences. Because tenure and promotion often utilize standardized course evaluations which do not capture the role of the professor as cognitive coach who lets go of much of the classroom and content control in HIPs, I think individual faculty, especially if contingent or untenured, should have a conversation with their Chair, Provost or Academic Officer, and the faculty evaluation body at your school about expectations for tenure and promotion and the rewards and risks of HIPs in their teaching but high-risk can be high-reward, for professors and students.

See also: Assignments; Experiential Learning; Senior Seminar; Student Evaluations of Instruction; Undergraduate Research

22

Honors

K. Merinda Simmons

As with many other elements of undergraduate teaching (like "writing," for example), "honors" is something that has both colloquial and institutional connotations. Colloquially, the category hovers amorphously as a designation conferred upon high-achieving students who maintain a certain grade point average or prove themselves academically exceptional. Even more broadly, it serves to some as a general badge of being smart. Institutionally, however, the meaning and function of "honors" is very specific to the college or university applying it to the curricular makeup of a degree program. Despite its "s," it sometimes functions more as a singular noun than a plural one, but it carries a host of different possibilities and applications. A significant part of early-career teaching is the process of becoming versed in institutional idiosyncrasies and attending to those structural concerns while crafting one's own pedagogy. The honors classroom is one site of such work.

Whither and wherefore does honors exist as a specific designation or site in the first place? What kind of entity is it (whether the designation itself or, perhaps, a unit on campus, such as an Honors Program or Honors College), and who are its stakeholders? For that matter, what are its stakes? The Venn diagram of possible responses to these questions has its share of overlapping circles, but every college or university crafts its own particular answer to suit its unique purposes. No one would blame an early-career faculty member for assuming that the aims of an honors program are strictly pedagogical. Despite the massive changes in higher education over the last fifty-plus years, there remains a romantic image of the academy—one that provides a home to, among other things, idealistic characterizations of honors programs and honors students. That image depicts students as entrepreneurs in the intellectual marketplace, eager to acquire a wide breadth of knowledge solely for the sake of self-betterment as they prepare to be citizens of the world.

Maybe, in some instances, the curricular and programmatic structures in place do strive to prioritize the learning experiences of those entrepreneurial students. Regardless, one would do well to take a closer look at the marketplace itself. Even in the contexts of small liberal arts colleges, where teaching may receive more direct resources or focus, administrators generally decide what learning experiences are necessary (thus being required for a degree program), valuable (thus counting for credit, maybe as an elective), and unnecessary in a degree program. To extend the marketplace metaphor, they control the products that are bought and sold, and they determine what counts as capital in the first place (as well as its worth). So in some contexts, at certain institutions or in certain programs, a strong emphasis on teaching might result in a common set of learning objectives or specific components on syllabi for all honors classes among various departments offering such courses. Perhaps all honors courses have a research or writing requirement, and so on. In other settings, an honors program might control and teach all its content in-house, creating its own courses that satisfy the full honors curriculum. And in yet other scenarios, the meaning of honors is less about the makeup of a course or program and more about an institutional selling point. Certainly, the term and designation mean something different to the students who enroll, the parents who pay tuition, the faculty who teach, and the administrators who oversee various units across a campus. Regardless, the marketing value of an honors program is very much at play in the choices made about what that program should look like and how it should run.

At a big state-funded school like the one where I work, there is an entire undergraduate Honors College unto itself that plays a strong role in recruiting students—among them, out-of-state students. Within the colossus of a student body that is upwards of forty thousand, honors classes boast small numbers and personal attention from professors. The Honors College implicitly suggests the ability to let students "have it all": a robust community of Greek clubs and exciting football games, along with small seminars in an academically rigorous liberal arts program, all nestled within an R1 research university. It has its own application process for students as well, using criteria like certain test scores or an application essay and a specific high school GPA. As a College (a particular designation all its own), it has its own Dean, registrar, programming and recruitment staff, and teaching faculty. What's more, outside its general University Honors Program, it offers a variety of specific experiences in coordination with other Colleges: an interdisciplinary living/learning community and a pre-med institute within the College of Arts and Sciences, its own computer-based honors program, STEM and creative programs within the College of Business, and tracks within the College of Engineering and the College of Education. What does any of that have to do with an undergraduate religious studies class? Well, various courses taught within departments can receive an Honors (H) designation, allowing them to count toward the total number of credit hours required by the Honors College of its students (thereby bringing honors students into a department's orbit, if only to help satisfy their honors program's requirements). So, as with other course designations, like Writing, there are elements to which faculty of any discipline—religious studies included—must attend. And it helps to know whether those elements are determined by administrators, departments, or the teachers themselves.

Since the Honors College at my institution does not set a universal curriculum in its own right, departments and their faculty can more or less shape honors classes to suit their purposes. So, just as honors is not a universal category across college and university campuses, neither is it always the same across departments on the same campus. In the religious studies department here, our H-designated course is REL 105: Honors Introduction to Religious Studies. The class is, to be sure, far smaller and more discussion-based than our large-enrollment REL 100, which seats over a hundred students. Outside of that practical distinction, however, the honors sections are not so very different from the regular Introduction. This is because the focus in REL 100 for myself and many of my colleagues is on critical thinking skills that students can apply broadly to a number of different examples and data sets. I emphasize those same skills in the honors course, asking students to get curious about their own behavior, the labels they use to organize society, and the myriad ways something called religion functions for people.

Tackling those kinds of questions and topics in an honors setting, therefore, does not look like giving them more pages to read or more facts to memorize. More productive, it seems to me, is approaching the honors class as an opportunity to spend extra time inviting and listening to students grapple with those broader issues and applications in real time. The smaller class size (twenty or so) makes certain things possible, like essays, open-ended test questions, presentations, and so on, but those assignments are not so much the point. They can certainly be helpful in getting students to demonstrate and explain their thought processes with a bit more depth, of course. The implicit process along the way, however, is that of engaging with students more individually or directly. That sometimes translates into recruiting majors—the honors program is not a major and so students still need to find majors and minors in the usual disciplines—but it always at the very least sees them leaving the religious studies classroom with a new way of approaching the rest of their studies.

Like many other departments, within the religious studies major itself we have invented our own honors process for students in their junior and senior years, something quite apart from those students admitted to the campus's Honors College. It entails working with a faculty advisor (by way of an independent study course titled "Honors Research") to turn a seminar paper into a full article-length essay. Each student who does so then presents their work before faculty and peers. The process is not affiliated with the Honors College—it's just a great chance for our majors to expand their research, gain some formal presentation experience, and build an even stronger sense of community within the department.

In other words, "honors" does not necessarily signify something content-specific. Of course, this approach represents a perspective shaped by working at a large flagship state university with the kinds of dynamics described earlier. Whatever the setting, however, one would be wise to consider "honors"—whether as a program unto itself, a course designation, a specific curricular track, a recruitment strategy, a bit of transcript filigree, all of the above, or something else entirely—in the broader context of an institution's particular demands and priorities. Doing so helps to identify one's own strategy in relation to honors students across the spectrum.

See also: Critical Thinking; Curriculum; Introduction v. Survey; Writing

23

Introduction vs. Survey

Vaia Touna

A primary concern when it comes to teaching any course is what to include and what to leave out. Even more so when it comes to teaching an introductory course, regardless the field or the discipline that we happen to teach from, because there are so many things that we think are important for our students to know and to learn. As a result, introductory courses tend to be modeled around a survey method whereby the focus is on description, in covering a huge amount of information with little detail in order to expose students to as much material as possible, whether it's historical periods, important names, traditions, etc. that are considered foundational to a field or discipline (think here, for example, of the classic survey of English literature in which so many undergraduate students enroll, covering everything from *Beowulf* in the early eighth century to Margaret Atwood). This particular model, though, has been debated for quite a while now, not only within Religious Studies but across the Humanities in general. For although there is something useful about a survey model, as I will explain later, I will mostly focus instead on an alternative way of teaching the introductory course that I have used for my classes, which is modelled around a more critical, or theoretical approach, if you will, rather than a purely descriptive method that's largely concerned with coverage.

There are some practical things that need to be taken into consideration in the planning of a lower-level course that, for many of its students, is the first exposure to a subject or a discipline. In North America, for example, universities follow a liberal education system whereby students, although they may choose a specific study area in which they specialize (known as their major), are required to take a number of mandatory courses from across fields and disciplines known as "the core" or "the general education curriculum," doing so in order to meet the degree requirements of their program. This is quite different than, for example, a more specialized education that is common in

European universities, certainly in the Greek higher education system in which I was trained early on, where all of the credit hours of a four-year degree will be in a specific study area, be it Theology, History, Law, Psychology, etc. That means that in the North American system, and more specifically in the U.S. where I happen to teach, especially in small departments like Religious Studies (meaning that there is usually a small number of students that will choose it as their major), the students who will enroll in any given course will *not* be primarily Religious Studies majors. Instead, they will be enrolling in a small number of lower-level courses outside their specialty in order to satisfy their school's so-called core requirements, so as to broaden their undergraduate education, as it is usually argued. Furthermore, there is a huge possibility that many of these students will only take one course in Religious Studies through their undergraduate years, and that course more than likely would be the intro course.

So, unlike higher education in European universities, where a field/discipline, at least in most situations, has the luxury to build their curriculum in an eight-semester span, knowing that their students will move gradually through the program, that is not the case in most higher education departments in North America. Surely, there are intro courses and upper-level seminars that are meant to do different things in U.S. colleges, but the student population and thus dynamic, as I described already, in any given class is usually quite mixed, consisting both of students within the major but also of students whose major, in many situations, lies well outside even of the Humanities. So, there may be students attending the course whose major is in Engineering, or Nursing, or Business, etc. Another important issue that I think we need to take into consideration when we are planning these courses, given the current job market, is the increasingly relevant concern of what someone can *do* with an undergraduate Humanities degree. Those of us who work within these fields may think of our object of study as self-evidently important and therefore assume that this enduring value ought to be enough for someone to enroll in our courses and get a degree in this or that field. The problem, though, with such a mentality is that we fail or give too little attention to incorporating into our syllabi ways to help our students translate the many skills and tools that they are acquiring by taking a course in the Humanities (or even earning a Humanities degree), in order to use them in any career path that they may choose to follow. In fact, these skills may actually make them quite competitive in the job market, as I usually stress at the first day of my intro course.

Therefore, in planning all of my courses, especially the intro course, I do take those things into account. In other words, I feel that I have an obligation to make my course worthwhile to all of my students, regardless of its particular disciplinary content. The hope is that they will take away something that they will be able to use well beyond our class, that is, those transferable skills that

I attach to the goals and objectives of the course. I have in mind skills like communication, critical thinking (i.e., the ability to analyze, interpret, and explain), problem solving, along with reading and writing, of course. At the same time, given that the intro course is in many situations the first course that students will have the opportunity to expose themselves to the academic study of religion (or any field for that matter)—a field that is usually quite different from what they expect it to be—it can also be a great opportunity to attract majors.

Taking all these into consideration, then, the question is: which of the so many things that we want to teach to our students should we eventually choose to include in our syllabus? Jonathan Z. Smith, a well-known and influential scholar of religion, in a lecture that he gave entitled "The Introductory Course: Less is Better" (included as the Afterword to this volume), said that "*there is nothing that must be taught*, there is nothing that cannot be left out," which is a phrase that has deeply influenced my thinking and my approach to teaching. In many ways it has also freed me from the pressure of what I "must" teach, especially in my introductory course, which, in agreement with Smith, I find to be both the most important and at the same time the most challenging course in any field or discipline. Of course, as with any course there are many possibilities on what and how one chooses to teach but one of the dominant debates, at least within Religious Studies, is whether (as discussed in my opening) the introductory course should be a survey, for example of world religions (as many students assume when they enroll in the intro class), or should it be a course with a more critical edge to it, dedicated to initiating students to theoretical issues like, for example, definition and classification. I do take seriously Smith's observation that an introduction is an initiation, bringing a newcomer into the field, as it were. Undoubtedly, there are good reasons for why anyone might choose between these two options, but it all comes down to what the professor wants such a course to do for them and their students.

My intro course as I teach it is therefore an initiation to and about the study of religion, but students soon understand that it is also about being curious as to *how* and *why* people use names and designations, how they define and classify things, asking what do those definitions and classifications allow them to do in the world, and so the examples that we end up discussing in class are not only related to religion (however one defines it). The goal, through this variety of examples, is that students will understand that definition and classification are tools that people use, which can help students to understand not only how both work in relation to religion but also how to see them functioning in other situations. They therefore understand that knowledge and its application is not isolated; by looking at how, for example, classifying something *as* religion works, students come to realize that we are studying how people organize their worlds, and then it is easy for them to start making connections with the class material by bringing to class their own examples of how classification works.

An intro course doesn't mean that it lacks survey elements, that is, descriptive, historical information or foundational concepts, and key scholars, but they all function for the purpose of a more general objective which is none other than helping students to develop a more critical thinking approach. Here I take "critical," in the Greek etymological sense of the word, as I learned from my supervisor Willi Braun, that is, the will to distinguish and decide (κρίνειν) between opinions, on the basis of reasons (κριτήρια) that are themselves the result of a critical (κριτική) process. And this is the basis upon which my intro course is structured.

In other words, creating but then also teaching such an intro course is about choice: realistically speaking I *can't* teach them everything, but I *can* teach students a model for how to read critically and how to write argumentatively and persuasively, and how to engage in analysis and interpretation. So, even in my large enrollment classes I try to incorporate elements that will allow my students to train in those very skills. For example, I have used weekly discussion assignments which are based on short readings that we read together, and then students discuss in groups (allowing them to engage in analysis and interpretations as well as communication, even in large classes). I used open book exams to allow my students (as I tell them) to demonstrate in their answers not only *what* they have learned in the course but also their ability *to use* and *to synthesize* that knowledge to make convincing arguments of their own.

Even the descriptive elements that I choose to include in my syllabus serve as examples both to discuss a broader issue in the study of human phenomena, for example, how definition and classification work; but also, to train them in some practical skill like for example to practice problem solving. The gain of such an approach is that it can make the Intro to Religious Studies a course of relevance to students from a variety of majors, regardless their reason for enrolling, because it is *not* about prioritizing memorization of "important" facts but, rather, it emphasizes the mastery of *tools* and *skills* that can be transferred both to other classes but also to any career path they choose to follow after their graduation. In the end, as Smith wrote, "our task . . . is not to introduce or teach our field for its own sake, but to use our field in the service of the broader and more fundamental enterprise of liberal learning" (2018: 18).

What I have found in approaching the intro with this more theoretical or critical twist is that students come to appreciate that it helps them "think," as they usually write in the course evaluations (which I take to mean that it makes them ask different questions, helps them have a more critical approach to things, because it complicates for them taken-for-granted ideas and opens up for them the possibility of new ideas). The last time that I taught the intro course, in the fall of 2022, I had a student (a Business major) who, at end of the last class, came up to me to tell me that he found the course very interesting, so much so that, although it was not what he thought it would be (meaning, it was not a survey of world religions), he decided to enroll in another Religious Studies course (not mine); as he went on to say: "I feel I have a better background on how to study religion and at the same time I liked how this course made me think." In the end, initiating them to a new field by opening for my students an appetite for more, while helping them think, is a good enough accomplishment for an intro course.

See also: Assessment; Critical Thinking; Examples; Large Lectures; Recruiting Majors; Syllabi; Transferable Skills

24

Large Lectures

Steven Ramey

Large lecture classes present challenges for a variety of the pedagogical emphases that many who teach in the humanities consider imperative. Those challenges, though, are not insurmountable, and large lectures can become a strategic site to address the contemporary dynamics of the humanities in current university structures, depending on the specific institution. In decisions about the viability of a program and the allocation of resources, including new faculty lines, two common measures that administrators consider are credit hour production and the number of majors enrolled or graduated. Obviously, the large lecture can enhance a department's credit hour production, if 50, 75, 100 or more students enroll in one section.

That can come at a cost, however, if it siphons off students from other sections. Having one professor teach one hundred in one class also becomes an easy way to reduce faculty, instead of employing instructors to teach those 100 students in four separate sections, enrolling 25 each, which requires more faculty. Thus, for the interests of a department and its faculty, increasing offerings of large lectures has to proceed carefully, where sufficient demand from students exists (either out of necessity if the institution is pressed to seat all incoming students or because a course is especially popular) that make an increase of overall department enrollment possible. However, in some circumstances, offering a large lecture can take some of the administrative pressure off of smaller classes. For, depending on the administration, some less well enrolled classes might then be given a pass if the overall credit hour production of the unit is strong or increasing.

From a multi-year perspective, rather than a single semester view, offering large lectures has the potential to influence the number of students enrolling in other, subsequent courses and also the number of majors. In my experience at public institutions, few students come planning to major in Religious Studies. Thus, an introductory course (sometimes termed a gateway course) becomes a primary avenue for recruiting a student to take another course, and then another, and then, maybe, declare a minor, and finally upgrade to a major. Having increased capacity to enroll more students in a gateway or introductory course (especially at an institution where such courses are one of many options in a General Education curriculum and not a stand-alone requirement) gives you an opportunity to meet more students and possibly to encourage some to pursue other courses in Religious Studies. Of course, the opposite is also true: it risks turning away potential majors if they experience the course as a boring and passive large lecture course.

Therefore, if a large lecture is a useful option given a department's context, teaching it well becomes especially vital, and that requires intentional planning. Assigning this task to someone with limited classroom experience is often a bad choice, whether that person is a grad student, an adjunct, or an early career scholar. For many people, the experience gained from teaching a smaller version of the course a few times makes the transition to a large lecture considerably easier and more successful. Overall, though, the large lecture is best when assigned to the best instructors, both in terms of their passion for the course and their pedagogical expertise. Viewing the large lecture as an unfortunate assignment to be foisted on those with less seniority institutionally (and thus less classroom experience) sets it up for failure long term.

The large lecture obviously requires adjustments as compared to smaller classes. Naturally, long essay tests and final papers become unmanageable to grade effectively, and individual student presentations are not feasible with 100 (or more) students, especially considering the anxiety that speaking before a larger group generates for some students. Pair and share discussion assignments (involving discussion partners sharing with the larger class) also become impractical, and many large venues, with unmovable chairs, make group work harder. Thus, the challenge is finding ways to make the class sessions and assignments pedagogically productive and engaging while also being feasible for an instructor working with a large number of students. Despite these challenges, the large lecture classroom does not have to be a purely one-way presentation of information and multiple-choice tests.

Contextual dynamics become one element in figuring out the possibilities. If your institution has graduate students, having a teaching assistant opens up greater possibilities for course management and grading. If your institution is only undergraduate, recruiting a major to help in the large lecture, perhaps as a paid assistant (if the department has access to such resources) and/or an intern receiving course credit via an independent study course (providing a useful CV line, depending on their long-term interests and goals), is one type of solution. Whether a grad student or an undergraduate, consideration of what they are prepared to or even able to contribute and what workload is appropriate become factors in these decisions about course design, certainly.

Over the years I have employed a variety of strategies to make the large lecture class educationally productive (given that my own department values the role that such courses play in the life of the unit). Rather than straight lecture, incorporating group discussion is vital. Sometimes I have broken the class into groups of five or six to discuss a question and then even write a paragraph as a group, all related to a question that applies elements discussed in that class session. At other times, I have used large group discussion, which requires both patience for the lecturer to wait for a response and courage from the students. Typically, the percentage who actually raise their hand and respond is not the same as it would be in a 25-student classroom, to be sure, but some will respond, and others will be thinking about the question, even if they are unwilling to answer themselves. (I intentionally choose not to call on people who do not volunteer in that large of a classroom.)

The discussion periods, whether in small groups or the class as a whole, provide a benefit by also breaking up the monotony of listening to one person lecture. Strategically organizing each class session to have segments featuring different pedagogical forms is important (even in smaller classes). Researchers debate the relevant attention span of contemporary students in lectures, but I find it useful to break each class session into shorter sections (whether students fully realize this pattern or not). In a regular class session, I play music or a video before class that is related to the topic of the day (e.g., Vedic chanting or Sufi qawwali), and then start class with a discussion building on the clip or its context and relevance, doing so in a way that leads into the material that we are addressing that day. After such a segment, which may be three minutes or twelve (I do not stress too much over the length of a segment), I shift to class announcements and general questions. In this approach, I follow the advice to use the start of the class for important information that you want students to understand, as their attention is generally greater at that point. While announcements are important, they involve a different level of attention and also provide a natural shift in class time. After the announcements, I move to the next segment of the day's plan.

In addition, I generally have at least one video clip in every class, which also serves to break the lecture into sections, and I usually invite discussion of the clip from students. This discussion includes questions and observations, but typically shifts to an analysis of the representation in the video. What choices did the speakers and the videographer make? How could this same topic be presented differently? Asking consistent questions such as these helps students to know what to expect in discussions and helps them to develop the critical analysis skills that we often emphasize as important educational outcomes—even in the large lecture courses. In fact, that has become one of the main objectives in my regularly taught large Religions of the World course:

to analyze critically representations of each religion, rather than accepting any representation as the complete or authoritative image.

Success in inviting discussion involves a number of factors. On the first day of class, I attempt to set the tone for the semester, using video clips from a music video depicting India and a clip from an Indiana Jones film, to talk about exoticization of various cultures; but in the presentation of these videos, I invite students to talk about what they see. Easy, open-ended questions set the tone for a constructive discussion, as opposed to quiz-like questions that students might fear getting wrong. An advisor at UNC Chapel Hill (where I completed my PhD) once recommended simply showing an image (such as a home shrine in India) and then asking students what they see in it. This encourages their active participation, not only speaking in class but also actively observing the photo rather than seeing it as fluff that won't be on the test. Doing things like that from the first day sets an expectation for the class as a whole, which is especially important due to the assumption students may have that a large enrollment class will be passive learning only. Again, not everyone will participate in this, but the success of the large lecture builds on the dozen or so students who will regularly answer discussion questions (plus others occasionally), which keeps the class progressing without being a one-way presentation.

Assignments are also tricky. Short essays can be very effective in requiring a bit more analysis than a multiple-choice question. Because having students write things in their own words is pedagogically useful, I have used in-class writing assignments, where students compose a paragraph that answers a prompt building on an issue from that class session. When collected, I have at times simply given credit for attendance to anyone who submitted such an assignment. This functioned to encourage attendance, which is an issue in large enrollment classes, and especially challenging in the midst of a pandemic. After all, the pedagogical purpose was not to correct their reflection but to get students to attempt to put things into their own words. While extensive feedback on all student writing is ideal, getting them to write an answer and receive credit for the effort is better than simply relying on a multiple-choice exam, and such grading techniques become one method to manage the larger enrollment.

In a related fashion, with an assistant, grading a paragraph essay on a test is manageable, especially if one person is grading perhaps 75 essays, not 200. I usually give the question to students ahead of time, as the objective is getting them to think about the issues and develop ideas, rather than catching students unprepared with a surprise question (these are not so-called pop quizzes, after all). If students meet and discuss the question, that is even better. Strategizing together can enhance engagement and learning.

Group presentations can also work, but I recommend that they be presented with only the members of the group present, rather than before the whole class. Thus, it is a challenge to schedule. With two TAs and 150 students,

I have routinely arranged for each group to meet with either myself or a TA to do their presentation, thus requiring three separate locations. It is also a challenge to stay on schedule for these group presentations, and any schedule must include time for a group's members to leave and the next to enter and get started (something I learned from experience). Thus, I also prohibited them from using PowerPoint for these presentations (due to locations and timing) and also had strict limits on the length of a presentation. During the pandemic, I shifted this to an individual essay, up to 750 words. Either of these approaches has challenges to manage the grading, but a set of 750-word essays have not proven to be too onerous for one person to grade 50 or 75 of these and to return them to students in a reasonable period of time. Five-minute audio or video presentations can also work (given the ease of recording and editing on phones), though sometimes accessing a format that a student submits has added a level of challenge. Having groups of three submit a five-minute video presentation would also be a way to balance group work, presentation experience, and grading.

One of the significant challenges of large classes is dealing with absences. I generally record my lectures and make them available to students via university-supported tools like Blackboard, noting for students that the recording is seldom as reliable as being physically present. Doing that, and not taking attendance, has meant some students seldom come to class, which diminishes their learning. In the context of a pandemic, however, that seemed to be the less problematic approach of the potential strategies. The in-class writing assignment was an earlier strategy to encourage class attendance (happening in about one out of every two or three class sessions). Online quizzes due before class, on reading and class material, also served as an accountability measure. However, these activities lead to the question of making up missed work, whether excused or not. My policy, which is far from perfect, has been to refuse make-ups on quizzes and in class assignments. Instead, I add extra points into the course (as much as 5% of the total points possible) as bonus points for those who do not miss and make up opportunities for those who do miss, whatever the reason. Someone with a significant, extended excused absence may require a different accommodation.

No grading policy or class structure will be perfect, especially considering the variety of learning styles, skills, and situations for our students. The large enrollment course, though, can address some of these variations in ways that both encourage higher orders of engagement while maintaining a manageable class—if such an enrollment strategy is beneficial in the larger university context.

See also: Accommodations; Assessment; Attendance; Grading; Learning Management Systems; Teaching Assistants

25

Learning Management Systems (LMS)

Russell T. McCutcheon

In a setting where decreasing government funding has led to more and more of higher education's costs either being cut or shifted to students and their families (via tuition and fees, at least in those national setting where they are charged), the inevitable implication is that cost-conscious administrators have opted to do whatever they could to manage campus expenses to recruit, educate, and credential students. While one of those by now well-documented measures has been to increasingly hire instructors who are off the tenure-track (and who are therefore paid considerably less and cost an institution far less in terms of their benefits) another has been to increase enrollment and class sizes, whether in-person or taught online in what can sometimes be rather large classes taught by a small number of (often contract or grad student) instructors. Though large lectures often come with the additional costs of graduate teaching assistants (who may receive a tuition waiver and/or stipend and benefits for their work), assigned to assist with the course (such as assisting with the grading or offering weekly discussion/tutorial sections that run in tandem with the lectures), their compensation is nowhere near to what it would cost the school to hire more tenure-track faculty to teach additional but smaller sections of the course so as to prevent the need for 300 or 400 (or larger) seat large lectures. The point? Courses with very large enrollments, though certainly hurting a school's student–faculty ratio (something that adversely impacts the rankings that many universities now chase in their efforts to recruit students), can be understood by the senior admin to make financial sense. It is from out of this context—i.e., decreasing financial support for a school and then increasing class sizes (and even increasing teaching duties for some instructors, who may teach four or even five different courses [or preps, i.e., preparations] per semester)—that third party vendors have developed, and then sold to universities, a set of password-protected software tools that are now collectively known as a learning management system (LMS), which can either be hosted locally by the school or on the vendor's own site. Though each goes by its own branded names (e.g., Blackboard, Canvas, and Moodle are currently the most popular), with different campuses contracting these services from different companies, they all generally collect together and provide a variety of tools and resources commonly used in running either a distance education course or an in-person lecture. A subset of what are often known as content management systems (CMS)—which includes an instructor opting on their own to associate something like a WordPress or Slack site with their course—an LMS is accessible to students and instructors alike, whether via a desktop and laptop or a mobile device (instructors have greater access, of course, and thus an ability to create and post content as well as edit a variety of settings); they include everything from grade books, syllabi, and daily readings (posted either as html or PDFs or as links to items posted elsewhere online) to embedded video content, a variety of testing instruments (i.e., short and long answer, multiple choice, fill in the blank, etc.), and even automated grading and discussion boards where students can post and comment on each other's writings which, in many cases, are in reply to prompts posted by the Instructor that can then be graded. In some cases, these tools then interact with a campus's own computing system, such as final grades being posted directly from a course's LMS to the university's own system.

The role that universities enhancing their prior distance learning courses via remote technology (sometimes collectively known as e-learning now—the move to online distance ed is a significant shift from just twenty or so years ago when mailing a textbook and hardcopy question packet often constituted a typical distance course at a university) played in the eventual widespread application of a LMS across campus is clear, as has been the challenge of a single instructor managing large in-person lecture classes, where it would take much if not all of the class's scheduled meeting time just to return individual assignments to all students in attendance that day. No doubt, using technology to centralize much of the work of managing a large class has been a key strategy in helping many students enrolled in such courses to be successful. And we would be remiss not to mention these online tools' crucial assistance, even for those faculty members who were critical of them, when hastily devised COVID-19 protocols back in spring 2020 forced in-person classes to move abruptly to a completely remote status. But despite the admittedly helpful role LMSs played in such circumstances, some faculty nonetheless remain critical of this development, inasmuch as it is seen as a symptom of recent and far wider, structural changes in higher education—changes that, at least in the view of such faculty, hamper the educational experience, e.g., large lectures where it is far more difficult, if not impossible, to focus on certain aspects of the class that faculty may deem as important, such as working on extended research and writing assignments, and in which conveying so-called content, as opposed to, let's say, a style of reasoning or skills in problem solving, has become dominant (i.e., course material that must be managed so as to be effectively delivered to students). Thus, the importance of the ease that an LMS introduces into the tasks of running such a class could be said to mask larger challenges in current higher education that deserve attention.

But, at least when judged from the point of view of a typical faculty member asked to teach a large number of mid-sized courses, let alone one or maybe more large lecture classes, each semester (i.e., classes with an enrollment of between 75 and, say, 400), the variety of centralized and integrated tools offered by an LMS will surely come in handy, especially if the faculty member can select and use just those services that strike them as helpful, given whatever their course's requirements and goals may be. For instance, even utilizing just the grade book feature allows a faculty member to ensure that all students know their current standing in the class, inasmuch as students see the graded results of just their work for each assignment that they've submitted, eliminating surprises at the end of the class (provided that students login to view it, that is—and, we should add, also know how to tabulate their current standing in the class [something that requires a level of basic math aptitude that, surprisingly perhaps, may be, as in may be beyond the capabilities of some students]). And, should such an instructor wish to offer, let's say, some sort of testing *outside of class time*, then their students will be able to complete the work with a variety of restrictions established by the faculty member (e.g., each question appears on the screen for a specific amount of time that discourages rummaging through books for assistance). Although a variety of more strenuous measures are also possible (e.g., cameras that monitor where a remote student is looking while they take an online test on their computer or so-called lockdown browsers that prevent students from using the computer during a test to go elsewhere on the internet), some faculty will just acknowledge the limitations of this medium and allow for the sort of open book tests that we've long seen as a viable option in many university classes. (If you think of it, even doctoral comprehensive exams are now open book tests now, once they made the switch from being an in-person piece of writing by hand that took place within two to three hours to a take-home assignment completed on a laptop and submitted within 24 hours.)

And so, hearkening back to the early mass media scholar Marshall McLuhan's once famous phrase, "the medium is the message," it is difficult to offer suggestions for how best to employ an LMS in various settings when the very existence of this medium normalizes a number of prior conditions on a university campus that have led to the need for such tools, i.e., situations in which many faculty may focus on the retention of so-called facts and may never even learn the names of the students enrolled in large sections or interact with them in class on a one-on-one basis. Much like assessment initiatives over the past two decades, where the issue has been how an instructor can know if they're getting through to a student who is one of several hundred enrolled in a large lecture (a setting where it may even be impossible just to take attendance, should the professor be inclined to do so, without an electronic system responding to student input from their smart phone), the appearance of a LMS on a university campus is evidence of specific moment in late modernity and a specific phase in the history of higher education. While this observation is not meant to naively wax nostalgic for small liberal arts colleges or the sort of undergraduate seminars that some schools can just no longer afford to offer (except when subsidized by the work of inexpensive contingent labor), it is meant to invite instructors to consider the larger structural issues that the presence of an LMS signifies and the type of class/learning that their use presupposes—considerations that may assist the faculty member to decide how their time and energy is best used if seeking to be an effective teacher but also an invested member of a larger community with whatever degree of shared governance that may exist. For, not unlike student evaluations of teaching, there may exist faculty committees that provide input to the chair or the more senior administration on not just the choice of LMS used on a campus but also the situations in which such tools are seen as necessary—input that may assist others on the campus who are undoubtedly also working to be successful in what are sometimes trying conditions.

But thinking more locally, the LMS can indeed provide the basis to allocate specific classroom tasks to teaching assistants (if any are assigned to the instructor) or the freedom for a busy faculty member to automate some aspects of the class (such as grading a true/false quiz). The potential time-savings aspects of these centralized tools is not to be minimized, of course, but the cost of instrumentalizing education in this manner involves faculty and students alike, at least at certain colleges, largely interacting with each other through a digitally-mediated interface (i.e., discussion boards). While this may be a necessary cost in a remote course—and, to be sure, distance education has played a long and crucial role in the history of higher education—having such media underwrite sometimes increasingly large in-person lectures may be a cost worth rethinking. For now a variety of other strategies must also be devised and deployed to engage and retain those students who understandably may react poorly to the somewhat impersonal natural of such classrooms.[1]

See also: Assessment; Attendance; Honors; Large Lectures; Online/Remote Courses; Student Evaluations of Teaching; Undergraduate Research; Writing

---

[1]My thanks to my colleague Nathan Loewen for very helpful suggestions on an earlier version of this entry.

26

Library Resources

Emily D. Crews

Early in the first semester when I was an instructor at the University of Alabama, I set aside a day to take each of my three Introduction to the Study of Religion classes on a tour of the university library. We walked out of our classroom and across the street to the Amelia Gorgas Library, where we gathered in an unruly mass in the front lobby, until the reference librarian assigned to our Department came to fetch us. After a session in their computer lab, where the librarian showed students how to navigate the library's collection and various research databases, we went into the basement to walk through the stacks. I gave each student a random call number that corresponded to a book in the Religious Studies section and asked them to find it, check it out, and take it home to peruse. They were to bring it to the next class session, where they would share some facts or ideas they had gathered from skimming it. I would in turn use the data from their searches—what topics they thought would be included within Religious Studies, how they would categorize the books' subject matter, what sorts of assumptions or expectations were supported or fractured by the experience—as the foundation for a first pass at a conversation about the task of classification and its role in the history of the field.

Now, it's time for a confession: I didn't undertake this project out of a love of university libraries or a conviction that knowledge of their inner workings is essential for students' intellectual growth. Instead, the project was a sort of desperate attempt on the part of a new instructor, used to the pace and brevity of the quarter system, to fill what felt like endless weeks of a semester-long course. It was also an experiment in how I might use the resources around me to illustrate the central claims of the Intro course (with, I'll admit, the useful byproduct of helping me to learn my way around a new campus and community). I had no grand expectations for the exercise, and was happy when, at the end of the tour, none of the students had snuck out early or seemed deathly bored.

When I polled students about the experience in the next class session, many of them offered responses that dramatic articles in *The Chronicle of Higher Ed* or other such publications had told me might be the case: that they had never checked out a book while they had been at college; that most of them had never been into the stacks; that very few had spent time in the library at all aside from occasional group study sessions. Hardly any did research with search engines that were not Google, and virtually none knew how the books in the basement were arranged. These bright, talented Honors College students did not have much use for the library, they told me, when the internet made everything immediately available in the palm of their hands.

This is the point at which one might expect this author, a lifelong book nerd who got her own library card at three years old and her PhD., well, some years later, to bemoan the state of the world and "kids these days." Indeed, the debate about the role of libraries in contemporary societies is a live one, within and beyond the university and students' comments about our library visit were representative of a larger moment in higher education. Questions about the potential obsolescence of print culture; the viability of in-person, hands-on research; and the corporatization of university education are all on the minds of many of us who read, write, research, and teach for a living.

Still, what I discovered on our library tour was not that students didn't care about learning or that they were doomed to live a life of endless scrolling. Instead, many of them simply hadn't been given a compelling reason to try or value something else. This is not to say that they had not had wonderful, talented teachers or that the university had failed them; instead, it was that few had explicitly articulated the value of the library for their students' generation of thinkers, and in language that was compelling and convincing.

Since that first semester at Alabama, I have spent a fair amount of time in libraries with my students—and in museums and galleries and other spaces that allow for a powerful extension of the space and logic of the classroom. The conclusion that I've come to is that if we, as intellectuals, are committed to such spaces persisting as viable venues for the production and maintenance of knowledge, we must not assume that anyone who doesn't share our perspective is backward, blind, or lost. Instead, we must offer our students a legitimate justification for the library's value, in the same way we would do for any other argument we want to make: in clear language, with evidence, and with the aim of persuasion.

These days I make two arguments about libraries to students: that they are a places to experience wonder and to make material the questions that we ask in our classes.

First, perhaps the greatest affective potential of the library is its ability to astound students with the breadth of knowledge that exists in the world, and the concomitant sense of possibility that it inspires. The sheer size of a university library—even a small one—can offer the opportunity for students to meditate on the things humans have asked, learned, written, printed, bound, and shelved. This is the power of taking students into the stacks. Sometimes I give students an assignment, like the task of finding a random book by its call number, as I mentioned above, or a kind of treasure hunt to find a book by a certain author or on a certain topic. More often, though, I have asked them to wander the stacks with no aim in mind, but with the expectation that they are completely silent. They are not to speak or be spoken to, but instead to take notice of their emotional and intellectual responses to being among centuries of human knowledge. This may sound naïve or heady in a way that only an elite college student may find compelling (and perhaps not even then). This is a fair critique, and one that I respect. Still, I have had surprising success with this exercise with diverse sets of students. When they reflect on the experience, they often remark on the rarity of silence in their lives, how the hushed nature of the stacks makes them better able to think or experience wonder, and how much they are able to engage their senses (especially sight and smell) when they are lost among the books.

Second, this last note about the senses is a crucial element of the other value of the library: it can help students to concretize and make material (sometimes literally) the ideas and questions that we discuss in our classes. The concept of classification is easily taught by asking students why a book is shelved in one section and not another. The history of a field can be told by asking students to create a taxonomy of topics in a certain area. Having students catalog the number of books by certain authors can help to reflect on canon—who is part of it and who is not.

I have found libraries' special collections divisions to be especially effective at making the intellectual material. At the University of Chicago's Special Collections, for instance, students can engage with one of the earliest extant manuscripts of Homer's *The Iliad*. The properties of the text—that it was written in Greek around the beginning of the first century of the common era—are apparent in its tattered, physical form, especially if one has been taught to observe the details that indicate time and culture of origin. Students can examine the ink, trace the lines of the columns with their eyes, even touch the document's deteriorating surface through its plastic covering. The same topics that I enumerated above—classification, definition, translation, canon, the history of the field—can be taught through engaging with the item of the manuscript.

There is, of course, more to say about the resources that a library can (or cannot) provide to students in the twenty-first century. Issues of race, class, immigration, and ability, among others, complicate students' access to and comfort with the library. Instructors' prerogatives and institutional contexts will determine whether a day or a class period spent in quiet contemplation in the stacks is a worthy use of class time. For my part, the library has become a collaborator in my teaching. I have given it a role in welcoming students into the pursuit and production of knowledge. Helping them to become accustomed to the architectural and social space of the library has been a pleasure and a privilege I hope to have for many years to come.

See also: Accessibility; Assignments; Class Participation; Critical Thinking; Digital Humanities; Experiential Learning; Group Work; High-Impact Practices; Primary vs. Secondary Resources; Readings

27

Office Hours

Leslie Dorrough Smith

For many, if not most, faculty, holding office hours is a requirement of their jobs, and the ostensible reason that they exist is to carve out time for students to ask questions about any course-related needs. I say "ostensible" because office hours can be much more than a simple forum for answering student queries. As I'll elaborate below, meeting students in the context of office hours can address a much larger series of concerns and obstacles that they may face across their time at college, and there are substantial benefits for instructors, as well.

At the outset, perhaps it needs to be said that students don't necessarily know what office hours are, or even where their instructor's office (or other designated meeting place) is. I take care during the first week of class to elaborate on both matters. I tell them that office hours are a designated time when I am on campus and consistently available to them to assist with any concern related to the course or campus life, but that with some advance notice I can meet with them at many other times, as well. Again, this may seem like information that doesn't need to be said, but younger students still adjusting to the culture shock of college life often benefit from this type of information. (And it never hurts more established students to have a reminder that help is available.)

Individualized attention is a key function of office hours. Meeting individually with students gives them additional time and an instructor's undivided focus as well as a more private setting for conversation, particularly when something personal or sensitive needs to be addressed. While we often invoke the importance of this type of privacy when referencing students who are in crisis or who need to discuss disability accommodations, etc., we shouldn't forget that, for many students, talking about their own lack of understanding of course material feels very sensitive, indeed. We take for granted that their ignorance is normal (after all, this is why they're students!), but they often don't feel the same way, and there are many who experience considerable shame at not understanding the material. Office hours thus provides them with the opportunity to ask questions, review course content, share concerns, and address any number of other issues that they prefer to handle without their peers looking on.

Because they may be somewhat uncomfortable or intimidated by meeting with me alone, a major goal I have during office hours is building rapport. When a student comes in I always make sure to ask them something about themselves that's not directly related to our class topic at the moment. When I meet with students near the end of the semester, for instance, I often inquire about their stress level, knowing that finals are around the corner. That gives them the chance not only to let off some steam about how they're feeling, but also gives me some insight into what their needs might be and how they're coping. Alternately, when I find out a student's major, I will often ask if they've had a favorite class or topic, and that information can also help me think of examples from my class that connect with their pre-existing interests. Moreover, having the chance to talk to students individually may allow them to overcome some misgivings about me, and I, in turn, learn more about experiences they have that affect their success but are sometimes easy for me to overlook. Knowing more about their busy and often complicated lives allows me to create interventions and changes to an assignment that don't substantially inconvenience me but can make their lives considerably easier.

Beyond building rapport, another reason why I believe office hours are so important is that the time allows *me* to ask questions of students in a more personalized way. I've found that many students who are struggling in a class have often resigned themselves to a certain degree of confusion or frustration that may keep them from knowing what types of questions to ask. As the person who knows what concepts tend to be most difficult, what connections I most want to see them make, etc., I can ask them about their experiences in the course that will help me understand their potential gaps in learning. For instance, if students are willing, I may ask them to use their notes (which are hopefully present in the meeting) to explain a particular concept. This helps me know not just if they understand the concept, but also how robust their notetaking skills are. In other cases, though, my questions are more general, like "What is the biggest concern you have about this assignment?" or "Are there specific things going on that are keeping you from doing as well as you'd like?" Those questions can assist me with connecting students with various services on campus that can alleviate some of their academic or even personal struggles.

Sometimes office hours show me how I need to improve an aspect of my teaching. This can happen when, for instance, it becomes clear that students are confused about an assignment that I didn't explain well. In other cases, a problem with a piece of technology (such as a learning management system) becomes much clearer to me once a student has the time to describe in detail what they're experiencing. Most commonly, though, I find that while students may be able to regurgitate certain ideas, they may have little sense of how to apply them or where else they are applicable. Realizing this through office hours discussions gives me insight into planning engaging activities and future assignments that can make the lessons from the material easier to understand.

There is a more far-reaching function behind office hours, though, that combines both the issues of rapport and student learning. Having a meaningful connection with one's faculty provides students a vital tether to the institution when they may feel that they have few reasons to remain. We know that many students (particularly first-generation) who drop out do so because they never felt like they belonged. Through simple conversation, office hours can give us the opportunity to act as something like translators who can help make sense of various college norms and practices. For instance, I was recently working with a first-time, first-generation student who was concerned about whether she could leave a class session to use the restroom without first seeking out my permission. This is something I'm unsure I've ever discussed with students before; I take it for granted that they will just leave on their own. Her question provided a great reminder that all cultural norms must be learned, and that we are all outsiders at some point.

Office hours serve many valuable functions for everyone, then, but motivating students to show up for them is its own struggle. Time is an obvious factor in this, as is possible student shame or intimidation. When I was an undergraduate, I had a professor who required that each student visit him once during the first month or so of the course. That requirement did its job, at least for me—I was somewhat intimidated by him at first, but then I felt much more comfortable and enthusiastic about the course after the meeting. However, finding the time to meet with each of one of our students individually, particularly early on in the semester, is something most of us can't hope to accomplish with the other labor parameters we face. There are, fortunately, other ways to promote office hours as a means of instructor-student communication.

A simple thing that can be done is to remind students that you're available. I reiterate multiple times across the semester that I am eager to talk individually so that they understand that the original invitation during syllabus day was not merely a formality. I also get specific about what types of concerns might bring them to my office in the hopes that they if they personally relate to one of those scenarios, then it might prompt them to visit me.

After the first exam, for example, I often tell students that if they felt like they made their best effort and yet received a disappointing score then a conversation with me might be in order. In other cases, I indicate that if they are having trouble verbalizing a particular concept then we need to meet. Still yet, it's possible to use office hours to establish a study group with designated topics or themes where students can prepare for assignments with the instructor present, which can then lead to even further meetings down the road, if needed. Giving students a pre-defined topic for discussion during office hours can make them feel as if they have a specific reason to come, which is often far more motivating than the nebulous sense that a class is hard or uninteresting.

Another tactic I use is to incorporate individual meetings into the class structure. Sometimes I set aside a class period to work on a final paper proposal where students work in groups, which gives me the opportunity to interact with each group's members. I can then ask a student who seems to be struggling if they'd like to meet with me personally, and I can schedule the appointment then and there if they're willing. I have also made it a consistent practice before an exam or project to devote a class period or two to nothing other than individual student meetings in lieu of lecture. I time these in fifteen-minute increments over a few hours. While these are optional, I have many students show up during these times, and again, their enthusiasm for attending is often piqued because there is a specific topic to discuss. Finally, some faculty have syllabus statements that list attendance at office hours as a determining factor in considering borderline grades.

Many parties benefit from the interactions that take place during office hours. Instructors can receive valuable information about how their course is working for students in a setting that provides real-time feedback so that course corrections can be made. Students benefit not just from asking questions about the course material, but also by practicing the ever-important skill of self-advocacy. No matter students' initial reason for attending, though, the ability to communicate individually with an instructor helps cement the notion that they belong, which is a foundational element to their college success.

See also: Attendance; Class Participation; High-Impact Practices; Recruiting Majors; Syllabi

28

Online/Remote Courses

Steffen Führding

In the spring of 2020, online teaching became a widely discussed topic at universities around the world. Before the Coronavirus pandemic, this topic had been in the shadows, at least in the German context and at my university. In Lower Saxony, my home state in the northwest of Germany, the first lockdown was imposed on March 16. As part of that lockdown, universities were closed. The university administration asked instructors at short notice to change their courses to online formats for the semester starting in mid-April. Efforts were quickly made to organize support services and to build and expand eLearning resources. At the beginning of the summer semester, for example, no video conferencing system would have had the capacity to implement synchronous online teaching in a relatively trouble-free manner. Nevertheless, even if such a system had been available, many lecturers would have needed much more competence to use it.

We therefore had to change our courses to a completely new format in a short time. Initially, there was little guidance and assistance, so very different concepts and models of remote instruction emerged. They ranged from courses in which instructors provided students with texts and assignments via email or virtual learning environment (VLE), to more sophisticated formats that made greater use of the limited eLearning resources available. Videos were recorded in one's home office and then made available to students via different platforms; online tests and remote learning modules were crafted. In many cases, these were asynchronous formats (i.e., not working with the student live though remote) because the appropriate equipment for synchronous online teaching was not available (to a sufficient degree). The situation quickly changed and improved, however, after the turbulent initial weeks. Appropriate technical resources were acquired and expanded. In addition, not only the technical but also the didactic support offered was significantly increased and improved. This same situation played out in university after university around the world.

The fact that the pandemic had caught us so unprepared is probably because there have hardly been any opportunities for distance learning, at least in German universities in the past. There were and are a few particular institutions for this, though the German university mostly understood and still understands itself as a presence university. Online teaching in the narrower sense was therefore limited to individual institutions and activities before the pandemic. One of these activities is an online introductory course for methods of qualitative research on religion, which I developed and implemented with a colleague and a small team as early as 2012. The starting point for this was our experience in corresponding face-to-face teaching settings. We had been teaching research learning seminars at our campuses for quite some time; in these seminars, students acquired methodological knowledge and practiced this knowledge in their own discrete projects. We noticed, though, that these types of courses were very time-consuming to teach, especially the supervision of their practical aspects. Often there needed to be more time for this. Acquiring the theoretical knowledge about qualitative research (i.e., methodology and methods), on the other hand, seemed to be less of a problem. This insight led to the development of a blended learning concept for our methods courses. We outsourced the theoretical input to videos; students can watch these online and work through them at their own pace, with additional online material and self-assessments. We then clarify questions in face-to-face sessions. However, these sessions are now mainly used for the practical elaboration of a student's project and the reflection on their research. It is also possible to leave out the practical parts. Then the course can be used as an online theoretical introduction to the topic.

This kind of engagement with online teaching was very different from what many of us experienced in the spring of 2020. For we developed the methods course as a team over a longer period. In addition, there was funding to support this development work and other resources were available for it as well. It was, therefore, a larger project that could not simply be implemented in this way for normal operations. This is also linked to a significant disadvantage of the course, which also applies to less comprehensive online courses: the materials developed have only a limited half-life. The more elaborate the materials are designed, the greater is the effort to adapt and keep them up to date. Since the pandemic, I have therefore experimented with several different online formats, all less elaborately designed than this methods course. In the following, I will discuss some of these formats exemplary for different design possibilities of online courses.

First, however, I would like to address a fundamental insight many colleagues made back in the spring of 2020. This insight is as simple as it is far-reaching. A topic planned for face-to-face teaching cannot simply be transferred one-to-one to the digital space. Moving the physical seminar room to a Zoom meeting room and simply continuing as planned *does not work*. Above all, the forms and opportunities for interaction are different in the online setting and are also more limited. Direct exchange and discussions are more difficult here. Also, group dynamics and social processes that can be created in face-to-face teaching do not work in this context. As an online synchronous teacher, I lack forms of nonverbal feedback that I can easily get in the seminar room by just looking around at the students. Looking at the virtual tiles on a Zoom screen cannot replace this. At my university, I was also frequently confronted with students who did not turn on their cameras. In many sessions, I was looking at a black screen. This made teaching difficult, as feedback and even nonverbal cues were lacking concerning how far students could follow the class or whether they were even "with it." The reasons for leaving the cameras off were many, to be sure. Among them, many students lacked the appropriate technology at the beginning of the pandemic (or even an appropriate setting from which to attend remote classes). Although this has improved significantly since then, this fact points to a fundamental problem with online teaching. Online courses do have the advantage of allowing participants from far-flung areas to attend. At the same time, however, participation requires appropriate technical equipment, sufficient bandwidth, and stable Internet availability. This is not the case in all parts of the world or even in all parts of Germany. These aspects must be taken into account when planning online courses. Beyond such technical considerations, planning online courses involves similar issues as any other course design. Basically, I need to consider the goals that I want to achieve with my course, what I want students to learn, and how I can accomplish that. The appropriate format should be chosen and designed based on these considerations.

Leaving aside the so-called "enrichment concept," online teaching can be roughly divided into two categories: pure online courses (virtual courses) and integrative or hybrid courses. I classify the latter two formats as online teaching in the narrower sense. The enrichment concept provides students with material parallel to the face-to-face course via the VLE (virtual learning environment, such as a learning management system). Virtual formats are purely online. These include the so-called Massive Open Online Courses (MOOCs), which had already achieved popularity before the pandemic. Among others, examples from the humanities and social sciences can be found on the edX platform (https://www.edx.org/). Integrative or hybrid courses bring together online and face-to-face phases. They are, therefore, often referred to as blended-learning courses. In blended learning arrangements, online and presence portions alternate. The online phases can be used to deepen or apply content acquired in the face-to-face sessions (e.g., by writing wiki entries or blog posts). Alternatively, you can turn the process around. In the so-called inverted or flipped classroom approach, students work out the basic content themselves in the online phases. For this purpose, the instructor provides appropriate materials (texts, videos, podcasts, etc.) and instructions. The face-to-face meetings are then used to deepen or practice the acquired content. For example, I designed a course on introducing academic work standards in this way. For the online phases, I recorded videos and compiled other materials (in this case, mainly texts). These convey central knowledge about aspects of academic work (e.g., how to formulate an academic question, design a term paper, or cite correctly). In the face-to-face sessions, we deepen this content with concrete exercises. In addition, this is the place where students can ask their questions.

As a rule, the online parts of blended learning courses are processed asynchronously. Completely virtual courses can be designed synchronously, asynchronously, or in a mixed form. In my view, lectures, in particular, lend themselves to asynchronous scenarios. You can record the lectures and make them available to the students via the VLE. Questions can be asked and answered via an online discussion forum, for example. This has the advantage that students can watch the lectures when it suits them and at their own pace. In addition, it is possible to view parts of the lecture that need to be better understood several times. Nevertheless, open questions can be clarified via the forum. Of course, holding a lecture synchronously would also be conceivable; questions could then be asked via the chat, for example (perhaps with someone other than the lecturer managing the chat). However, as many experienced, a fatigue effect occurs more quickly on the computer than during face-to-face classes. Therefore, the participants of live-streamed events often take less with them. This must be taken into account during planning. Lectures should therefore be made shorter. In addition, they should be broken up by using intermediate activities (e.g., short quizzes on the content via appropriate tools). From my point of view, the advantage of synchronous lectures is primarily that I, as a teacher, do not have to adjust my work too fundamentally. I lecture in front of an audience, even if the audience is only present virtually. This is different when recording videos for asynchronous formats. In this case, I record the lecture without an audience. That was and still is a strange feeling, at least for me. The important thing with the videos or podcasts is not to let them get too long so that students can follow along well. It is better to provide two or three shorter recordings on the topic than one longer one.

If an event focuses on debating or agreeing on the meaning of the content, synchronous settings are more suitable. They have the advantage that immediate feedback is possible. Another advantage is that they provide students with a clear time structure. My experience shows that remote course participants often have difficulties with self-directed learning processes. That is why it is crucial to have precise time guidelines and remind students of them, even in asynchronous formats. Another critical aspect is enabling communication among students, not just with the instructor. This may be easier in synchronous formats because of the virtual plenary meetings. Enabling joint collaboration increases social inclusion and, thus, student motivation.

In my experience, hybrid formats—combining asynchronous and synchronous elements—work best for online seminars. Here, you can combine the strengths of both areas well. In an online seminar on "Religion and the State," for instance, the goal was to work out how different representatives of political theory conceptualize religion, the state, and the relationship between the two. For this purpose, small groups were formed, each dealing independently and on their own responsibility with one theorist. Their task was to write a wiki contribution according to predefined criteria within a set period. In addition, the working groups were assigned the task of giving each other feedback on the wiki contribution (each group was responsible for a different one). This input was used to revise the contributions once again. The criterion-driven feedback was done via a feedback table/matrix, which had to be filled in by the group and posted as a file in the VLE. This work was all done asynchronously and in small groups. We used intervening live meetings to discuss the assignment and to clarify formal and content issues. The last part of the online course was conducted synchronously and was designed as a role play. In the form of a virtual symposium, the participants slipped into the role of their respective "theorists" and discussed their positions on the topic together. As a lecturer, I accompanied the working groups throughout the course. In addition to the joint virtual plenary sessions, I offered regular online office hours for the working groups to keep in touch with them about the progress of their work. This approach helps students to better structure and organize their work steps. At the same time, it increases their commitment to cooperation and strengthens social integration, at least in the working group (the latter being a real challenge outside of in-person learning). This contributes significantly to motivation and helps to minimize student dropout. This online course did not require creating larger materials such as videos, podcasts, or tests. It was, therefore, no more costly in terms of my own preparation than a traditional face-to-face seminar. However, the support for the students through consultation hours, feedback rounds, etc., was significantly above the average level.

The effort mentioned above is an aspect that must be kept in mind when planning online courses. Creating materials can be time-consuming and often only "pays off" when used several times. At the same time, many materials have a limited half-life and must be revised regularly. Virtual courses without instructor or tutor support are less labor-intensive once created, except for maintenance. However, they also tend to have a high dropout rate because engaging and motivating students in such venues can be a real challenge. If one supervises an online course, the effort is therefore usually greater than in a comparable face-to-face course since questions and problems often cannot simply be resolved on the sidelines of the course but, instead, require extra forums (which means additional work and time). Therefore, I prefer blended-learning arrangements, for the interaction of face-to-face and online parts can significantly add value to a course. Which format one finally decides on depends, on the one hand, on the requirements of the respective institution. It is advisable to find out what these framework conditions look like and what support options are available locally. But on the other hand, the intended teaching and learning objectives can also help to determine the format.

See also: Accessibility; Assignments; Learning Management Systems

29

Peer Tutors

Russell T. McCutcheon

Like many of the items discussed in this volume, the topic of peer tutoring can be approached in at least two ways: examining the context of higher education that has made this an appealing option for some instructors or discussing the strategies that can make this initiative most effective; these are not mutually exclusive ways into the topic, of course, since the former makes plain the practical conditions that have led to discussions of the latter. So, with that in mind, we'll first consider some of the structural conditions of current higher education and then examine strategies for effective peer tutoring—an approach I would recommend to anyone trying to understand any of the many initiatives and expectations within the modern university, regardless the national setting.

Because of shrinking contributions from governments toward public education, followed by rising tuition costs over recent decades (thereby passing a greater share of a students' education costs directly back to students themselves, at least in nations where tuition is paid by students), the ability to continually recruit new students (i.e., new revenue sources) but also to retain, engage, and eventually and efficiently graduate current students has continually taken on increasing importance on university campuses. (In those settings where tuition is not charged to students because the state covers the costs of education through the taxation system, institutions are generally funded per student, so the ability to bring in new students, possibly growing the campus population, remains a crucial way to increase revenues, along with enhancing external grant funding, of course.) So the ability to assist students to be successful, sometimes in an environment of large and possibly somewhat impersonal classes, while also engaging them and therefore assisting them to develop practical skills that may be of use in future careers, has received much attention, resulting in, among other strategies, an initiative known as peer tutoring (usually focused on assistance with the work of a specific class) or sometimes peer mentoring (often concerned with broader topics, such as professionalization and career preparation). In the best cases it results in student-to-student tutoring, whether both students are enrolled in the same course or when one who recently excelled and completed the course returns to work outside class time with those who are now enrolled. Whether it is done for pay (should the unit have such spare resources), voluntarily (for the experience and thus recorded on the tutor's resume), or for course credit (in which the unit possibly has an upper-level course in which student tutors can register while working with their peers), successful peer tutoring programs will depend on considerable attention from a faculty member, to prepare and debrief with student tutors to ensure that those receiving their assistance are hearing a unified and accurate message across the lectures and the tutoring. While much the same needs to happen in the case of graduate teaching assistants, the additional experience of most graduate students assigned to work with undergraduates likely makes the faculty member's duty to prepare graduate teaching assistants somewhat different from readying undergraduate students to take a leadership role with their own peers (especially if the program is between students enrolled in the same class at the same time).

So while coordinated, collaborative learning has surely characterized the undergraduate classroom for a considerable period of time, the now branded notion of peer tutoring (i.e., it is an item that is easily found online at the sites of a host of education product vendors) can be seen as a fairly recent development; it aims both (i) to provide assistance to students in academic need in settings that are not capable of funding the sort of graduate teaching assistants who once ran tutorials, recitations, or discussions sections that would ran parallel to the class and complement it and (ii) to provide practical and documentable work experience for the undergraduate tutors which they may in turn use to help credential themselves in preparation for their own next steps (e.g., applying to jobs or graduate school). In this way the institution of peer tutoring could be seen to be part of the wider phenomenon of continually shifting pre-professionalization to earlier and earlier stages of college or even high school.

Though often administered by the faculty member and connected to specific classes, on many campuses peer tutoring is now also linked to various centralized administrative initiatives, run by various student life or advising staff, aimed at increasing a school's retention and graduate rates (not to mention helping to generate empirical data to satisfy a campus's various assessment and credentialing initiatives), such as we commonly see in the supervised student tutors who may staff a campus-wide tutoring center, where students either drop-in or make appointments to receive assistance for specific classes or even assignments (often for those standard introductory classes whose syllabi and textbooks change little if any from year to year, e.g., first year chemistry, math, biology, English lit, etc.; often, success in such courses can be a strong predictor of overall success in a bachelor's degree, hence a tutoring center's frequent focus on specific first-year classes). When approached properly, such learning centers—or, as they're sometimes called, centers for academic success or student success—work closely with the academic units whose content they address (e.g., with faculty in those departments both vetting the students who are annually applying to become tutors and regularly confirming the approach taken, and material covered, in these tutorial sessions); but, all depending on the campus, there can sometimes be no necessary coordination or perhaps even contact between the two, such that the chair, undergraduate coordinator, or even faculty member teaching the class may have little input into or knowledge of what goes on between such a center's tutors and the students using their services. Such a disjoint can be explained by the fact that the centralization of such services may sometimes further administrative interests that are distinct from department or even faculty interests (e.g., they may be seen as part of the campus's recruitment efforts, to assure incoming students and their families that students can find academic support outside of their scheduled lectures or labs), something that may be especially evident when the academic unit lacks sufficient resources to offer the kind of well-staffed and required tutorial sections in which a different generation of undergraduate students would have been required to enroll (i.e., a Monday/Wednesday lecture course with a fifty-minute required tutorial section, led by a graduate student, on the Friday).

Be this as it may, an instructor may still decide to implement a peer tutoring system of their own in one or more of the courses that they teach, in which the expertise of high achieving current or recent undergraduate students can benefit others in the course (under the presumption that peer communication can, at times, be far more effective). Something to bear in mind when developing such programs, however, is that unless such tutoring sessions take place during class time and thus in the presence of the course's instructor of record, there may very well be a liability issue that the faculty member must take into account, especially if the tutors and students meet outside of class time, whether in such locations as a campus library, a residence hall, a coffee shop, etc. As an official part of the course and thus a university requirement, the faculty member will likely need to consider a campus's policies for such sanctioned meetings, probably requiring the tutors to have gone through some sort of training, whether for pedagogy or, as is more likely the case today, the sort of ethics training expected of incoming graduate teaching assistants and new faculty members. So, apart from the sort of weekly meetings that a faculty member may decide to have with their tutors (to ensure that they are all on the same page for new course material and able to debrief on possible challenges that they may have experienced in recent tutorial sessions), the faculty member opting to institute a peer tutoring program in their classes would be wise to talk to their department's undergraduate director or chair, perhaps even an associate dean responsible for personnel issues, to ensure that such an initiative is in line with their campus's expectations for the level of training of those in varying positions of leadership and responsibility. For, despite possibly being a volunteer, any student sanctioned by the faculty member as a tutor carries authority that, in the worst case, can indeed be abused.

Otherwise, peer tutoring should be focused, such as concerning a specific assignment or discrete skill, since the tutor is best not seen as a shadow faculty member in command of all course material. The relationship between tutors and student can be assigned by the faculty member and persist all throughout the semester or, instead, it can be far more flexible, student-initiated, and result in students being identified at the start of the semester as a tutoring resource while leaving it up to others in the class to seek them out as needed—which should make plain that peer tutoring is no one thing and exists across a spectrum of models. In fact, it could even take the form of a faculty member soliciting advice on such things as notetaking or test preparation from specific students in the class and then distributing it anonymously to the rest of the class, as advice from their peers—something the instructor could even review and discuss as part of their lecture, never singling out the authors, of course.

A wise approach would be one that takes into account a wide variety of factors that influence how each student learns best, with whatever model of peer tutoring that you adopt being seen as but one of the strategies employed to assist students who are experiencing difficulties in the course. Ensuring that the tutors are themselves well supported—whether that entails some training as well as regular opportunities to reflect on their experiences, not to mention eventually able to obtain letters of reference to reflect the work they've done as tutors—is essential for the success of such programs; all of which means that peer tutoring programs, if done well, should not be seen by the faculty member as necessarily being a timesaver for them; instead, while perhaps transferring a small portion of their work it brings new work along with it—work well worth the effort for the effect it can have on both tutors and the students with whom they work.

See also: Assessment; Teaching Assistants

30

Prerequisites

Steffen Führding

> The reader is invited to direct his mind to a moment of deeply-felt religious experience, as little as possible qualified by other forms of consciousness. Whoever cannot do this, whoever knows no such moments in his experience, is requested to read no further; for it is not easy to discuss questions of religious psychology with one who can recollect the emotions of his adolescence, the discomforts of indigestion, or, say, social feelings, but cannot recall any intrinsically religious feelings.
>
> OTTO 1924: 8

The systematic theologian and one of the founding figures of the study of religion, Rudolf Otto, famously argued for the existence of a specific religious musicality or sensibility as a prerequisite for studying religion. Even if Otto's views are still more widespread than many members of our discipline (or should I say field?) want to admit today, there is an agreement in most institutes of religious studies that one's religiosity is not a prerequisite for the academic study of religion. A look at relevant institute websites supports this assessment. "You do not have to wear a toga to study ancient Rome. And you do not have to be religious to study religion" (https://religion.ua.edu/).

At my institute, too, it is explicitly pointed out that one's religious convictions do not play a role in the study program; religious awareness or experience is certainly not a prerequisite for admission. What is recommended, however, is an interest in historical, empirical, and social science issues as well as in religion and culture. However, this is optional for the study program and falls into the recommendations area. In Germany, the institutes can only influence concrete prerequisites for admission to a degree program to a minimal extent. The prerequisites are laid down in the admission regulations that the universities issue. The institutes (or what might be called departments in other settings) only have a certain say in subject-specific regulations. At my university, the only requirement for admission to a bachelor's program in the academic study of religion is that you have a recognized university entrance qualification. For master's programs, the situation is somewhat different. Here, it is usually required that you have a bachelor's degree closely related to the content of the intended master's program. In some cases, specific language or methodological skills are also required.

Against this background, in our introductory courses for bachelor's students, we assume that beginners come to us without any knowledge of religious studies. We basically start from scratch. But this is only true in theory; in practice, we often start in the "minus" range. After all, our students come to us with all kinds of folk ideas about what religion is or does. They have all sorts of opinions about religion in general and in specific, about the so-called religious traditions in particular, and the spectrum of this prior knowledge ranges from anti-religious to affirmative attitudes. And so, some students choose the study program to acquire knowledge that they hope will expose religion as a fantasy or a problem in one way or another, while others want to deepen their faith. The largest group of our students, however, sees religion as an important social factor that offers great potential for peaceful coexistence—if only enough is known about it. What's more, the World Religions Paradigm (WRP) strongly influences all of these preconceptions and attitudes. Therefore, among our tasks at the beginning of any course is often an "Unlearning Religion" process; the goal is to have students reflect on the everyday notion of religion and everything related to this fuzzy concept and to overcome such preconceptions as much as possible in favor of a critical religious studies approach. I often teach together with colleagues from sociology, where I hear very similar things from them regarding concepts like society, etc., and so the "problem" that students start their studies with their everyday conceptions is not a peculiarity of religious studies.

At the course level, the departments have more influence on setting prerequisites for individual courses than on general admission to a degree program. In the natural and technical sciences, it is common practice to set prerequisites for taking courses. For example, in mathematics, one may only take the Algebra II course only once one can demonstrate knowledge of the Algebra I course. However, in most religious studies programs that I know of—just as in many other humanities and social science programs—there are no such prerequisites or, if so, only minimal ones. Where I work we strongly recommend that our students first complete introductory courses before taking "in-depth" courses. However, this is not strictly required as a rule and after completing the introductory course such recommendations usually no longer exist. One of the reasons for this is that our content and thus courses often do not build on each other systematically to the same extent as the mathematics example mentioned above. In my opinion, this is often a characteristic of humanities and social sciences subjects. In these fields the focus is generally not on imparting relatively fixed stocks of knowledge and, in a stricter sense, skills and competencies. Instead, our subjects are usually organized around examining specific bodies of knowledge (that is, content). These bodies of knowledge are contested and fluid; they are subject to constant discussion and (re)interpretation (e.g., a course on Islam or a course on ritual). Therefore, the consecutive construction of curricula and the prescriptions of prerequisites are, to some extent, arbitrary and not appropriate. This is especially true when programs are designed broadly rather than in a specialized manner. There is no objective reason why a course on the role of religion in mass media must be taken before or after a course on theories of secularization from a global perspective. The topics are often taught on the same level and are therefore not hierarchically dependent.

At my institute, therefore, we do not understand in-depth courses as dealing in-depth with a specific topic that one has already (necessarily) dealt with in an introductory way in a previous course. The difference between first-level courses is, instead, that in the in-depth courses it is presupposed (or I should better say assumed?) that students are more familiar with academic thinking and work skills. In introductory courses, students have been given an initial toolkit of how scholars approach their "bodies of knowledge" and how reflection and negotiation of knowledge occurs. Ideally, students will then use these tools to approach entirely new topics in the in-depth courses.

Moreover, since our courses are not only aimed at students of our field or discipline but are often taken by students of other disciplines (as an elective, for example), it would be challenging to implement strict—especially content-related—prerequisites, for now they might prevent students from enrolling in classes that they might otherwise have taken, merely because they had not already completed a prior course that they never intended to take (given that their studies, or what some call majors, are mainly in another discipline). In this case, prerequisites might hurt a unit's overall enrollment (which is among the metrics administrations use to judge performance and viability). Furthermore, as described already, it would also not be appropriate to the subject matter. As instructors, however, this circumstance repeatedly confronts us with the challenge of dealing with heterogeneous learning groups all in one classroom—heterogeneous not only in terms of personalities and performance but also concerning the students' prior, and thus shared, knowledge. Therefore, I make it a point in my courses to get to know the respective status of the group in terms of their previous experience and "attitudes" toward the topic at the beginning of the semester. Brainstorming or problem-centered discussion formats on essential aspects of the course can therefore be very helpful here. And, with this in mind, when designing courses, different preconditions must be considered as much as possible.

Variable assignment formats, for example, can be used to pick up and engage students who are coming from (sometimes very) different starting points. At the same time, one should be aware that bringing everyone along is not always possible—even if that should, of course, be the ideal goal.

It would be desirable for one's course in the second- or upper-level area if all of the students knew, for instance, the relevant theories, methods, or research discussions that animate a field. However, it is much more important to me that students bring curiosity, openness, and a willingness to engage with the content. I consider this attitude toward studying in general and individual courses in particular to be the central prerequisite to all of my courses. However, curiosity, openness, etc., cannot be laid down in any of the class's regulations or expectations. The students must bring them along of their own accord. Nevertheless, as a lecturer, I can promote them through my own actions in the course and through its design and requirements.

See also Assignments; Curriculum; Seminars; Syllabi

31

Primary vs. Secondary Sources

Craig Martin

Why and when to use either primary or secondary sources fundamentally depends on one's pedagogical aims in a course. Is the goal to help students learn and recall basic names, places, dates, and historical facts? Or is the goal to help students learn how to read and analyze a text, situate it in a historical context, and attend to the social and political biases the text inevitably reflects? For instance, one might teach students that the Bhagavad Gita was written in India about two thousand years ago, and that it recounts a conversation between a god Krishna and a warrior Arjuna about the class-specific duties one owes to Brahman; for those purposes, reading a summary of the Gita in a secondary source might be sufficient. By contrast, one might wish to teach students that the Gita was likely written by someone in the upper classes in ancient India, that the authority of the author's (or authors') claims is amplified by putting them in the mouth of the god Krishna, and that the purpose of the text seems to be to discourage members of the lower classes from attempting to rise above their assigned station; if that is one's pedagogical goal, having students spend a great deal of time with the primary text might be more useful than reading a summary in a secondary source. (As will be clear, I almost always favor spending more time with primary than secondary sources in class; that bias shapes the discussion that follows.)

Before beginning, it is worth briefly pointing out that whether a source is "primary" or "secondary" is not the result of some intrinsic features of the text itself, but is, rather, observer-dependent. While I understand it might be necessary to simplify such matters in introductory courses, wherein students learn what these terms mean in the first place, I'm always slightly frustrated that students apparently come away with the view that primary sources are always primary and secondary sources are always secondary. By contrast, it seems clear that primary sources are always secondary *with respect to* some other, prior texts, and that texts that were once viewed as secondary sources can always be viewed as primary in the classroom or in one's scholarship. While it would usually be considered a primary source, arguably the Gita might be used as a secondary source insofar as it appears to offer commentary on the teachings of the Upanishads—particularly insofar as the Gita offers several rather pointed criticisms of Upanishadic orthodoxies (e.g., see the opening comments of Chapters 3 and 5). Alternatively, Gandhi's commentary on the Gita seems obviously a secondary source—it's a *commentary on* the Gita, after all; however, one might also treat Gandhi's commentary as a primary text that sheds light not so much on the Gita as the religious, social, and political context of India in the 1920s. All of that is to say: whether a text is primary or secondary depends on how one is approaching the text, *not* on features of the text itself.

In any case, using what we commonly know as secondary sources is often necessary when it comes to teaching about primary sources that are too difficult for students to read, or which would take more time to elucidate in class than one has. For instance, were I teaching a course on modern European philosophers and their views on religion, I would include a discussion of G.W.F. Hegel, particularly what he says about religion in his famous *Phenomenology of Spirit*. However, that text is one that even doctoral candidates struggle to understand and interpret. Consequently, resorting to a summary in a secondary source might be the only means of covering such a text in a reasonable amount of time in an undergraduate course.

Similarly, secondary sources might be necessary when there would be too many primary sources for students to read in order to grasp the material. In my course on religion and capitalism, I spend the last section of the semester looking at how "spirituality" self-help literature arguably functions to legitimate the capitalist mode of production (particularly as much of it focuses on how one can and should adjust one's self or accommodate one's self to the demands of one's workplace when self and work come into conflict). Unfortunately, substantiating these claims about "spirituality" requires taking into account claims found in and across several self-help books. Needless to say, I cannot have students read entire books by Eckhart Tolle, Deepak Chopra, and the Dalai Lama in the span of three weeks (the time devoted to this topic in my course). Instead, for the sake of expediency I assign secondary sources that summarize and analyze such primary sources.

Sometimes what we usually call secondary sources—like textbooks—can be treated as conversation partners, so as to give the instructor the opportunity to consider different possible frames for the course content. I think one of the things that makes veteran instructors stand out is their ability not only to teach *what* the textbook says, but also to teach *why* the textbook puts the narrative together the way it does, *what* that narrative leaves out, and *why* other textbooks might construct alternative narratives. In my ethics class, for example, I use a textbook with which I significantly disagree at several points. Why not discard it for another textbook? In part because it becomes a dialogical foil for my lectures. In class, I can point students to why I disagree with the way the author presents the material in some chapters, why I would present it differently, and so forth. In those cases, secondary sources are extremely useful because they permit meta-level reflections on the course content—something many faculty tackle in undergraduate courses if they're trying not just to convey "the facts" but also to promote the skills commonly grouped together as critical thinking.

In other instances, I find the use of primary sources absolutely necessary, particularly when students might come to class with a number of assumptions or stereotypical views of a text. It is easy enough to find students who hold the simplistic view that the gospels basically teach that Jesus was born, was crucified and then raised from the dead, and that between birth and death he taught his followers to love one another, help the poor, and seek salvation through "belief" in him and his divinity. Of course, parts of the gospels support such a narrative. However, when diving into the primary texts themselves—the plural is important here, for there are multiple primary sources in this case, not all of which agree with each other—and walking through them in class, it is difficult to unsee that Jesus spends a lot of time making apocalyptic claims that never came true, that he encourages his followers to become eunuchs, that he says one cannot be a true follower if one does not hate one's family, that the Jews follow the devil and his lies, etc. Or, consider reading Rudolf Otto: the idea that religion is really about inward experience and that organized religion is just a later add-on fits neatly with many students' common-sense views on religion. However, I find that when I assign Otto's work and we actually see that the whole text works toward the Euro-centric, even racist goal of ranking religions according to how well they reflect supposedly authentic religious experience (i.e., Christianity first, then Judaism, Islam, and the primitive religions [the latter of which he says are more pre-religions than actual religions]), we end up with something that chafes against many of their sensibilities rather than confirming their common sense. Challenging students' assumptions and stereotypes about the primary texts might therefore only be possible through what we often call a close reading of those texts.

Similarly, students often come to class prepared to approach the past through what historians call "presentism"—the tendency to project the present onto the past and to interpret the past through contemporary values and assumptions. For instance, many North American students come to class with a great deal of prior exposure to twenty-first-century Christianity, and they may have difficulty seeing that Christians from the first century to the twentieth were quite different in many ways. This is one reason why, when teaching about how nineteenth-century American Christians appealed to the Bible in order to justify slavery and the racial hierarchies that existed at the time, I ask students to read parts of a book by a Christian racist—James Sloan—that was published in 1857. Coming into the course, students tend to think that, insofar as Jesus taught people to love their neighbors, Christian racism must be completely hypocritical and results from clear misinterpretations of the Bible. However, Sloan's book offers readers a mountain of biblical citations that directly or indirectly support institutions of slavery. It is therefore difficult for students to think "Christians who supported slavery were 100% hypocritical" after they've read a book by a Christian who faithfully cites explicitly pro-slavery passages from the Bible. The result is that their presentist assumptions about Christians—that they've always resembled twenty-first century Christians—are difficult to maintain after sustained engagement with the assigned primary source.

Similarly, reading primary texts helps to inoculate students from developing monolithic views of cultural traditions. Simplified narratives make it easy for students to see continuity across tradition. If their primary frame for thinking about "religion" is Christianity, they might assume that all religions have a foundational sacred text, and that the development of the tradition involves nothing more than various manifestations of the essence found therein. By contrast, when I teach Hinduism, I point out that what we find in the Vedas is different from what we find in the Upanishads, and what we find in the Upanishads is different from what we find in the Gita, and what we find in contemporary devotional practices might show little connection to any of these texts. At the end of the course, when I ask my students what these texts or practices have in common, it is a difficult question for them to answer—and, consequently, they are less likely to come away with a monolithic view of South Asian traditions. The take-away? The groups that we study are far more complicated than we might have at first assumed.

I would argue that reading primary texts is also great simply because they are often alien and bizarre to modern readers. Why does the Lotus Sutra say the Buddha had a laser shooting from his unibrow? Why does the biography of Muhammad say that his mother's belly functioned as a spotlight that illuminated castles in distant lands while she was pregnant with him? Why does Leviticus say that we can "clean" the temple by throwing animal blood around on everything? Why do the Upanishads say that you can tell whether someone is lying by handing them a red-hot axe and seeing if it burns their hands or not? Making the familiar strange—one of the most entertaining things about the job, at least for me—is so much easier with primary texts; secondary texts all too often domesticate the material for modern audiences, leaving out what is most alien or off-putting, and including only what suits contemporary sentiments.

The last case I will make for including primary texts in undergraduate courses is that one cannot do a close reading when working from secondary sources. If, in my politics and religion class, we want to understand a particular Supreme Court ruling on a first amendment matter, we will have to look at the language in the ruling itself. What legal concepts are brought to bear on the matter? How are those concepts defined, or, if they are not, what can we discern about the implied definition from how they are being used? How are those legal concepts being used in this ruling in a way that might be different from how they have been used in the past or in different legal cases? That sort of close reading seems to require having the primary texts in front of oneself.

In sum, reasons to use secondary sources include the following:

- primary texts might be too difficult for undergraduates to read and interpret;
- the content from primary sources might be so extensive that summaries in secondary texts might be necessary to comprehend the material; and
- secondary sources can be used as foils or dialogical partners in meta-level discussions about how the course content is organized.

Reasons to use primary sources include the following:

- reading primary sources may unsettle students' common-sense views or stereotypes about the content;
- the use of primary sources may make students' tendency toward presentism more difficult, as reading sources from the past helps to make it clear that the past is usually very different from the present;
- spending time with undomesticated primary sources may make the monolithic narratives in secondary sources more difficult to swallow;
- primary texts often make it easy to "make the familiar strange"; and
- sometimes a close reading is the only way to understand the content with any depth.

Ultimately, both primary and secondary sources are essential to teaching, but reflective instructors should always carefully consider *why* and *when* to choose one over the other.

See also: Examples; Readings; Syllabi

32

Professionalization

Richard Newton

I come from a family that very much values higher education—even when higher education didn't value them back. My grandfather hailed from the Ozarks and loved the University of Arkansas as an idea. I have vivid memories of him wearing Razorback Red, just as I can recall the moment when he told me that he did not—scratch that, *could not*—attend due to Jim Crow laws in the U.S. My father was from Topeka, Kansas; his elementary school is now the Brown v. Board of Education National Historical Park. While I took for granted that he would go on to study at the University of Michigan, serve as a military officer, later work at a Fortune 500 company and retire from a position in city administration, I'll never forget when my grandmother told me that none of this was a forgone conclusion. For when he was a teenager, my Grandma Rosie was on the fence about letting him study so far away. Unbeknownst to him, the turning point in her decision was a test. He had told my grandmother that he'd be coming home late because he needed to burn the proverbial midnight oil at the library. My grandmother allowed it, but spied on him from the stacks to confirm that he was doing what he said he'd do. According to her, that's when she decided he was ready to leave home for higher education. She could trust that he was going to work.

Work was important to my Grandma Rosie. Though she would never describe herself this way, a class history project on early twentieth-century U.S. government and economics helped me to realize that she was indeed—no kidding—a "Rosie the Riveter." Like many women in Second World War era Kansas, she was working in an armament factory as part of Franklin D. Roosevelt's New Deal "alphabet agencies." So it's not hard to imagine her appreciation for hands-on practicality. I gather that she expected my father to exude a similar work ethic. If he was going to college, then he better know he had a job to do.

I share all of this because religious studies teachers don't have a great track record of expecting as much of our students. We hear "STEM" (i.e., science, technology, engineering, and mathematics) and wring our hands at a job market that doesn't value our course of study. We see pre-professional programs and think we can't compete. Even in comparison to other programs in the humanities and social sciences, we have the struggle of finding avenues to the workforce that don't circle back to "religion-as-ministry" cliches that are myopic even when applicable. More often than not, the academic study of religion doubles down on the importance of the abstract life of the mind—whether in the verbiage of critical thinking or vocational discernment. Neither of these things are outright objectionable to me. But too often they're the high-falutin' sighs of resignation uttered in response to the question of the hour: "What can you do with a religious studies degree?" If we're going to break out of the malaise, then we need a reality check.

For starters, I'm not convinced that the pipeline to professionalism outside of the humanities is nearly as smooth as we assume. I've lived in a few college towns now, and in all of them my professional-class neighbors have reminded me that they are often working in jobs alongside college graduates whose educations don't intrinsically align with their careers. And here in Alabama, the town-gown divide is not nearly as pronounced as you might think. I have heard quite a few mechanics, carpenters, and other so-called blue-collar laborers wonder aloud about why their young co-workers went to college just to do the same job that they are doing.

Why would we be surprised by this when my friend in organic chemistry is charged to teach in a manner where some of his bright eyed, would-be pre-med students will surely fail? How many smart kids never manage to jump the hurdle of Calculus III to get to those engineering courses that they came to college to take? From the lawyer who struggles with speech and communication to the business majors who can't for the life of them calculate a tip, we should never forget that professionalization is more than a set of classes. It's an ethos that requires elbow-grease on the part of students and faculty.

Our hermeneutics of suspicion about the professionalization fetish in higher ed today should prompt us to create an environment where departments answer the question: "What can't you do with the study of religion?" As faculty, we should mentor and advise students "to study religion and find out" (as we've come to say at the University of Alabama) that the applicability of their education is only limited by their inventiveness, curiosity, and creativity. We then have to develop opportunities and encounters that challenge students to work their education into pathways of success.

One easy place to start is to expose students to your department as a professional environment. Our programs are not just ethereal realms where the ideal versions of our scholarship reside. There are memos, spreadsheets, letters, meeting agendas, job interviews, and catered events going on. People have to do that work. Why would we hide that from students? I'm not suggesting that you give students a faculty line and top-secret human resources clearance. But you might be able to hire majors and minors to become student workers in the department. Maybe you create an in-house internship program where students get credit for creating the snazzy announcements, newsletter mailouts, and registration course lists that you use to foster a sense of departmental identity. These experiences are not only resume-worthy but answer the fear employers have about Gen-Z's unawareness of legacy office settings. Give your students a leg up by acculturating them into your department as a work environment.

As much as colleges and universities highlight academic pre-professional programs, most of the spaces have considerable professional resources on the student affairs side of campus administration. The irony is that career centers, writing centers, and internship offices are underutilized. Instead of re-inventing the wheel, collaborate with them by hosting professional coffee breaks or luncheons. Book a meeting room and have students bring their cafeteria trays and brown bags to these sessions. Topics could include resume-building (and, yes, a resume and a CV are not the same thing), networking, interview tips, dressing for success, professional etiquette, informational interviews, meeting and dining, and whatever else you and these experts think would help your students succeed tomorrow.

Beyond extra-departmental resources, consider bringing back alumni who have made the professional case for the study of religion in their own careers. Here at the University of Alabama, we often invite former students to participate in a public conversation on life during and after the program. We've had graduates who've talked about everything from going to graduate school in and beyond the academic study of religion, to starting their own business and working in the tech sector to doing non-profit work and going to law school or med school. Each time a different faculty member asks questions to help the alum narrate their journey. We call this program "There and Back Again: A Grad's Tale" or "Grad Tales" for short.

And it's not the Tolkien reference that make these events fantastic. It is the organic way that current students begin to ask honest and insightful questions to someone who can genuinely relate (i.e., ideal guests are not too much older than the students themselves). The event becomes a place where some students will get their start at practicing professional conversations, and others will witness how it can be done. Who knows? Maybe some of your alumni will help you to host one of the aforementioned workshops—and alums usually feel pretty honored to be asked.

As far as current students are concerned, we have a lot more curricular flexibility for professionalization than we know what to do with. The academic study of religion has no accreditation standards or professional competency requirements. Nothing is keeping us from filling that lacuna with our own departmental initiatives.

Capstone courses often wrap with some thesis exercise or comprehensive project. Given that the next step for most of our graduating students is some sort of entre into professional life, why not use that ultimate teaching–learning moment for professional preparation? Instead of having students writing theses on the order of a small tome, why not have them write a solid short article commensurate with a writing sample for graduate school or some other project of utility to them? In other words, if we don't start thinking creatively about the professional payoff of what our students do in our programs, they will unnecessarily struggle to do so.

For me, the goal of professionalization is to enhance students' ability to leverage their skills, knowledge, and work ethic in eventually securing gainful employment. It may never be too late to have these conversations with students, yet I prefer thinking about this potential from the jump. Student presentations, paper writing, hands-on projects—these are all possible opportunities for students to gain and sharpen tools that they may need later. I say as much to them as I teach with the hope that they will come to narrate their professional journeys in their own words. I can't help but think of a cohort of senior capstone students from the Class of 2014. In our seminar, students were required to create a portfolio project that they understood as showcasing what they learned as students of religion and that they could draw upon in their first steps out of college. One student had lost her father to cancer when she was a child. Since then she had worked hard to enter the medical profession to join the fight against pancreatic cancer. For her senior project, she analyzed the language people use to narrate cancer, treatment, and grief in the hope that it would help her to be more responsive caregiver. She is now an oncology-certified nurse.

Another student had already learned to podcast and edit video as part of an internship with me. For a capstone project, she developed a companion video series for essays in Brad Stoddard and Craig Martin's edited volume *Stereotyping Religion: Critiquing Clichés* (2017). She studied the most popular genres of social media and news media videos that go viral (e.g., comedic, infographics, talking heads, documentary-style) and then emulated them for her YouTube series. Not only has that series been used in classes by professors outside her school, but she's now working as a radio journalist, news producer, and internet media domain expert on, among other topics, religion. It's worth noting that she was not a journalism student. She developed these skills while working in the humanities, specifically religious studies. And in a prior year, a colleague of mine mentored a social work/religious studies double-major. The student created a resource kit of potential considerations for serving clients of various religious backgrounds. The challenge was how to do so without replicating the problematics of the world religions paradigm and other essentialist frameworks. She could begin her first days with the confidence of having spent considerable time working through a complex topic that many struggle to make sense of in polite conversation and professional settings. Students in similar courses of study have since done such projects as they make for handy resources to have for those disorienting first moments on the job.

If you're skeptical about the ethos that I've been encouraging here, believe me when I tell you that I once shared your reservations. What turned me was the overwhelmingly positive feedback from my students who took the above opportunities seriously. There is a common thread in their stories: the student of religion comes ready with a resume to an interview; the interviewers see the requisite experience, spy "religion," and get curious; the student talks about the value that the study of religion adds; the interviewers agree, often sharing about the memorable religion classes they took way back when; rapport is built; a position is offered. I've heard these testimonies from graduates from small private colleges to large public universities.

When we realize that few people simply fall into their jobs and their careers, then we can begin helping our students to better determine how they are going to work for what they want. We have nothing but opportunity to help them do this if we decide that the study of religion is worthwhile—because its skills are so widely applicable. But if we aren't confident in what we are offering, neither will students (or prospective employers) be.

See also: Assignments; Critical Thinking; High-Impact Practices; Senior Seminars; Transferrable Skills

33

Public Humanities

Richard Newton

I love the phrase "public humanities." To me, it invites the order of questioning that makes for vivacious academic work. The academic study of religion is neither a place for secrets, nor is it one for the private hoarding of knowledge. It is, like any other academic discipline, a space for thinking aloud about a subject matter in a manner that helps us home in on what we know and what we don't. So we would do well to think about our teaching as preparation for leading a better and wider conversation about the relevance of the study of religion in and outside of the academy. And given that most of the students we have in class will not have the luxury of an entire undergraduate course of study, let alone a graduate one, dedicated to such discussions, we don't have a moment to lose in equipping students to foster a richer discourse.

When I reflect on the pedagogy of the public humanities, the first thing that I ask myself is who might benefit from seeing *how* my students think and *what* my students know. In media parlance, content is held in tension with audience. Because my students' learning is my primary concern as an instructor, I think it's wise to begin with considering the content of a humanities education first. Sometimes our students are focused on learning things that are more-or-less public knowledge (e.g., matters of literacy, survey understandings, encyclopedic facts). Sometimes our students are sharpening the way in which they think about a subject matter (e.g., theoretical frameworks, methodological approaches). Scholars in the field know that at some level both are subject to debate, and a debate of consequence at that. Students presumably get a taste of that debate in our classes. So as students come to understand the stakes, who can benefit from being privy to this perspective? That is a potential audience whom we might prepare students to engage.

For example, I've regularly taught courses on African American religion in predominantly white institutions of higher education. Both on and just around our campus, the general historical knowledge of this subject matter is really low. This means that there's an opportunity for my students to share information that they they've learned that would likely be new to those around them. To accomplish this, I've had students create a pop-up museum on African American religion where each student curates a mini-exhibit on what they've learned. Each student takes a conventional subject in an introductory religious studies textbook (e.g., violence, ethics, texts, truth-claims) and makes that the theme of their exhibit. Each exhibit has to make use of media artifacts from a digital archive or special collection. Here students have included everything from music clippings and YouTube video to materials from the campus archives. Because the class's primary student learning outcome revolves around how we might theorize African American religion, students shared their own theses on this by 3D printing an object that they take as exemplary of their exhibit. All of these items were accompanied by panes of short text that had captions and brief explanations about what that item helps to illustrate. These were, of course, informed by students' bibliographic research.

Now, none of this is intrinsically public, but I think you could see how it already meets a need of potential interest to the broader community in my students' context. What is most important, however, is the richness of the knowledge production in which students are engaged. And what is more is that they are doing so with the intent of reproducing that knowledge outside of the classroom. They have to do the work of making a complex assemblage of ideas and materials into something intelligible to a different audience.

Meanwhile my job was to bring students to the kind of audience that would help them rise to the occasion. My students could likely name student learning outcomes met through the pop-up museum, but they probably aren't aware of how I constructed the audience that would help them to meet their educational goals. The campus librarians and archivists who helped them access materials were now invested, as was the instructional technologist who was fascinated by how a humanities class was creatively using the underused but nevertheless expensive 3D printer that the library had purchased. Because we had to reserve a public campus atrium space, we were on the radar of the campus community outreach liaison who works with media relations. Thus students, faculty, staff, and community members came, saw, and interacted with what my students created with (and in a way, for) them.

But that atrium isn't the only place to hold such events. Since so much of today's public interactions happen online, this is also a great place to have students share their intellectual wares. Blogs, podcasts, videos, and social media channels provide spaces for students to present their work to audiences well beyond the classroom and even a campus. There is a temptation to equate *virality* with success when the goal should instead be adding *vitality* to your classroom and your students' connection to the world outside of it. Rather than asking how do you get eyeballs and clicks on student work, give some thought to how you can optimize the type of work your students are creating for public consumption. Yes, students might create a video of facts that they learned about a religious community, but maybe a blog post detailing how scholars of religion think about the politics of identity in said community might be more intriguing. With little difficulty you could have students post a traditional essay assignment on a blog platform, but instead you might create a podcast conversation between students on topics they've recently researched. Even an unedited discussion, bookended with some music might bring a more dynamic and interesting result. The key is to use the mundane assignment to challenge students to create something that shows what they've learned in a manner that they would be proud to share with strangers, friends, family, community members, government leaders, and any other audience one can conceive.

Now here I must pause because most of my own religious studies teachers once cautioned me *against* putting my thoughts online, for wider public consumption. They feared that my thinking was too nascent and unrefined for public consumption. They worried that I might get attention from audiences that might be unfriendly or downright hostile to me. And they thought that, as a budding academic, I had too much to lose by putting out my thinking for all to see. After all, what if someone were to plagiarize my next big idea? We would do well to hear their concerns, and I do not begrudge their hesitance. At the same time, however, I think their reservations could be taken to miss the point of public humanities. After all, knowledge is always under construction. Learning is never finished. Critical thinking is going to put us at odds with conventional wisdom and its apologists. And while an idea may be able to be taken or even reproduced, the journey to forming and then articulating a perspective is where actual learning takes place. I say this with confidence because my former students tell me so. They tell me about what they've done with class lessons, sometimes even years after the fact. As the now-memed singer Tay Money once said: "[they] understood the assignment."

When looking for a place to start, I encourage faculty colleagues to take a syllabus and retool an assignment for which you can imagine a broader public—one of their own conception or that of their students. Determine the kind of deliverables a student might provide to show *what* they know and/or *how* they know it. Then carve out the requisite time for students to develop, create, revise, and present their work. This last piece is a matter of figuring out *how much* time is needed as much as it is *when* in the semester. Because I want students to be at their most competent, I generally devote the last quarter to last third of the semester to public humanities tasks. Practically, that means I've introduced most content by this point. And I've discussed this project enough throughout the semester that they are confident to get started once we reach that portion of the semester.

Brainstorming begins with me asking students to share with me the things that they know best. What piece of course material most captured their attention? What kind of media, project, or experience (whether in or outside of class) did they have access to or command over to tell their friends about what they've learned in class? What one thing do they wish to remember from this class twenty years from now? I ask students to answer those three questions, and then I tell them to go build something that conveys that.

Students and faculty alike can get hung up on tools and know-how. But don't. A good grade and a good assignment correlate with their ability to further students on that aforementioned journey of perspective. At this point, I have a number of *bon mots* I share to help encourage this. Boomer's know you have to break a few eggs to make omelet. Gen-X can relate to leaving a Wile E. Coyote-shaped hole through the mountainside to purse what they want. Gen-Y and Millennials will remember Ms. Frizzle's advice to students boarding the Magic School Bus: "Take Chances. Make mistakes. Get Messy!" And though most of my students are now from Gen-Z and beyond, their fears are assuaged when I tell them that their phones have more computing power than the machines that took the first astronauts to the moon. My classroom is the lab, workshop, makerspace, and study to create the thing somebody doesn't know they need. If they fail, no big deal as long as they fail gloriously, having learned something along the way.

I don't give students much guidance beyond a list of the competencies or learning outcomes that I expect students to demonstrate over the course of their project. The reason is that I want their creativity to meet their knowledge and know-how. Unless I'm making a point of teaching students how to use a specific digital tool or some sort of media technique, I don't stress over platform requirements. Personal devices increasingly come with What-You-See-Is-What-You-Get or "WYSIWYG" programs for designing podcasts, films, blogs, and even interactive presentations. And with streaming video tutorials, it's never been easier for students to explore (and this is before you steer them toward campus resources on how to use the tools available on your campus). As a faculty member, you don't have to be a power user of any particular tool—though sharing your expertise and favorite examples never hurts. You just need to create the conditions to reward the initiative and experimentation of students working on these great public humanities projects.

We've hinted at the ways students can succeed with these projects, but what happens when a students' work doesn't result in something that they (or you) are proud to share? As much as you are the cheerleader of student ingenuity, you are also the quality controller and master of ceremonies. Over the course of the project, you'll have to check how students are doing. If you and they are confident, then build an audience that will honor the students work (e.g., invite more colleagues, think about getting the wider community involved, determine how to help students showcase their work on social media and in their own networks). But if you or they are unconfident, then you need to figure out how to bring students to a worthwhile perspective. You may be helping them lower their expectations or tailoring the project's scope. Perhaps you determine that a public display is not realistic and that the student needs to focus on the minimal amount of work needed to pass the class. All of these are marks of vitality even when they couldn't be further from virality.

This leads me to my final admonition, and that is to remember that your students are *your* public. If you are helping them with what you know, then you cannot fail. So break some eggs, get messy, and leave a Wile E. Coyote-shaped hole in your classroom. In time and with a little perspective, you just might find that your lessons have a wider audience than you thought.

See also: Digital Humanities; Examples; Final Examinations; Introduction vs. Survey

34

Readings

Craig Martin

Teaching a new course for the first time and wondering what readings you should assign? What must you include? What can be left out? In general, I am in agreement with Jonathan Z. Smith, who once famously argued that, when it comes to undergraduate courses, "*there is nothing that must be taught*, there is nothing that cannot be left out" (original emphasis; see the Afterword). As I interpret his claim, what he means is that a course's content should ultimately be set by the aims of the instructor, not by the more or less standardized table of contents found in typical textbooks. Have you been assigned "World Religions"? If so, perhaps you should ask yourself *what lessons do you want students to learn*? While a world religions textbook might cover the basic content of Judaism, Christianity, Islam, Hinduism, and Buddhism (for example: Where was Jesus born and how did he die? In what century did the Buddha teach and what are the four noble truths? What does the Qur'an mean when it refers to the "people of the book"? etc.), an instructor might instead choose a substantially different agenda—as do Christopher R. Cotter and David G. Robertson in *After World Religions* (2016) and Leslie Dorrough Smith and Steven W. Ramey in *Religions of the World* (2023)— focusing on *dismantling* the world religions paradigm (WRP) rather than using it to frame the course content. In that case, the instructor might not talk much about the content of Judaism, Christianity, etc., unless discussing how that content gets shoehorned into the WRP. Accordingly, one's reading choices for students should perhaps be based on one's unique or idiosyncratic goals for the course, rather than what you might find on a Wikipedia page after searching for the course's title.

To offer an example from one of my courses, in "Islam & Western Imperialism" I start the course by having students read four or five pages about the life of Muhammad from a random world religions textbook on my office shelves. In part, I do so because I want them to learn the outlines of the standard narrative. However, in class I point to the fact that these authors cite no sources, and nor do they point to how we might have arrived at that narrative or where it might have come from. Where *does* this narrative come from? It turns out that we have very few primary sources from the time period of Muhammad's life and the early caliphate. We read the so-called "constitution of Medina" that Muhammad purportedly made with the tribes at Medina, we read several suras from the Qur'an, we read selections from an early hadith collection, and we read a handful of narratives from the earliest extant biography of Muhammad, attributed to Ibn Ishaq and edited by Ibn Hisham. Only one of those four sources has any narrative content about Muhammad's life; the story in the textbook is apparently based almost entirely on Ibn Ishaq's biography, *but that text reads like folklore*—the stories are more like Aesop's fables, Homer's Odyssey, or the Epic of Gilgamesh than books by modern historians. Using Ibn Ishaq's folklore as the basis for our history of early Islam would be like claiming Judaism started with Adam, Eve, and a talking serpent. At the end of this unit of my course, the students have learned the textbook's standard narrative, yes, but—and far more importantly—they have also learned the lesson that popular narratives about religious traditions' origins aren't typically supported by the sort of evidence modern historiography usually requires. The reading selections I choose (i.e., the textbook excerpt, the Qur'an, the hadith, the constitution of Medina, and selections from Ibn Ishaq's biography) therefore reflect that particular pedagogical and historiographical aim. If I had different aims—for instance, if I wanted to trace how popular Muslim narratives about Muhammad were adapted across the globe as Islam spread—then I might not have assigned *any* of those things, opting instead for rather different texts. Once again, instead of using a textbook's table of contents to organize one's course, come up with a list of theoretical lessons that you want your students to learn, and then choose the particular readings that support those particular goals or which build toward them. The resulting curriculum will probably be rather different from how other instructors teach the course, but that is okay: as J. Z. Smith argued, there is nothing that *must* be taught (see the Afterword to this volume).

Of course, for a number of reasons not all instructors have such freedom when putting together course readings. First, some colleges, faculties, or departments may have standardized syllabi for particular courses, in which case all instructors might be required to use the same textbook that everyone else uses, perhaps even following the same weekly class schedule. You might be obligated to use Cunningham and Kelsay's phenomenology-oriented text, *The Sacred Quest: An Invitation to the Study of Religion*, even if you have no use for concepts like "the sacred" or "the quest for salvation" in your own scholarship. However, even when that is the case, you might be able to subvert the framework of the textbook—doing so strategically, if needs be—by assigning supplementary materials. Some instructors I've talked to who've been in this situation used the assigned textbook not primarily as an authority but as a perpetual foil for meta-level conversations about different approaches within the field; by pairing the textbook with supplementary readings that problematized the textbook's paradigm, they could pass back and forth between the more critical reading and the textbook, using the latter as data for illustration purposes.

Second, if your particular course is a prerequisite for later courses a student in your program might take, it might in fact be necessary—with all due respect to Smith—for some things to be included. For instance, if your department has a largely content-based world religions curriculum, it might be necessary in REL 101 to ensure that all students have been exposed to, say, the five pillars of Islam, the Buddha's four noble truths, etc. If instructors teaching REL 201 are going to assume students already know about such things before coming into their course, it benefits you to find that out and assign readings that meet the needs of the course, as situated within the overall program framework.

What should you do with the readings when you get to class? I always encourage instructors to reflect on their pedagogical strengths. For instance, when it comes to my strengths, I think I am more dynamic in the classroom when elucidating difficult texts (perhaps because, as a Bible major in college, my early training was nothing but constant historical-critical contextualizing and close readings of dense and alien texts that resisted easy interpretation). I am at my best when I assign a reading that I know students will struggle with; but then, in class, I'll conversationally walk them through the text's historical context, point out the intellectual debates the author was engaging in, demystify the technical vocabulary in the reading, show them what the author's implied goals were and how the text works toward those ends, and then engage students in a discussion about why these matters might still be worth taking into consideration. A selection from Kant's *Groundwork of the Metaphysics of Morals*? No problem. The students arrive to class flummoxed by the reading—not all readings are meant to be easy to understand upon first tackling them—but they leave class wondering how they could have missed what now seems so self-evident.

By contrast, I struggle to teach readings where the significance of the text is relatively easy to identify. When I assign something that is simple to grasp, when students come to class I don't really have anything to add: "Did you notice the author said x, y, and z? You did? Alright, I guess we're done then . . . ." However, other instructors might have different strengths. If facilitating class discussion is your strength, easy and accessible readings might be perfect, because perhaps in class what you'll do—instead of explication—is spend time socratically teasing out connections between the reading and other course content, students' prior knowledge, competing perspectives, etc. Since I often teach things that undergraduate students have little prior knowledge of (e.g., it's unlikely that any of them have heard of Kant, let alone have read *Groundwork of the Metaphysics of Morals*), there's often no prior knowledge to tease out—and that's okay, because I'm great at exegeting the text for them. But if that's not your strength, do something different. *If you have the freedom to do so, always play to your own strengths.* When we play to our strengths, we're more dynamic and enthusiastic, and that enthusiasm is often infectious.

It is sometimes inevitable that I must teach a text that is so accessible that I might not know what to say about it in class. When that happens, I sometimes shift my pedagogical strategy from contextualization and explication to inviting students to exercise their reading and summarizing skills. For instance, I might generate, before class, a worksheet with four or five questions about the excerpt that they read for class that day; once in class, I pass it out and ask them—in small groups—to look for the answers in the reading assignment. Case in point: I sometimes teach a book about suicide terrorism in my Islam class, but it is extremely accessible. When we get to that text, several class sessions are devoted to students finding and summarizing with precision the answers to the questions about the parts of the chapter that I think are most important, rather than me walking them through the text myself.

It is worth mentioning that students seem to appreciate it when instructors intersperse more accessible readings among the more difficult ones. If I can, in each course I try to move back and forth between readings of various difficulty levels (although I confess I'm not always successful, sadly). This has several benefits. First, students tend to get frustrated when the course content is perpetually difficult; this can cause fatigue or burnout, possibly resulting in some students just giving up on the readings altogether. Second, switching up the reading difficulty permits me to invite some meta-level reflections on the course content. I find that with just a little prompting, students will complain about the difficult readings and express relief when we arrive at the more accessible ones. On the one hand, this permits us to talk about what in particular they found difficult and why; in my opinion, generating any such meta-level reflections about their learning experience is intrinsically valuable (in addition, permitting them to vent about the difficult readings—especially when I can say I found them difficult as well—is a way of generating rapport with the students in the course). On the other hand, it permits me at times to point out that perhaps the accessible readings they liked were written at a ninth-grade reading level, while the more difficult ones were written at a college level; there is real value in getting them to realize that college is hard, that to some extent it's *supposed to be hard*, and that it is by doing hard things that we stretch our brains. In my opinion, the ability to break up, digest and understand, and then critically engage rather technical texts is one of the most valuable skills students acquire in exchange for their (rather expensive) investment in higher education.

The last thing that I would like to mention is that colleagues in the academy, our students, and the wider public are increasingly policing the identity politics of one's bibliographies. This is often for very good reasons: it seems quite obviously problematic if, in the twenty-first century, students are taking courses on, for instance, African American women's history but only reading books or essays written by white, male historians. Consequently, it is always worth paying attention to such things as the gender, race, ethnicity, or nationality of the authors one assigns—maybe even their career stages. If the course's readings are top-heavy when it comes to members of privileged groups, then perhaps it would be beneficial to look for a more diverse cast of contributors to the syllabus.

See also: Curriculum; Examples; Group Work; Prerequisites; Primary vs. Secondary Sources; Theory

35

Recruiting Majors

Richard Newton

Religious Studies was a pre-professional degree for me. I count myself among the fortunate few who majored in religious studies with the intent of becoming a teacher-scholar. Of that few, I am part of an even smaller group—one composed of those successful in securing full-time employment in the field. So I declared my major at 18, thinking that the courses I would soon take would be necessary preparation for my eventual career. But as impactful as those classroom experiences were, I am convinced that the very best preparation that I received took place in those business meetings and department conversations where I joined faculty. Recruiting majors was always on the agenda. Those conversations taught me that there would be no profession without recruiting majors.

It also taught me that students, professors, and administrators are often not on the same page regarding the significance of the Religious Studies major. And that's okay for students because they can find another major. And it's okay for administrators because they have many other matters deserving attention. But for professors in the field, a dearth of majors is game over, since tracking the number of majors is, in many schools, the way to assess the health of a department. To have the chance to do what we do best, we need to understand what I'll just call the *major* problem and how students, colleagues, and administrators can help us address it.

In my experience, the major problem is best understood as a perfect historical storm that manifests somewhat differently depending upon context. In regard to curriculum, "religion" no longer holds its onetime place as "the fourth R" in the canon of "Reading, Writing, and Arithmetic." Here in the U.S., many church-affiliated private schools once required students to take a religion course—usually an introduction to the so-called world religions and/or biblical studies. But this requirement is now under threat as such schools rework general education requirements to make space for first-year experiences, internships, service learning, and pre-professional programs that often have demanding credit hour and course requirements.

In this way, private school faculty are now experiencing the woes long endured by their colleagues in public universities. Not only do public school faculty usually lack a mandate for their courses in the study of religion, they also must compete with other departments in the humanities and social sciences that offer their own courses on religion (e.g., does your English Department have a course on "The English Bible as Literature"?). Furthermore, these other departments often have the advantage of brand name recognition—for instance, students come to university already having a grasp of what History is all about as a field—some with the added benefit of a corollary subject taught in high school (unlike many countries in Europe, Religious Studies majors in the U.S. are not training for a public-school career in Religious Education [RE]). Thus, departments of religious studies have an uphill battle when making their presence known to students. If units want to connect with students, whether just to possibly gain them as a student in a course or as a major, then they need to understand where students are and where students will go within the university structure. For this reason, I recommend doing an ethnography of undergraduate student life.

To start with, study a campus map, browse around, and observe where students congregate. Take stock of the student center, the intramural fields, a campus quad, the cafeteria, the library. Learn how students go to see and be seen as part of the student body. These are potential sites where your department can catch students' attention.

Calendar the rhythm of student life on your campus. How and when do students register for classes? Are most students commuting or are they residential? Who takes classes at what times? Are their peak hours for co-curricular activities such as game days, parties, or big campus events? Are there times when little programming is going on at your institution? This is all data with which you can determine where to place recruitment energy and resources—after all, our time as faculty members is limited, what with the various things the career, let alone our lives away from campus, expects of us so wisely investing it is key.

It is easy to think of the major problem as a lost cause, especially given how understaffed and underfunded our units typically are. But trust that limitations have the potential to breed the creativity required to make a little go a long way. I find that the key is focusing recruitment efforts where students are and other departments aren't. "Stealing" majors from other units doesn't serve students or the institutions they come to call home (it's a zero sum game, after all). But fostering the kind of space, programs, and resources that offer something different or complementary enriches campus life. Those niches are where small programs (which the study of religion often is) can build a reputation for being where students want to go, especially those unsatisfied or uncommitted students.

For example, in my first year of full-time teaching, I quickly learned that a large number at my small school had no idea our department even existed. Course enrollment was happenstance. Students enjoyed the classes once there, but they had no idea that we had a major. So in an attempt to reintroduce ourselves, my department decided to bring our classes to them. From our ethnography of the ebb and flow of campus life we learned that, on Tuesday and Thursday, most departments do not teach classes after 3:30. And between then and the 5:30 dinner rush at the cafeteria, students usually hang out. They eat snacks. They work out. They look for things to do to pass the time. Additionally, we learned that students start pre-gaming for the weekend on Thursday afternoons (and were recovering from the weekend on Mondays). Meanwhile co-curricular programs seemed to own Wednesday. This left us with our window of opportunity—Thursday at 3:30. So we decided to put on pop-up classes in the Student Center. Each month for a semester, a different faculty member would give an engaging or timely lecture on some broad topic that would engage students. We covered Star Wars and Asian myths, fake ID Cards and the politics of scripture, uses of sexuality in the Bible, and the religious history of America's most notable public figures. This would show that we were the department that students didn't know they were missing. We just had to figure out how to get students there.

Department faculty asked the students currently in our classes for suggestions, and they did not disappoint. They recommended that we get the student government committee for activities to make themed banners to hang in the student center. So amidst hanging advertisements for intramural sports, trivia nights, and theme parties, there was one academic department bold enough to boast fun classes. Students scratched their heads wondering what those religious studies faculty had to say about space ships, getting carded, biblical sensuality, and celebrity faith-life. Now they knew we were building something. The question was whether students would come? According to informal class surveys, students would—for the right food. Admittedly, this was a tricky proposition because we had a very limited budget. But since we scheduled the event to precede the cafeteria dinner rush, we decided to go with snacks. We got a hold of the campus catering menu and had our current students identify the most-popular yet least-offered foods. In seconds they unanimously gave us a list that included buffalo wings and deconstructed gyros. We went back to campus catering and had them price a small plate appetize for our budget. And we advertised the snack with each talk. Between food and extra credit, we packed out our large meeting space. Students sat around large tables eating and chatting about religious studies. Meanwhile our department made a statement.

What really became key was making sure that this statement was being echoed outside of the meeting space and beyond the event. That's why we invited the campus newspaper to cover it and we invited deans, academic advisors, and other faculty colleagues to come for the event. We quickly became a department—if not *the* department—that was known to be connected to students. I'm not sure if course enrollments and majors increased solely because of these events, but I do know within a year that students could articulate this narrative of faculty–student connection, and that's not nothing.

Extra-curricular events can be a great way to show activity, but in order for students to take the step to make a *major* investment, they need assurance that the departmental unit has a level of permanence to make that investment worthwhile. No matter how great an event or a class may be, students need the departmental unit to become an institutional home. Prior to serving as Undergraduate Director of the Department of Religious Studies at the University of Alabama, I watched this psycho-social space online, from afar. Long before I had visited the post-Civil War southern gothic building that houses the department, I therefore had a mental picture of it from the logo circulating on their social media accounts. I recognized it from their substantial website and busy blog. I knew it from the coffee mugs, buttons, and newsletters shown to me by anyone who had spent time there, either as a student or a guest. As I list these imprints, I hope it becomes clear that the logo isn't simply a graphic design The logo is a mark of literal and figurative real estate. It communicates institution—Émile Durkheim told us as much long ago.

The department should therefore be understood as more than a page in the academic catalog. It is a constructed community that gives students a place to hang their hat and stay awhile. But we have to build it for them to come. The department student association can create an imprimatur to recruit and honor those students who are contributing to the department's programmatic institution just as departmental honors tracks and honor society chapter inductions mark academic commitment. Crafting the potential for belonging is crucial for conveying the department as an entity with *major* staying power.

Make it as easy as possible for students to enter into your course stream so you can do the work of keeping them there onto the finish. What can you do to advise them toward that goal? I say, honor the work that they did prior to finding your program and be the first to ask how to help them pursue their post-college aspirations. Vibrant departments do not need to be the answer to all of students' professional questions. They do however join students in pursuing them. Being the program that helps students make the most of the career center, the writing center, and all the other hidden gems on campus can go a long way. And maybe that is the best place to start.

Even if you were to infuse a ton of money into a department's budget, those monies won't translate into majors in a sustainable way if you don't have the goods. The goods—in their rawest form—are the relationships that lead students and faculty to keep conversations going after class. They are the little nuggets of connection where students re-learn that university life is better because you all get together from time to time. And the best of university life is missed when you're apart for too long.

That *major* potential is there in your program. Maybe you don't have a lounge (yet?), but you get hungry and your students get hungry and I'm sure you can scrounge up some chairs for a brown bag a lunch somewhere. Or I bet you could fold a sheet of paper, write "Reserved for the Religious Studies Student Association," and place it on a lunch table in your campus cafeteria. Ask a few of your most interested current students to meet you there periodically. Invite them to bring a friend too. And start picking their brains. The next time doesn't have to be a lunch. Book a classroom and ask a student to come ready to teach you all how to play their favorite game or you show them a good movie they've never seen. That alone is an activity. If someone springs for snacks, that's a party!

And "voilà!" You just started it.

Now if you're not sure what "it" is, it's the foundation for your *major* solution. Build from this. You don't need a building for your department to be the place to be. Keep investing in your program and your program's capacity to show students that you have a place for them. Start with the ones you already have in your program and in your classes. Work to keep them there (what the administration calls retention) by rewarding their presence and giving them reasons to come back. Maybe those are the officers you appoint for your Religious Studies Students Association. And perhaps the high-achievers among them are the charter members of your chapter of Theta Alpha Kappa honor society for the study of religion?

As you think about your context, your students, and your campus ethnography, I bet you'll find some major solutions hiding in plain sight.

See also: Core Curriculum/General Education; Extra Credit; High-Impact Practices; Honors

36

Seminars

Steffen Führding

Small learning groups which, together with a professor, actively work on and discuss topics or problems from a discipline or a research field: this is how one imagines seminars. In addition, seminars are considered to be the type of course in which scholarly thinking and work are practiced to an exceptional degree. The main activities of reading, questioning, presenting, discussing, and writing are in the center of learning.

In this understanding, the course-type "seminar" dates back to the first half of the nineteenth century. Learning focused on discourse, and academic foundations were then established in an area now known as Germany. The introduction of the seminar as a teaching format was part of a fundamental educational reform that took place at this time. Beginning in the 1880s, the format was imported to the United States and gradually implemented at research-oriented universities. While seminars were initially aimed at advanced students, they soon found their way into lower-level courses.

In the German-speaking university context, seminar courses are widespread. They often outnumber lectures in a degree program—at least in the humanities and social sciences. They are aimed at different groups of students, from beginners to exam candidates, and therefore differ significantly in form and design. At my university, the description of a seminar formulated at the beginning of this chapter applies most closely to seminars aimed at advanced students.

In the spring of 2006, I had to teach my first two seminars. As a student of religious studies and history, I had already attended many seminars. However, I had no experience as a teacher. In Germany at that time, it was not common to be prepared for the role of a university teacher. There was little or no support. That has changed somewhat only within the last years. So, in preparing these first two seminars, I drew primarily on my experiences as a student. I took my cue from teachers who had impressed me both positively and negatively and tried to incorporate those experiences into the planning. Even today I believe that this is not a wrong way to reflect on your own teaching concepts. Nevertheless, above all, I recommend the exchange with colleagues. And indeed, some further training in university didactics cannot hurt, nor can reading books like the one you're reading right now.

During my teaching career I quickly learned that not all seminars are the same. I teach several seminars on a regular basis. When a teaching concept has proven itself, I use it again. If necessary, I adjust something at one point or another. If I notice that a text is too difficult, I replace it. If a teaching method turns out not to be effective, I change it. On the whole, however, the concept remains the same. And yet no two seminars are the same. This is first and foremost because the students who attend the seminar are different each time. They bring different prerequisites and expectations with them. But also, the time of day or the room in which the event takes place impacts its success. The importance of these factors became clear to me only gradually. Today, I try to take them into account in my planning. In seminars, for example, where mutual interaction is essential, and students often have to move around the classroom, I try to ensure that I get a classroom that allows this form of interaction. I remember a seminar for which I had planned quite a bit of group work during the sessions. Unfortunately, the room assigned to me was too small, and the seating was fixed, so, the group work elements I had planned were not feasible. This impacted the seminar participants' mood and motivation because they soon realized something was not working. I quickly had to redesign the seminar concept fundamentally because my plans did not work in this setting.

Seminars also differ with regard to the target group: it makes a big difference whether the students are beginners or advanced students. If the students come from your own discipline, the seminar has to be planned differently—and also run differently—than if you have many students from other areas. In my opinion, courses with beginners need clearer guidelines and a tighter framework. In that case I write a course description and especially the remarks on requirements and expectations in a much more detailed manner. The step from school to university is quite large—at least in the German context. University students are expected to be much more independent and responsible than at school. So the syllabus makes it easier for first-year students to find their way around and offers more orientation. Seminars with advanced students open up other possibilities. These courses can be made more open and more oriented toward the ideal of a seminar as a place of shared scholarly discourse in which faculty and students both participate.

The number of participants in such classes also has a significant impact on the seminar. In the German context, seminars often have twenty, thirty, or even more students. This seems to be a difference to seminars in some other places in the world, where they may be limited to smaller group sizes.

The list of factors influencing the successful implementation of a seminar could be continued. Some of the mentioned aspects are, of course, also valid for lectures. In my experience, however, many contextual factors strongly influence the success of seminars—more so than in lectures—because the engagement of the students and the shared discourse between the instructor and students are essential. This discursive character and the active role that students (should) take are the unifying elements of seminars, despite all the differences that may arise from such factors as class size, location, preparation of the students, etc. The challenge is to enable—and to motivate—students to take an active role in their learning. The way one achieves this is closely related to the factors mentioned above. But it is not always successful.

For me, a seminar has been most successful when I notice that I have stimulated the students—at least some of them—to think, having triggered a further development of their perspective on the class's topic. Such processes are more accessible to observe and guide in smaller groups than in larger settings, but it is still possible. At the beginning of the semester, I spend quite a bit of time in my courses in getting an impression of the seminar participants' prior knowledge, ideas, and attitudes about the topic. Simple brainstorming sessions on the main content or concepts are an excellent way to do this. In my seminar on Introduction to Religious Studies—with an average of thirty-five students; usually, in the German context, a seminar has up to fourteen sessions spread over the semester, with each lasting ninety minutes once a week—I often start by having the students watch a short YouTube video of the so-called "Eagle Dance" of a Zuni group. Students are given the task of writing down in bullet points, and submitting, what they see there and what this video might have to do with the seminar's topic. These notes provide an Instructor with insights into the students' expectations of the seminar. I can also read a lot here about their ideas of religion, culture, and other aspects central to Religious Studies. For me, this "information" is an important starting and even anchor point for the seminar. It is true that I have to disappoint most of the expectations that are formulated here, although, at the same time, I take them seriously and refer to them again at different points in the seminar to clarify central aspects of the seminar or the field. In this way, it is possible to establish a personal connection to the topic for everyone, even in the case of what at first seems like unwieldy topics, and to increase their motivation in dealing with the issue. Real-life examples fulfill the same function. In doing so, you have to be careful not to assume too much about the reality of your own life, as I have noticed over the years. Events that are important to me may no longer work for younger generations to illustrate things. For instance, I belong to a generation of students that was strongly influenced by the attacks of September 11, 2001. For all the suffering that was (and is) associated with these attacks, they brought attention to Religious Studies and seemingly increased its relevance to society. But today I teach students for whom these events are history, of which they have no memories of their own. Often, therefore, the examples no longer work to engage the students to the same extent as they did just a few years ago.

For engaging the students is central to every seminar. This type, of course, thrives on the participation of the students. If you manage to make the participants see the class as "their" seminar, much has been gained. Understanding the seminar as one's own means that the participants become aware that the success of the course and the added value they can derive from it fundamentally depends on their own participation. As a lecturer, I can support this "appropriation process"—as mentioned above—for example, through appropriate teaching methods. It is also necessary to allow enough space for the students' concerns and questions. This facilitates the process of appropriation and promotes (intrinsic) motivation.

However, this approach also harbors dangers. There is a fine line between giving participants the freedom and the opportunity to help shape the seminar, on the one hand, and, on the other, undermining your role as the Instructor. As a lecturer, you should therefore consider in advance how far the participants can help shape the seminar—and make these limits transparent: students' concerns often lead to exciting discussions and can lead to productive results. Sometimes, however, they lead away from the actual topic and the learning objectives that have been set. It is therefore crucial to deal with this area of tension. This is true not least because the content-related objectives do not depend solely on the lecturer's own ideas and plans. Instead, examination regulations and module descriptions, among other things, specify certain goals and content that must be adhered to.

You should also be prepared for the opposite case. Individuals or whole groups may avoid participation and remain passive. Including criteria for active participation as part of the seminar's evaluation criteria could therefore prevent this problem. However, if the inclusion of the students is successful, the seminar offers the chance for "deep learning." Thoughts and positions on the topic can be reconstructed and understood, for example, through the joint, intensive reading and discussion of texts and topics. This provides the opportunity to situate them in their own disciplinary context and to question them critically. This is an important step in tracing the development of an idea, a topic, a paradigm, or entire research fields or disciplines. In the process, contradictions and unanswered questions also come to light. Learning that scholarship is centrally about developing and asking questions and practicing how to ask and work on questions in the respective disciplinary context is a central aspect of seminars. Since—as already indicated—academic questioning has been influenced by the respective context, that is, by the perspectives of the respective fields or disciplines, seminars are central places of "disciplining" and initiation. Here the participants learn the rules of the respective discipline and gradually become part of it. This gives the professor a particular role—despite the strong centering on the role of the students. We university teachers are role models for our students and represent our discipline. Being aware of this role and repeatedly reflecting it is central, in addition to all the other aspects mentioned.

You have to develop your own teaching style to be successful. Even then, you don't always succeed in bringing all of your students along. Not all of them want to or can get involved in the journey. Not everyone likes what I do in my seminars and how I do it. And some of them let me know in the obligatory evaluation at the end of the semester. I would be lying if I said it does not bother me, but critical engagement with such feedback is essential. This also applies to dealing with other expectations placed on you from the outside. They can help you to develop steadily. At the same time, however, as the Instructor one should stay true to oneself and also make the seminar one's "own" within the framework of the given possibilities. In my experience, it makes it easier to give students their own space in the courses, to motivate them to participate actively, and in the end, to offer seminars from which both students and lecturers benefit.

See also: Assignments; Class Participation; Examples; Group Work; Senior Seminars; Syllabi

37

Senior Seminars

Rita Lester

Senior seminars can occupy pride of place in the undergraduate curriculum. For students, the research carried out with a supervising or mentoring faculty is the culmination of their undergraduate education and preparation for jobs, prestigious scholarships, graduate school and other competitive applications. For the department, these courses can provide direct and indirect data for assessment analyses on department learning goals, how/where those goals are achieved (or not). For faculty, teaching a senior seminar is a feedback loop for what prior courses help students to realize our learning goals and what should be rethought, either in our courses or department learning goals. Maybe no other course, except possibly first-year seminars, are such heavy lifting for undergraduate professors.

Although I have argued elsewhere that administrative permission to conduct faculty searches, such as proposals submitted to Academic Planning Committees or Deans which make recommendations to a campus's chief Academic Officer (e.g., a Provost) about hiring, should include not just the numbers of prospective majors/minors the position could recruit but also the number of general education students and first-year seminar students to be taught, so-called service departments like Religious Studies or Philosophy and Religion are often assessed on the senior student work. For example, at my small, liberal arts university, the senior seminar is the opportunity for students, professors, and administrative assessment staff (and subsequently higher learning accreditation organizations), to see how the major accomplishes not only department learning goals, but the goals of the university curriculum. And for this last reason, I think the best way to get all department members on the same page about department learning goals is for everyone in the department who is tenure or tenure-track to be the professor of record for the senior seminar. If possible, I think this is best if the role of the professor of record (i.e., the course counts as part of their teaching load) rotates annually through such courses and in the case of combined departments (such as Philosophy and Religion), it should rotate between the faculty in those disciplines, with all students having second readers in their specific area for supervising, mentoring, and content collaboration.

What is accomplished in the senior seminar is shaped by the department's learning goals, usually expressed in an assessment plan that is itself anchored to a mission statement. What experiences or products count and how many credits or semesters are required to earn the degree? Some departments, even ones at the same school, may conduct the senior seminar as an independent study or accept internships outside the department as alternatives to research, but all three forms (seminar, independent study, or internship) can be the setting and occasion to produce writing that will be presented publicly (if this is part of such senior seminars). In my department, the senior seminar is a two-semester sequence capstone taken in the students' last year that includes vocational reflection on both the general curriculum and the specific course of major study, crafting personal statements for what is next professionally (modeled on Fulbright and graduate school statements), and the polished final writing of a research project (which may or may not have included an internship) that is presented publicly at a university-wide research symposium.

Assessment plans require that departments set goals for learning outcome and I think that we learn plenty from showing those goals to students in the major, asking if and where they think the goals were accomplished and collecting data from those courses or experiences by asking them to show evidence of their learning using such things as digital portfolios. I wonder what the impact would be on student learning if faculty, in the senior seminar, set individual learning goals in consultation with each student given the variety of things that they each want to do next. In my department's major in the last ten years, we have graduated students who go on to be eye doctors, ministers, politicians, reporters, lawyers, physicians, police, prison guards, therapists, and coffee shop managers, as well teachers. They work in theatre, funeral homes, and community non-profits. A few go abroad with teaching or research Fulbright fellowships or critical language scholarship awards (e.g., Boren, Gilman) to places like Ukraine, Jordan, Indonesia, and Spain. One worked on social media for Al-Jazeera and another builds tiny houses. All this to say, departmental prescriptive learning goals may or may not capture what learning our students value most or what learning ends up being the most valuable to them.

Vocational reflection on the major course of study has been recently boosted by The Council of Independent Colleges and the Lilly Endowment through a program called NetVUE. Although invoking religious vocation (as in theological exploration or calling), two of the three stated goals of this vocation reflection initiative are to help colleges assist students to "develop more effective links between developing a philosophy of life and preparing for a career" and to "build connections with community partners ... and organizations." Reconsidering curated digital portfolios as an early assignment to reflect on the common themes of their intellectual and academic journey (expectations, likes and loves), we ask that a student articulate how the senior research project is a logical culminating subject given their previous preparation and work. The argument is novel, but the project is not *ex nihilo*. This reminds me of how, after listening to Jason Ānanda Josephson-Storm on the *Religious Studies Project* podcast of May 14, 2018, "From Static Categories to Rivers of Theories," he encouraged his listeners to see his three seemingly unrelated publications (*The Invention of Religion in Japan*, *The Myth of Disenchantment*, and *Metamoderism: The Future of Theory*) as intertwined or related, like nesting dolls whose nascent ideas existed in the body of the previous work. Grant funded or not, faculty are often the conversation partners with their students for work and career exploration in the major. Even if the students do pursue religious studies in graduate school, there is increasing recognition and planning for work and career outside of the academy. For example, the Director of the Encounter World Religions Centre has a PhD in religion from the University of Toronto and runs a non-profit with a mission statement not unlike many religion departments: to increase our literacy of diverse religious, secular, and spiritual identities, and transform our response to differences from one of threat to opportunity, from fear to curiosity, exploration, and growth.

Upon working with our campus Fulbright committee, it occurred to me that personal statements, statements of purpose, or even application cover letters are the kinds of professional writing that undergraduates need. And they are the hardest things to write! Producing a concise personal statement for an application requires the ability to talk meaningfully about what you have done, what you want to do, and how they are connected. Like most writing, it benefits from workshopping, a clear editor/mentor, a rigorous revision process, and a public sharing. When setting a senior seminar's due dates for such statements, consider the timing of applications the students may be submitting. It has been my experience that these statements are most useful for students if ready in time for applications, which are often due by or during the first semester of their senior year (Fulbright applications are due by mid-October for the following year, but graduate program deadlines tend to fall, at the earliest, toward the end of the calendar year).

When I was an undergraduate and graduate student, the only output considered was the polished thesis and dissertation writing, but today I think it is a more promising practice to understand writing not as a big final "test" but as a way of discovering the heart of the student's intellectual interests and as a turning toward next goals (e.g., vocation, employment, or further schooling). This is why many departments accept intensive internships for senior projects, but the hour requirements per internships credit can range widely (from 45 to 300 hours). Along with the number of hours per credit for internships, the required length of the research paper varies from program to program, even at one small school. Because I teach and have chaired both programs, I know that Philosophy and Religion aims for fifteen pages, but in Gender Studies, the goal is twenty-five pages. The general curriculum impacts this goal as well. As research writing is replaced with project-based learning in our first-year seminars and writing instruction is embedded into various disciplines (e.g., writing in biology, writing in psychology, etc.) this may increase the need for more writing instruction in the senior seminar (as well as in lower-level courses in the major) or it may increase the number of students who pick an internship or a project instead of research paper because, although still research based, that writing is more organically connected to activities, organizations, and more public (or campus) issues.

As the American Association of Colleges and Universities (AACU) shows, this public-facing sharing of research or reflective (i.e., on an internship or project) writing is important for community building and life-work skills. It is less about seniors as public intellectuals, whatever that means, and more about showing one's work! We research, in whatever discipline, to use our knowledge and skills to try to solve a problem, to reconceptualize for the purposes of improving something. And this public sharing, open to discussion and critique (which I think the arts model does very well), provides for students a taste of what professionals do. It prepares our students to hear, evaluate, and contribute to the larger conversations, be they scholarly, vocational, professional, or civic. At my university, we set aside one Wednesday in the spring when all classes are cancelled and seniors from every program and major, along with internships and any recipient of award funding, present and engage the community (non-university folks welcome) with their own original research or reflection on their experience.

It does not have to be a campus-wide symposium to be public-facing, of course, for it could easily be a department colloquy open to campus/community or the assignment could require that seniors submit their research paper to national or regional conferences open to undergraduate submissions, such as the Philosophy and Religion Undergraduate Conference at Truman State, the No Limits Gender Studies conference at University of Nebraska, the recent University of North Carolina at Charlotte Religion conference (theme "Religion and Futurity"). The competitive nature of conferences is more authentically real-life that any course assignment and that itself might be a high-impact lesson.

For the senior seminar, do not make an idol of what has been done; instead, build flexibility into the design to reflect the wide variety of paths our students come from and are going to, and create/assess/revise your department learning goals to better design this course at the intersection of what students learn in the major and what they want to do with their lives.

See also: Assessment; Curriculum; High-Impact Practices

38

Student Evaluations of Instruction

Russell T. McCutcheon

When I was a student in Canada (beginning my undergraduate degree in the fall of 1980), the student government would annually produce reviews of faculty teaching by, as I recall it working at the University of Toronto while I was a graduate student, sending a student representative to each class, on a day prearranged with the faculty member, armed with evaluation forms that would be distributed to the students, to be completed in class, anonymously. The professor would leave the class during this time—more than likely arranging for the evaluations to be administered in the last ten or fifteen minutes of the lecture, enabling them just to leave for the day. Eventually, all of these quantitative scores and presumably a selection of qualitative comments—simply called something like class evaluations back then—would be assembled and distributed by student government in a printed softcover volume that anyone could acquire and, presumably, use as a resource in deciding their future classes. While there were no chili peppers to be given out to "hot" faculty—a onetime practice that the popular site ratemyprofessors.com ended back in the summer of 2018—the process was, much like that site, entirely out of the hands of faculty and the administration; it was therefore disconnected from the annual processes by which faculty are formally assessed (for such things as career progress through the ranks or annual raises). In fact, the old timers at my university, who have been retiring over the past decade or so, recall much earlier in their own careers when such evaluations were first implemented by the administration (in the early 1980s) but, significantly, they were not tied to formal assessments of faculty performance—in fact, the administration apparently assured faculty back then that such evaluations were merely informational, for faculty to receive feedback from student in their classes. But, at least in my experience, university administrators can't resist putting a ranked score to good use—more on that in a moment.

I open with these anecdotes to suggest that what some campuses now call student evaluations of instruction—which are now usually administered online and therefore outside of class time (a move that, in many cases, adversely impacts response rates, something for which faculty are sometimes faulted)—are rather more complicated than they may at first seem. For if we add to their history of being increasingly tied to the ways in which faculty performance and careers are assessed by university administrations the fact that a considerable amount of research has by now made plain that assessments of faculty by students can presuppose a number of assumptions that are now widely seen as rather problematic (e.g., common race and gender biases, whether implicit or quite explicit), then we see that citing a faculty member's score on a teaching evaluation as the reason for their promotion, dismissal, or raise, is not nearly as straightforward as it may seem. For, writing as a longtime department chair who has read all faculty members' student evaluations at the end of each semester, I can say that I've never seen a student comment on how a male faculty member dresses while I've seen plenty of such comments—admittedly sometimes very positive and seemingly innocent—among evaluations of female colleagues. (Readers should, at this point, ask what how one dresses has to do with how one teaches and why this is apparently only an issue for some students when it comes to their female instructors.) The challenge, then, is precisely what we, as faculty members and administrators, should be doing with the formalized but, as many have long known, seriously flawed student feedback that is now so deeply ingrained into university life that it is more than likely going nowhere anytime soon. After all, the research on their shortcomings is hardly a secret.

One of the challenges of our career is that success in the classroom is particularly difficult to measure—i.e., to quantify—and, sooner or later, those in charge will want a seemingly objective number that can be used to evaluate and, importantly, rank the performance of various faculty, for a variety of purposes. However, one does not have to be inclined as a classically Humanistic scholar to conclude that effective teaching can be more of an art than a science, inasmuch as it involves far more than conveying a string of memorizable facts (i.e., the proverbial "names of rivers and dates of wars" approach). Instead, it can involve inspiring and motivating sometimes disengaged students to be curious about things that they otherwise take for granted—especially in a field such as our own where, at least here in the U.S., the vast majority of the students whom we teach are majors in other fields, taking their sole course in the study of religion simply to satisfy some breadth requirement of the so-called Core Curriculum. And so the challenge of evaluating our teaching is very real. Over a couple decades ago the answer to this was not only to recruit peers to periodically visit our classes and comment for the record on our teaching but also to shift from evaluating *teaching* via traditional student evaluations (the so-called delivery of information) to assessing *learning* (i.e., whether the information was received, retained, and used). Rightly recognizing that student evaluations of teachers can often turn into popularity contests in which easy courses and undemanding faculty may score high while far more rigorous courses and demanding faculty can score far lower, there was a shift to increasingly fine-granted learning assessments, i.e., a final course grade is considered to be far too broad a measure, or so we're told, so we instead need to focus on specific assignments and how a student's performance on them reflects the acquisition of specific skills or competencies relevant to the class's goals (now called outcomes). For example, in some settings university students are able to register answers to class prompts instantaneously, via a small remote device or an app on their phone, which communicates with the multimedia system computer in the lecture hall, such that a faculty member can pose a question about something just taught and then immediately learn that, say, 35% of the class does not know the answer—prompting the instructor to repeat or review the material right on the spot, offering another pop quiz to demonstrate an increase in learning. That this technique usually takes place in very large and impersonal lecture halls, possibly in natural science lectures, is something not to overlook; for it makes plain the linkage between the rise of student learning assessments and the funding that determines, among other things, declining student–faculty ratios and increasing class sizes.

The backlash against quantifying teaching, coming especially from some faculty in the Humanities who often claim that their courses are designed to accomplish goals that are, again, unquantifiable (e.g., students will learn to appreciate this or that quality or thing) continues to this day, making plain that teaching evaluations is a site of considerable negotiation and sometimes contest in the modern university. But despite pushback and empirical evidence of their many problems, measurements of the student response to the teacher and the class continue, with students being asked if the instructor was timely, available, prepared for class, etc. So as to add some context to these reports, thereby trying to make them more useful, perhaps, additional questions have appeared over the years, such as inviting students to report the grade they expect in the course or how much work they put into the course and whether they had ever sought assistance form the professor or enrolled in such a course before. (Interestingly, early on it was apparent that asking just two questions—"What grade do you give the course?" and "What grade do you give the instructor?" yielded results not much different from far more complex questionnaires—something still known to admins since, at least on my campus, they sometimes focus only on the scores of just these two prompts.)

And because these scores—which are reported as comparative data, relative to the other faculty within the department, the college, and the university (such that one scores in this or that percentile)—are now helping to govern an individual's career advancement, they are now considered confidential, usually being available only to the faculty member themselves and their supervisor. In fact, at my own university, these scores are automatically uploaded into the online productivity reporting system that each faculty member must populate with data each year (e.g., number of courses and students, number of graduate students supervised, bibliographic information for all publications submitted, accepted, or published that year, along with all grant applications or awards, etc.)—a report which forms the basis of their chair's annual evaluation and raise recommendations. And so, in a world where we can easily count the number of peer review articles someone may have written in a year or the number of citations to their works, a teaching evaluation score based on student feedback has become a pretty appealing metric to use as a basis for comparisons among faculty—at least for administrators in a litigious environment who may be eager for a way to appear to be fair and objective when it comes to assessing faculty and determining their career progress.

But, returning to the earlier comment on assessing these assessments of our work in the classroom, it's an open secret that such metrics are hardly objective or neutral. We have long known that international faculty who speak with varying levels of accent can be unfairly criticized by students and that male faculty often receive drastically different sorts of comments than do their female colleagues. A student who once missed a faculty member at their weekly office hours may report that the instructor is difficult to meet outside class time and students with an overinflated sense in their ability may complain about their low grade, seeing in it as a failing on the part of the professor. Moreover, as readers may very well know, the most consequential teachers—an impact that can only become apparent many years after the conclusion of the class—are sometimes hardly those who students initially think did a good job, making plain that just what we mean by a successful class requires considerable attention; for, to select but a simple example, is success a class in which everyone earns an A (and thus a class in which student capabilities seem not to have been pressed very far) or a class in which many students fail (since the inevitable breadth of student preparation and abilities sometimes makes plain that not everyone is up to the task)?

This all leaves the instructor in the unenviable position of not really knowing what to do with the results of student teaching evaluations. More importantly, perhaps, the problem that an administrator has can be even more acute, since they are the ones who determine the consequences of these reviews. The only recommendation within the agency of faculty and their chairs is to read such reviews with an eye for patterns or trends (across one course or over a variety of courses), since the lone complaint can mean so many different things (including ill will on the part of the student) that it is unwise to take any action based on it alone. While recognizing that this or that perception exists among students is not without value (a perception that itself may need to be addressed by the faculty member in their future classes, even if they think it is incorrect), the already mentioned linkage of these evaluations to career progress means that a chair would be wise only to act based on repetition of the claim, which provides the basis for a conversation with the faculty member—one that begins with a question and not an accusation: "What did you make of your teaching evaluations this semester." For while there are indeed faculty who, as in all professions, sometimes need to make significant adjustments to the effort that goes into their work, in far more cases faculty members are very mindful of their students' needs and eager to put in place the conditions to assist with their success in the classroom—which means that they more than likely have already read the reviews and are considering how to adapt their teaching style to address the comment. Bracketing out for the time being the sorts of student complaints, whether or not conveyed via such evaluations, that trigger far different administrative processes (e.g., claims of harassment on the part of the instructor), the positive and the negative feedback from student teaching evaluations, though broadly helpful as a sampling of student perception, is a far too blunt device without nuance and one that must therefore be handled rather carefully if, as it often is, it is linked to performance reviews of the instructor.

See also: Academic Misconduct; Assessment; Large Lectures

39

Syllabi

Richard Newton

Ah, the much-bemoaned syllabus. So many students are averse to reading it. Faculty race to devise it just before the semester's start. Colleagues share it. Colleges and universities assess it. For something that causes such a fuss, the syllabus is a surprisingly mystifying document. But it doesn't have to be.

Like the classroom itself, the syllabus exists at the intersection of a number of interests. It needs to accomplish certain things for students, departments, and administrators. Your college likely has directives about the minimum requirements for syllabi: policies on late work; an explanation of your grading schema, and compliance statements regarding (at least in the U.S. where I work) the Americans with Disabilities Act (ADA), the Federal Education Rights and Privacy Act (FERPA), and the U.S. Department of Education's Office of Civil Rights (of which statutes like Title IX may be the most well-known). Post-COVID-19, your institution probably has new syllabus requirements for the role and rules of technology use. And there's always the Registrar's insistence that certain academic calendar dates have a place on your syllabus.

I lay this out at the start because this boilerplate information has little to do with the teaching of the study of religion. Every class—from biology to basket weaving—is going to have the above. However, that doesn't mean it is unimportant or irrelevant to you. The very term "boilerplate" comes from the industrial-looking metal typesets of syndicated news to which local newspaper outlets subscribed and printed in lieu of developing similar content themselves. It kept local presses from having to worry about what's happening "over there," allowing them to instead focus on what's happening in their domain. So too with the syllabus. The boilerplate addresses issues that your larger institutional setting has already handled or at least addressed to its satisfaction (e.g., what is the campus's severe weather policy?). Maybe this is all old news to you, but a surprising number of faculty get hung up on matters that are literally meant to be copy-and-pasted. Move on, I say, so you can focus on the syllabus as a resource for your teaching of the study of religion in only the way that you can within your program.

Sometimes colleagues get really excited about sharing syllabi. Personally, I don't think this is as useful an exercise as many people think. Sure, perusing a syllabus will give you a sense of what could be taught. You may even get some insight into how to teach an idea or two. But a good syllabus meets a local need, one particular to a program's setting. What do you need your course to do in your context? Have you been charged with teaching a specific skillset? Are there certain knowledge competencies that students are expected to have by term's end? Is your course a retrospective capstone that ties things together or is it an introductory course needed to make the case that that the study of religion is in fact interesting and worth students' time? To what extent is your course linked to other offerings? The always local answers to these questions inform the constraints and possibilities for relevant course development. With them and the boilerplate in mind, you are free to do whatever you want.

Yes, you need to spend time deciding what books to teach or what tests to give. But those "whats" are not as important for you as they are for bookstores and registrars. Being the expert that you are, I trust that you are smart enough to see that nearly any resource or assessment can work for your ends. And relative to everything else your students will be doing while in college—let alone after graduating from school—they aren't spending much time thinking about the "what" of your class either. The driver of your class is its core argument—and yes, I see a course as making a persuasive argument across a semester. Determine the research question and working thesis statement of your course. What case are you making? Everything you'll be doing in class will come back to this conversation. In formal syllabus parlance, the summary of that discussion is your course description.

The real work—and fun—of the syllabus is the "how." Given everything represented by the boilerplate information and your department's needs, how can you best make your course's case within the time constraints of a semester? There is no right answer—only answers that empower or impede you in executing the course.

Teach from a position of strength. Ask yourself where, in the past, you have been most effective in the act of instruction. If you've never taught a class of your own, think of the public speaking engagements that have elicited the most positive response. If you're developing an online or hybrid class, the thrust of the question is the same. Given a mode of instruction, where do you see yourself most helping students connect with material, not because of the content but because of the instruction? Build your classroom around setting up those moments in a way that leads students to exemplify, explore, work through your course description. Whether this is a repeatable activity (e.g., hands-on case study analysis, riveting class discussions, or exciting lectures) or one-off highlights (e.g., a compelling film, a field trip, or project), assume that this is going to make an appearance in your class in some appropriate manner.

What constitutes appropriate? Well, in addition to your course description, you've likely been given or have developed a set of student learning outcomes that you are expected to meet. This is that formal list of expectations that you and your department have for students successfully completing the course. Meeting these expectations will bring your students in alignment with your department's goals. An appropriate activity is one with an eye on positioning you to do your instructional best and an eye on what students need to accomplish while working with you. Every class moment won't be devoted to these in equal measure. But you will adjust your focus throughout the term to increasingly bring your course's thesis into students' view. The syllabus then becomes a plan for plotting out how you intend to progress toward your goals.

Disabuse yourself of having to assign that must-read article or book that everyone was talking about back in graduate school or citing in the field's premier journals. Your students—even those who have taken a few courses in our subject—will likely be ill-equipped to appreciate what that work accomplishes. And you probably have more appropriate resources at your command for raising an undergraduate student's understanding, interest, and curiosity about the study of religion. No one is served by assigning bibliography that students aren't going to read, essays they're ill-equipped to comprehend, or assignments you're not going to want to grade. The only required course materials are those that will provoke your students to think about the things that you are prepared to discuss. What will get that job done?

Not knowing your subject matter, I don't have stock answers for you. And honestly, you wouldn't want them even if I did. What you need is the confidence that comes with knowing what you're doing and why you're doing it. So instead of giving you a sample syllabus, I'm instead going to share some of the things that I think about in my syllabus design.

The syllabus is a lot of things, but its most important and unifying feature is that it should work for your teaching. So the syllabus, for me, is a manual of the course's logic. My students are surprised to learn that I haven't committed due dates, assignment word counts, and other details to memory. The syllabus is where I keep that information and so much more. The syllabus documents all that information so that I can focus on other, more pertinent, things. I expect it to operate similarly for my students. In fact, explaining this makes for a great first teaching moment.

By many standards, my syllabus is laughably long. I'll explain why later on, but it is so long that when I distribute it to students prior to the beginning of class, I tell them not to read it and just to bring it to class. I even jokingly admit that reading it now will give them the impression that this course is impossible when that couldn't be further from the truth. They just need to show up on the first day and trust me. This initial interaction communicates, yes, that the course is not a blowoff class. More importantly it frames our relationship as one of concern. My students know that I'm thinking about them and how they approach learning. This is my way of preparing them to receive whatever resides on the syllabus that they have yet to see.

So why is my syllabus so long? Because I include a calendar of all of the assignments and readings that require work on their part. I have initial descriptions of how to approach each deliverable as well as guidelines for how to prepare for class. And though I reserve the right to amend the syllabus (a point that I also include on the syllabus), my syllabi are pretty stable. I want students to be able to use this as a resource to plot out how they will direct their energies toward our learning outcomes, just as I am doing the same. To this end, I don't include policies or lessons that I'm not willing to hold myself to because I want to be free enough to adapt *how* I engage my students *where they are*.

Among the best things that I ever did was to include a "flex day" once a month—class sessions with topics still to be determined. I can use these to review course content or to follow up on one of those not-so-tangential tangents that can emerge in the classroom. And I've taught long enough to know that sometimes, students (and teachers) just need a day to catch a breath and catch up on work. I want students to know that there is a method to what they might perceive—especially in those first weeks—as madness. A detailed syllabus is Exhibit A in making that element of my course's case.

On the first day of class, I invite students to treat the syllabus like an automobile manual. Just as most motorists drive without ever reading an automobile manual cover to cover, one need not pour over the details of a syllabus during the first week of class. However, I explain that my role as a teacher is to draw their attention to things on the syllabus as they need to know them. In this metaphor I suppose I'm the indicator lights on the dashboard, signaling those matters worthy of further consideration for a smooth ride.

Now call me old school if you like, but I also share with students how it wasn't uncommon for drivers of bygone eras to log their oil changes and repairs in these manuals. Some would even consult the manual to carry out repairs themselves. The syllabus can—and in my class, should—be just a such a resource. As a class, I have the students pulling it out regularly to talk through where we've been, where we're going, and where there are sticking points in their learning. I might stop the class and ask students to circle or highlight a day or reading that they found (or I find) particularly challenging. We review in kind and thus the syllabus becomes a working document.

This is by no means the only way to devise or use a syllabus. Contra what I've laid above, some professors insist on single-sheet syllabi or graphically organized syllabi because they see these as engaging students more than the more classic document format. The question is how to make sure whatever you do helps students engage and meet the concerns of your department and institution.

Where I tend to detail all of the moving pieces prior to the start of the semester, colleagues of mine present rough schedule outlines, affording them the flexibility to adapt throughout the semester to what's happening in the room. What helps you to be present and persuasive as an instructor? If your syllabus is helping you do that, and it is enriching your institution's students and your department, then you probably have a syllabus that is working for you. If not, make it so.

See also: Assessment; Class Participation; Curriculum; Introduction vs. Survey

40

Teaching Assistants

Steven Ramey

The roles of graduate students (and occasionally undergraduates) as Teaching Assistants can vary significantly across departments. In predominately undergraduate institutions, occasionally a professor will perhaps have an advanced undergraduate, usually a senior major, who assists in a regular course, sometimes helping redesign a course or simply assist the professor in course logistics and (likely minimal) grading while gaining valuable experience. On the graduate student level, teaching assistants might be similar to the undergraduate teaching assistant described above, providing mainly logistical and grading assistance. In some course arrangements, a graduate student will have multiple discussion group sections that meet once a week to supplement the lectures, and in some institutions, graduate student teaching assistants, even in their first year, can be assigned to teach a course all on their own.

Whatever the structural context of a teaching assistant, the advisor should recognize this as an educational opportunity for the teaching assistant, an opportunity to train them in pedagogy, rather than only a source of labor to free the professor from certain tasks. Sharing with the graduate student the rationale for the course design, assignments, and specific lectures is therefore a useful experience. I remember fondly a professor while I was a doctoral student at UNC Chapel Hill, who was the instructor for a course outside my specialty where I was assigned to be the TA. He regularly explained why he arranged tests and lectures in the ways that he did. At Chapel Hill, each TA ran multiple discussion sections that each met once a week, and this professor not only visited the discussion sections on occasion (giving feedback to the TA afterwards as well as assisting in limited ways) but also gave his graduate students both structure and freedom in designing the sessions for each discussion section. He had a basic structure for what each session would discuss, with some sample activities, but he allowed us to modify that structure. He also drew on his years of teaching experience to share some advice with us, including a piece of wisdom that I still employ regularly: make sure that students leave each session with some bit of knowledge, an example, an explanation, an anecdote, that they did not have when they arrived. Thus, students remain more engaged because the discussion section included something new, beyond a simple review of the material in the readings and lectures.

Perhaps the most ubiquitous task that a teaching assistant manages is grading. When professors teach large enrollment courses, with or without discussion sections, grading essays and other assignments becomes the most tangible way that teaching assistants help (at least in my experience). But having a group of teaching assistants grade written assignments in a fair and consistent fashion is a challenge. It requires the professor to articulate, whether in an explicit grading rubric or another fashion, how to assess the assignment. Is proper grammar determinative in an essay? Clear descriptions or information? Specific formatting? Robust analysis? Articulating what makes an essay a 97 vs. a 92, or a C vs. a D, is especially difficult if the assignment is relatively new to the faculty member (who may just intuitively recognize the difference between an A+ and an A). I have continued the common practice, which some of my supervisors employed when I was a teaching assistant, of starting the grading of an assignment by meeting together with all of the teaching assistants and grading a sampling of essays. We pass several essays around the room, then discuss the various grades that we each would give, to move toward a consensus grade with as clear as possible standards. Such an exercise is rarely perfect, however; very good essays become fairly easy to assess, and high grades are easy to give out. But a bigger struggle comes with the student who misses a chunk of an essay assignment but gets the overall point, or the mediocre essay that barely gets the point but includes all the required elements.

Determining the amount of grading that is reasonable for a TA to be assigned is another challenge. I have sometimes expected too much of my teaching assistants, and at times I have recognized a need for me to step in and help a struggling teaching assistant complete the grading in a timely fashion. Designing assignments in ways that are easy to grade for TAs is also important. That said, I have also had graduate students recommend that they take on additional grading. After talking with some teaching assistants years ago, I instituted an essay on exams in my large enrollment course (100–150 students, working with one or two TAs). The teaching assistants who recommended the essay did so while discussing the difficulty distinguishing between those students who really understand the goal of the course (critical analysis) and those who can mainly repeat what they have heard (reflecting more rote memorization). To make it manageable to grade, though, these essays are only one-paragraph long, with only one essay per exam. Once a standard is set, most of them can be graded fairly quickly. On top of the length, I present students with the question ahead of time, as the point is not to catch the unprepared student but to encourage them to think about the material and formulate the answer. Some especially diligent (and often somewhat anxious) students will send the teaching assistant a draft ahead of time or meet with the teaching assistant prior to the exam to discuss their answer. Both of those are wonderful, in my opinion, as they demonstrate an engagement and willingness to learn (inspired primarily by the grade they hope to receive, which is one reason we have grades, no?). Providing the question ahead of time improves the quality of responses, of course, which smooths out the grading process, and it also makes the assignment of a low grade less troubling, as a poor answer suggests a student who either needs to take the course seriously or who needs to come and ask for assistance. A low grade can therefore motivate the appropriate response.

The success of this addition to the course is important to recognize. The essay questions encourage and assess student learning in some areas of the course better than, say, a multiple-choice test (it is a large lecture course, after all) and allows students whose test-taking skills are not geared toward multiple choice tests a better chance to succeed. This point illustrates the value of the TA as a course design consultant. While the feedback works best after the semester (and thus any changes are relevant for the next time teaching the course), their observations on the success of the course and their constructive criticisms can be extremely useful, as we so often teach without much substantive feedback from others invested in the educational project. And the more that professors and TAs discuss the pedagogical rationale and techniques of the course, the better their feedback can be.

Having teaching assistants engage undergraduates in office hours or other opportunities outside the classroom can also be important for both the undergraduates and the teaching assistant. I recently heard a major in my own department explain that she talked with one of my teaching assistants over Zoom (during the height of the pandemic) for an extended time, something that helped her decide to major in Religious Studies. One challenge, as with faculty office hours, is getting students to attend. While I have some anecdotal success stories, experimenting with other ways of encouraging engagement is a topic that I am currently discussing with my teaching assistants, with options including returning to a digital office hour option and describing office hours as a workshop for assignments and thus, by relabeling, encouraging students who want or need more engagement to attend.

Presenting lectures of their own (whether or not in a large enrollment course) is another challenge for a teaching assistant, as well as an opportunity for them to learn. When I had the chance to work with some teaching assistants who were completing dissertations in an adjacent department, I could not expect them to take on a day's regular lecture in a world religions course, but we found a topic on which they were confident (usually related to their dissertations) and then found a place for it to tie into the course. These were often a third to a half of a class session, giving the graduate student experience preparing and presenting a lecture. This naturally can generate apprehension for a graduate student new to teaching, regardless the size of the class. However, it was a low-stakes context, as I did not serve on their dissertation committee. Thus, even an unsuccessful lecture (which none of them were) would have been simply a learning opportunity without the risk of a negative reflection within their committee. With M.A. students in my own department, I have recognized that asking them to present a significant lecture on a topic that is outside of their expertise is similarly unfair. However, I have found it to be a rather productive challenge for less experienced teaching assistants to present a mini-lecture modeled on a very specific assignment: the analysis of a news article. For the teaching assistant, therefore, they do not have to be an expert on a specific religion but, instead, put together a brief presentation related to an undergraduate assignment. In fact, these mini-lectures are vital in the course to demonstrate to students what we want them to do in their own critical analysis of a news article, and having them presented by a TA can increase attention for some students, what with the inevitable shift in presentation dynamics. While the material presented is thus easily developed and mastered by the TA, the process of presenting in front of a class is often a challenge for an M.A. student, hopefully a productive challenge that builds their confidence. For these occasions to have the most learning potential for the teaching assistant, of course, preliminary discussions about the lecture and time afterwards for debriefing is very constructive.

Another area where graduate students can benefit from the experience of being a teaching assistant can be helping to design assessment questions. Because I have particular emphases in the types of questions that I prefer, I have chosen not to ask a TA to create the entire test. In some cases, I have therefore asked them to produce a few questions that I can then insert into the test (modifying as necessary). Encouraging teaching assistants to develop discussion questions for their own discussion sections or lectures is also an important skill. It can be difficult to articulate to students what makes a good question, but that is why giving them those opportunities is important. Since teaching is central in most any academic career, it is often in the teaching assistant position that important career training happens for those hoping to pursue a career as a professor. Therefore, including a range of opportunities, plus preliminary assistance and constructive feedback afterwards, are vital.

My focus has been on Teaching Assistants working with a professor in a course. This type of model has great potential to help the graduate student develop, whereas teaching an entire course on their own, especially early in their graduate work, often serves the interests of the institution more than the student themselves. If graduate students are brought to an institution primarily to provide instructional labor for a curriculum, thus freeing the budget from a full-time instructor's pay and benefits or freeing faculty from teaching, say, introductory undergraduate courses, the practice can generate significant problems. Graduate student burnout, attrition, and increased time-to-degree can occur in any program, but the added pressures of a heavy, solo teaching load compounds all of this. Naturally, some graduate students thrive under that freedom to teach on their own and the related pressure, but some exceptionally capable graduate students do not thrive in that environment.

The problems can extend further, though, if the burnout for the graduate student instructor and lack of teaching support and experience results in a poorer quality class for the undergraduates. For programs that rely on the introductory course to recruit majors and students for upper-level courses, pushing entry level courses onto inexperienced graduate students may be counterproductive for the department and the university as a whole. Of course, some new graduate students may be more successful in the classroom than some senior or early career faculty. A scholar's level of experience does not guarantee engaging and productive pedagogy, of course, but the anecdotal exceptions are not sufficient to dismiss the concern that more teaching experience typically improves the quality of a course. For me personally, the first time I taught a course by myself—and really any course that I teach for the first time—becomes an experiment with significant opportunity to improve. The late Jonathan Z. Smith of the University of Chicago argued that the most senior scholars should teach the most general courses within Religious Studies, because graduate education and research emphasizes such specialization that an advanced graduate student or early career professor is best equipped to teach advanced specialized courses. It therefore takes years within the discipline, decades even, to develop the breadth of examples that enhance an introductory course. From my own experience, I know that I understand more about religions outside of my main research area of South Asian religions after I have taught those religions multiple times in a Religions of the World survey. Each semester, I develop more familiarity with the concepts associated with a religion and examples and case studies that help students engage the material more fully and critically.

When done well, with consideration for the needs and vulnerability of graduate students, supervising a TA definitely adds work for the professor, while it also assists them with some of their duties. In some situations, it would be less time consuming to do tasks, such as lectures (whether a mini-lecture or full class lecture), themselves, but it is important for the training of the teaching assistant that the supervisor give them opportunities, with clear instructions, guidance, assistance, and feedback.

See also: Assessment; Final Examinations; Grading; Large Lectures

41

Theory

K. Merinda Simmons

I've described myself as a "social media slouch," not to be self-deprecating but to give what I think is a pretty honest description of this introvert's ambivalent relationship with the sensory input (or what feels at times like an onslaught) that comes courtesy of a web that is very much worldwide. One of the things that I appreciate or resent depending on the day is the unsolicited "memories" Facebook offers when I sign on. As it happens, the one that came up today was a post I wrote six years ago about "theory" in the introductory religious studies classroom. It went like this:

> Someone in my large-enrollment Intro course of 110 students stayed after class today to let me know how important and exciting it is to her that she has the chance to do some critical thinking in a structured way. She wanted to talk about how to transfer some of the ideas we're discussing to other domains in her studies and even career pursuits (only a sophomore but, of course, is thinking about the marketability of her interests, etc.). She's a great example of how important it is not to withhold theory from 100-level contexts and introduce it only in upper-level courses "once students have a foundation." It *is* the foundation for the upper-level work I want them to do later.

I still remember that moment. The student was an anthropology major who was early in her program. What that means for a lot of undergraduates at a place like the University of Alabama whose student population hovers at roughly 40,000 is that they're still taking required courses, often taught by graduate teaching assistants who have their own academic fish to fry or by professors who don't take the introductory classes as seriously as they do their upper-level seminars. This is a vast and unfair generalization, of course—there are scores of professors and grad students alike who invest heavily in their teaching (I assume you're in that cohort if you're reading this book). But that hadn't been the experience for the student who stopped to talk to me that day six years ago, and she's unfortunately not alone in that. She ultimately became a Religious Studies major and a student worker in our department's main office before going on to pursue a graduate degree in Consumer Sciences... But I'm getting ahead of myself.

The reason I admitted my occasionally less-than-enthusiastic involvement on social media is to explain just how dumbfounded I was when a relatively heated debate ensued on a thread about my post—a thread that racked up a whopping twenty-two comments (to be fair, it was on the timeline of a friend who shared it). That's a lot to this pseudo-user! I was pretty surprised to see that what I felt was a relatively innocuous "proud prof" post seemed to strike such a nerve. But as I sit here now writing this brief piece six years on, debates continue to swirl among scholars in religious studies about what the role of theory should or should not be in our research and in our classrooms. Where pedagogy is concerned, a couple of the issues that were present in that thread and that come up again and again are to do with 1) how much room theory should be included in a course's content and 2) when students are ready to read and incorporate it (i.e., how much prior study is required in order to fully understand or process theoretical texts).

Perhaps *the* biggest shift from my undergraduate to graduate work in literary studies was the move from courses surveying works of an uninterrogated Western canon to courses examining the power, ideologies, and politics that govern that very canon. The questions were no longer about an author's meaning but about their context, and the point of our discussions were motivated not so much by what a text is (an example of this or that poetic form, etc.) but more by *how* a text comes to be or mean anything at all. In that sense, my "light-bulb moment" did not illuminate a stable object sitting before me. Instead, it illuminated a vast structure I didn't even know I was in, revealing hallways to innumerable rooms that I could suddenly explore. The role of theory in the introductory classroom, as far as I'm concerned, is to shift students' gaze so that they begin to see an object of study as part of a wider network of social forces that shape the world (and the phenomena contained therein) as they know it. They need not wait until graduate school to make that shift.

Besides, the importance of the "stuff" I teach—or data, or whatever word one wants to use—is not as inherently obvious as I might want to think. Too often, our presumption in area studies or survey classes is that the area we're studying and surveying is not just beneficial but actually necessary to a liberal arts education. After spending so much of our own time, energy, and money becoming a trained specialist of that topic, how could it *not* be necessary? It had better be! But while that logic may help assuage our own academic anxieties, it doesn't do much to compel our students, many of whom are there to fulfill a curricular requirement. We do our students a favor when we draw attention to a course syllabus not as a "greatest hits" compilation but as a very specific claim about what *we* find particularly worth reading or discussing and why. Admitting our own editorial role from the outset—that we curate as much as present information—allows really interesting questions and debates to emerge among students who are invited to engage with the course material rather than merely receive or repeat it.

This pedagogical approach to undergraduate religious studies courses also shifts traditional classroom power dynamics in a really constructive way. Letting our undergrad (especially 100-level) students in on the conversation that is too often reserved for graduate students signals our treating them with an important level of intellectual respect. If there's one Student Learning Outcome shared (implicitly, of course) across all the classes I teach, it's that students become curious about their own behavior. I want them to start noticing the norms they've internalized, the norms that they easily take for granted. Applying what we read and discuss in class to their own lives, students can—if they're willing—start the difficult, often uncomfortable, but incredibly valuable process of taking themselves more seriously by subjecting themselves to their own modes of critical inquiry. As teachers, we get the privilege of facilitating that process and watching it unfold—a privilege that I find especially rewarding at the introductory level.

One of the reasons professors give for relegating theory only to upper-level and graduate courses *on theory* (often siloing it to a course topic all its own) is the amount of background necessary for students to process dense conceptual readings. This is a narrow/myopic view of what theory is, however. One need not plunge students into inscrutable jargon to get them thinking theoretically. My intro syllabus includes accessible snippets from classic thinkers like Karl Marx to contemporary ones like Craig Martin, sure. But the primary sources of "theory" for my students are everyday examples of how the ideas from those course readings play out in the world. So we'll read and talk about Mary Douglas's take on the classificatory structures deployed in ritual practice. But then I'll show them a news article on controversies surrounding seemingly neutral classifications like "milk" and "meat" thanks to non-dairy products' ad campaigns and the rapidly developing world of lab-grown proteins. We talk about who ultimately decides how such designations get assigned, as well as what the consequences are for consumers. These examples are what help my students "get" Douglas. In considering what gets to count as what in their grocery stores, students are "doing theory" whether they realize it or not. They are thinking about complex interrelationships of power and capital, and they're thinking about the role of naming in reflecting and governing those dynamics. It is a relatively easy task, then, for them to apply the same considerations to "religion"—who uses the term to name what, when, and how, and what the effects and functions of that term can be depending on context. Students start seeing the components of their social worlds animated by these dynamics—these labels that turn out not to be so innocent or neutral after all.

Often, students take our classes to meet broader degree requirements. This is especially true of introductory courses that fulfill part of the core credit hours students need in humanities, regardless of their degree program. In these settings, there may be only a small number of people enrolled who are majoring in something even remotely to do with the liberal arts. So it doesn't do anyone any good to approach these classes as stepping stones en route to upper-level seminars or graduate courses in religious studies. They are surely also that for those on that path, but they have to be able to stand on their own for the vast majority of those who aren't. That's why I find it so much more important to introduce students to critical thinking skills that cultivate and hone their curiosity than to ask them only to rehearse the ins and outs of a specific group or tradition. It's also why I think the dichotomy between data and theory—in whatever amount either is administered—is a false one.

The student I mentioned in my Facebook post is only one person, of course, but she reflects a trend I continue to notice in 100-level courses. The reason so many of our majors get recruited from REL 100, as she did, is not that they decide to become experts on early twentieth-century American Pentecostalism (or on meat-product marketing, for that matter). It's that they receive the tools necessary to see the world and the phenomena therein—"religious" or otherwise—in a new light. I call those tools "theory." As evidenced by the back-and-forth stemming from that post six years ago, and as evidenced by the debates still swirling in the field, many suggest that theory is, by definition, a dense set of specialized discourses that have no place in an introductory classroom because students aren't ready for it and/or because theory doesn't help them understand the real world. I have total respect for the specific turns and terminologies in theoretical interventions that require some prior knowledge and framing. But that's a different set of pedagogical concerns. At issue here is simply that theory—when introduced early and incrementally—is something students are ready and even hungry for, and it helps them not only understand but also live with more curiosity and engagement in the "real world." It also empowers them to explore and apply those curiosities to whatever their degree program might be, to wherever they might go when they leave our classes.

See also: Critical Thinking; Introduction vs. Survey; Transferable Skills

42

Transferable Skills

Steven Ramey

Articulating the transferable skills of a humanities degree has become a common way to encourage students to major in Religious Studies and other departments. Lists of transferable skills developed in the humanities and related fields are abundant from such humanities programs themselves and even from a campus's career center. These lists often include variations on the following:

- ability to gather and process information;
- creative thinking and problem solving;
- written and oral communication;
- logical and analytical thinking;
- ability to engage diverse perspectives; and
- "soft skills," such as interpersonal communication (including listening) and empathy.

Such lists also frequently draw on, or are justified by, reports from employers about the skills that they desire in new employees, referencing how humanities courses foster these abilities that are widely applicable (thus the transferable element). (For example, consider Google's Project Oxygen—an initiative dating from early 2009 that "began analyzing performance reviews, feedback surveys and nominations for top-manager awards" in order to "build better bosses," as a *New York Times* article succinctly phrased it [March 13, 2011, section BU, p. 1].) These arguments further note that the applicability of such skills is powerful and long-lasting, as few people now stay in the same career throughout their adult life, whether by choice or necessity.

Selling students on humanities courses and even majors with catchphrases like "Learn to think critically," or "Communication skills are marketable!" is part of the process, but in my experience, our articulations of the relevance of their work in our classes need to go further. First, making direct connections between skills developed in Religious Studies classrooms and specific contexts outside academia is stronger than an abstract assertion about an ability to "process information." The concrete examples can also build on student reports that they have used these skills already in their college career, applying them in a course in another department, for example. Second, all of these assertions need to be routinely integrated into the classroom rather than just emphasized as a sales pitch at a majors fair, parents' weekend (since career questions often involve parents), or advising session. Developing these discussions further, geared toward communicating with undergraduate (and even graduate) students, can involve a wide range of contributors and strategies.

For programs whose alumni predominately do not go into the study of religion (or even ministerial careers), the experience of alums is the first stop on the road to refining our discourse on transferable skills. Judging by my own department, our alums develop careers in many sectors, teaching in public schools, starting a business, working in marketing and sales, practicing medicine or law, etc. Their anecdotes on the relevance of the skills they gained in our classes—something departments can elicit from them in various ways (inviting them back, featuring an interview with them in a newsletter, inviting them to write for the unit's website or blog, etc.)—become far more effective examples than the more abstract assertions made by a faculty member, who is often long removed from the challenge of applying undergraduate training in diverse ways.

These alums have become an important source for my department, with several invited to discuss with undergraduates what the religious studies major prepared them to do. But frequently, these are not automatic or natural presentations to make. Often, the skills they have developed and routinely use are rather implicit to them, and so graduates of a program have to reflect back on their career and studies in order to identify different benefits, such as learning to read people through social analysis as a salesperson, breaking down a task to its various component parts in a lesson plan, locating resources (i.e., carrying out research) to learn a new skill, finding alternative readings of legal decisions to support their position, writing a clear business plan in order to secure a loan, etc. Listening to alumni, whom I recall presenting each of those anecdotes, has helped me to articulate better to students the benefits of the work that we do together in our classes and how it translates into skills for different contexts throughout their careers and their lives more generally. It therefore takes thought, practice, and analysis to begin to make a more convincing case for the value of a religious studies degree. And I certainly don't think that I have mastered the genre.

Since so many of our students do not pursue careers in the field, the specific information that they acquire from classes sometimes is less valuable than the skills that they acquire during their studies. The more that we can convey to our students explicit and concrete ways that they can recognize, the better our results will be. I often rely on critical thinking skills as a primary emphasis in my classes, but what does that mean to the typical 18-year-old incoming student I might teach in my introductory course? How can I make that less abstract, and thus clearer to a student who has probably heard others referring to "the value of critical thinking" in an abstract or general way?

One strategy that I have employed is to illustrate the everyday nature of what I mean by critical thinking. For example, showing a funny commercial (my go-to example has been a commercial from Domino's India, but that's an idiosyncrasy of my own research specialty) allows students to demonstrate their ability to recognize the ways that advertisers try to get something from viewers (that is, their patronage and thus their money). We then proceed to apply those same skills to other sources, such as news articles, documentary videos, and academic works representing religions in various ways, all in order to help students refine and deepen their ability to analyze information critically while emphasizing how these analytical skills help them to avoid being manipulated for other's ends. One way that we further complicate these analytical skills is to interrogate that language of bias that students will often employ as a critique of a news article. This leads to a discussion of stance and viewpoint, as well as the problem of assuming objectivity or neutrality as an achievable goal of good analysis.

Similar processes are possible for other skills related to analytical thinking. Studying various retellings of the *Ramayana* or *Journey to the West* is a central component of an upper-level undergraduate seminar that I often teach. In the class, it becomes explicit that we are considering the function of telling a story in a particular way and, by studying the variety of tellings, we recognize the role of creativity in generating multiple versions. Studies of identity and the labels that people use to affiliate with, or separate themselves from, others similarly helps students to recognize the complexity, and perhaps even ambiguity, of the world and thus the ways various constructions of difference influence social worlds. Through such work, we can talk about how social groups form and perpetuate themselves, which provides a method for social analysis that is useful in innumerable other contexts.

Through such exercises, I attempt to demonstrate the broader relevance of the work that we do in the classroom—work that seems to some students, at least at first, only to be relevant in the study of a particular ancient Indian epic. Making such connections explicit, and modeling them for students at a variety of sites (from commercials to epics), also helps students to engage the material (especially non-majors in General Education courses in colleges like my own) and even becomes a way to recruit majors. Some students, perhaps disappointed in their current major (or with the extra electives that are available to them), respond well to learning a different type of skill or way to think about the world than perhaps what they are using in their natural science or business courses, and making these processes more explicit extends that potential. In fact, the occasional report from a student that they used these skills in another class or in their own consumption of media becomes useful anecdotes to help other students recognize the skills that, whether they knew it or not, they have actually honed.

Such examples of broadly applicable skills that sometimes seem naturally to be relevant in our classes (e.g., comparison, interpretation, explanation) raise the question about our own course design. To what extent do we focus intentionally on teaching transferable skills? Reflecting on what we intend to accomplish in our classes can become a freeing moment, considering well ahead of time what students will take with them from a class (both ideally and realistically). Often, developing these various skills has greater long-term influence than memorizing terms or names, but it is easy to fall into the trap of teaching how we were taught. It excited us at the time (and thus led to a career in academia), enthralled by certain historical periods, groups, texts, or ideas, but that is not an effective educational model in today's world and falls flat in university environments where professional schools often have considerably more influence than do the programs often grouped together as the humanities. If our objective is to recreate our own experiences as a student, we have failed to advance or meet our students where they currently are (especially in General Education and introductory courses). So, that vocabulary test that requires students to memorize Sanskrit terms in a Hinduism course might not be the most effective form of testing in a world with Google in your pocket. However, if that type of testing is valuable to your course and its goals, then make that clear to students, articulating why this is something worth investing their time in, beyond the tyranny of a grade. Implicitly asserting that this is important "because I say so" or "I learned it this way" will not be convincing for students, administrators, parents, and others interested in (and sometimes questioning) the significance of what we teach.

Rethinking the curriculum is a hefty challenge in itself. If your department has the energy for it, great. If not, reflecting on individual assignments or the structure of one regular class is an excellent starting point for a faculty member, both in terms of refining how we highlight what we consider to be most important and then clearly articulating to our students the value of those elements. Small steps can lead to bigger results.

Recognizing a variety of transferable skills can also become an opportunity to expand the ways that we educate our students. Internships and other experiential learning opportunities can provide practical experiences that put to work the skills that we prompt our students to develop, doing so outside academia, which can lead directly to a future job for some. But these opportunities do not have to focus on work in a religious or social service organization—again the content or topics of our courses do not exhaust how we talk about their relevance. If religious studies coursework develops the range of skills that we have been discussing, then an internship in all sorts of contexts (publishing, museums, student services, to name a few) is not only relevant but can be vital to reinforce with students the range of things that they can now do.

Expanding the notion of transferable skills also needs to recognize the range of skills that are important in our academic careers as well. Presenting information publicly not only relies on clear, accessible communication skills but today also basic web and editing skills for managing a blog or editing a podcast. Additional skills in coding, data visualizations, and machine learning, some of the areas important in the Digital Humanities, also expand the possibilities of transferable skills, thus extending the training traditionally associated with the humanities (e.g., reading, debating, and writing). In fact, in our M.A. degree at the University of Alabama (a program in which some students do indeed go on to doctoral studies while many others pursue a wide assortment of careers), we have expanded our program to include developing digital skills along with encouraging a range of internships (some involving digital work, some not).

Some wariness is warranted in an emphasis on transferable skills, however. The more we emphasize career trajectories, the more higher education can become equated to job training and career outcomes. Of course, that emphasis is not entirely in our control, as the public discourse and policy makers have largely adopted these ideas, not to mention our students themselves and their families. While full-scale resistance may be one approach (which itself risks uncritically promoting a nostalgic vision of "the life of the mind"), finding ways to balance the discourse on job training with a broader notion of transferable skills is useful. One type of balance involves reflecting on the transferable skills that we want to highlight. If we focus too quickly on the easily articulated and testable skills within our courses, the more abstract skills take a back seat. While better articulation to make skills less abstract is one of the strategies that I advocate, that does not mean giving up on anything that cannot be easily packaged. Students take from our courses life skills about living in a complex and diverse social world, skills that do not necessarily equate directly to a career or a measurable assessment. Yet these skills are also important for a functioning democracy, even as our students will apply them to a range of political interests, and these skills help people function in their family and social lives (though they might not be central to conversations at a holiday party or first date).

In this context, the concept of value added or bonus material is perhaps useful. We don't need to suppress important skills that students refine in our courses that are more difficult for us to articulate, measure, or instrumentalize. Yet, we can do both. We can outline and convey specific transferable skills that we develop in particular assignments in a course, while also accomplishing some of the less concrete educational objectives that may be more important for the future success of our students, in both their careers and life.

As a concluding example, both creative thinking and rhetorical skills can be refined in our classes, and we can make these apparent in explicit discussions of careers and transferable skills. In fact, discussing skills is an important moment to help students recognize the creativity that is necessary to communicate anything, something that they often develop intuitively as they analyze multiple interpretations as part of their work in our classes. This in turn helps students to recognize that creativity is not simply a transferable skill in problem solving but also a rhetorical skill in articulating ways that a college education, and especially a humanities major, relates to whatever task or job they are pursuing. Just as we cannot assume that our students automatically recognize the ways studying religious identity or textual analysis apply to a specific job, so too they cannot assume that a human resource officer or manager immediately or just naturally recognizes the ways that their humanities degree fosters skills relevant to a specific task or role. Making this explicit in a class, regardless the topic it may emphasize on paper, and helping students to refine their analytic and rhetorical skills in applying their studies to a range of contexts and careers is an important, added skill, that humanities coursework can develop and refine. As faculty, we need to develop these skills further in intentional and systematic ways, both for our own articulation of the relevant skills that our students develop in our classes and for the ability to encourage them to be ready to identify and convey their skill development to others more successfully.

See also: Assessment; Core Curriculum/General Education; Critical Thinking; Digital Humanities; Experiential Learning; High-Impact Practices; Public Humanities

43

Undergraduate Research

Suzanne Owen

Undergraduate research based on a scientific or philosophical enquiry first gained prominence from the early 1800s, particularly in Germany. In some cases, students would be employed by researchers to carry out some task—I had this opportunity myself as an undergraduate, working for one of my lecturers at the University of Edinburgh—but the main vehicle for student research in the modern university is the undergraduate dissertation, or thesis. Typically, the student would choose their own topic related to their course of study and meet regularly for one-to-one supervision with one of their lecturers.

Planning and writing an extended written assignment (usually between 8,000 and 12,000 words in length) has its own value as a sustained piece of research, and prepares students well for postgraduate study, but undergraduate research can also be embedded throughout the course of study. As many universities like ours have become more practice-oriented, with the stress on employability, undergraduate research can play an even greater role. This might be surprising but makes sense when the focus is on learning through doing, with "students as researchers."

As with any management-led learning and teaching initiative, it comes with special jargon. Various pedagogical models have passed through the university with terms such as "research-informed," teaching based on lecturer expertise, and "research-led," with students engaging in solving "real-world" problems. "Research-oriented" has been added as another type, where students reflect on the methods themselves. In coming across these terms, I discovered that I had been doing all of these for the past decade in my undergraduate modules, partly to adapt to what I perceived to be more engaging for students (and lecturers) and also with an eye toward developing in them a broader range of employability skills. Not every student goes on to further study or a teaching career in the subject.

The majority of students at my institution are first generation, from the north of England. Upon my arrival in September 2008, I was told that, in general, our students were unused to reading for classes. I expect this has become a wider phenomenon with the increase in the use of new media for finding information, much more widely available now than when I was a student. This led me to think: what could we as lecturers do to make attending a class more than what you can find on the Internet, and which was not over-reliant on students having done preparatory reading? Over the years, my classes became more analytical by evaluating and applying criteria to a topic during the session, and more practical, developing different research skills.

At the beginning, I'd set worthy essay titles where students would "compare and contrast," "evaluate and apply a theory," or "debate a problem" but I found that in some cases students would refer to dubious web sources. In the main, assignments were produced by reading existing research. A few years after I arrived, there was a push at my institution toward "students as researchers," to improve engagement and to develop their professional skills. This initiative can be understood in different ways, from students participating in staff research to undertaking original research for assignments, including their undergraduate thesis. There is scope also for students to disseminate their research, e.g., at student conferences, in blog posts, and so on.

However, I wanted students to understand the nature of research itself and how different methods produced different types of data. I also wanted students to reflect on methodological problems and their limitations, and that knowledge is neither complete nor neutral. As soon as I was able, I created new courses and assessments where students were required to create new data, which they were to integrate and compare with existing data. This enabled students to understand more about how research is conducted and how language can affect results, e.g., in a survey. I'll discuss two examples of undergraduate research my students do, one using social research methods and the other employing fieldwork. Both assessments are titled "reports" to signal that they are different from essays. While the basic essay structure is still the main component, the reports include other content such as charts, reflective observations, and appendices.

First, I should point out that one of the differences between undergraduate degrees in the UK, compared with the U.S., is that students begin studying their specialist subject from the outset. The UK humanities degree favors depth over breadth and critical analysis over general knowledge. Therefore, in a U.S.-style educational setting, these examples may better suit an upper-level undergraduate or first-year graduate class. However, they may be worth doing still, in a more limited form, as classroom exercises in a lower-level class. Both these examples below would be difficult to plagiarize or complete using current AI tools. The assessments are also enjoyable and interesting to read from a lecturer's point of view.

In my first example, I have a year-long lower-level module focused on theories and methods in the study of religion. I dedicate much of the second semester to employing and understanding social research methods, following a pattern I'd experienced when working on a couple of city council projects during my postgraduate studies. The students design a short questionnaire, using different types of closed questions and a couple of open-ended ones, on a topic related to the study of religion. Once I've approved their drafts, they send them to six participants (ideally, other students) and then conduct two follow-up interviews. Six is enough to produce some data without it becoming too much. The aim of this assignment, which is more akin to a pilot study, is to understand how different types of methods produce different results rather than to gain a comprehensive understanding of the chosen topic. In terms of research ethics, the module has undergone ethical review and I make sure students understand that participants must be aged 18 or over, etc., and have given consent. The questionnaire must state what it is for and that responses would be anonymized. We do a questionnaire together in class first, and they also practice interviews before doing their own. In particular, the students afterward often say how much they enjoyed doing the follow-up interviews, giving them confidence in a skill they might never have had the opportunity to do before.

The second of my examples is research using fieldwork methods. Fieldwork-based modules have become a mainstay of many religious studies degrees, as visiting places off-campus can be attractive to students, and they provide an important counterpoint to text-based studies of religion. In my module, students need to evaluate the visit and the group employing a selection of analytical lenses, such as gender combined with spatial analysis, identity with cultural, and so on. I organize the first couple of visits, which we do as a group, and then the students organize the final one either on their own or in small groups. This can be challenging, especially if they get no response to enquiries or are met with rudeness. I tell the students it is all data and to put it in the report, which should also include some reflection on fieldwork itself as a method (students produce mini-reports, between 500 and 1,000 words, after each of the organized visits and a longer one of about 2,500 words for the site visit of their choice). Recently, however, many Religious Studies programs have been transformed into Philosophy, Ethics and Religion degrees and this component can get squeezed out. Yet, fieldwork can be one of the most rewarding experiences for students, developing important life and employability skills.

Sophie Gilliat-Ray's 2016 article on employability skills gained through fieldwork identified three main areas of attributes: personal qualities, such as confidence and reflexivity; core skills such and written and verbal communication; and process skills, such as ethical sensitivity and planning

(134–5). As graduate outcomes become ever more significant in course rankings, it helps if the lecturer can guide students toward understanding the skills they've acquired and how to present them in applications for further study or employment.

In addition, a lecturer, or a group of students, could consider ways to showcase the original research produced in these assignments. Students may not otherwise realize the value of the research that they do at undergraduate level. As a class, their assignments could be presented as posters in a student symposium at the end of term. A selection of these could be edited for blog posts, or in some cases developed into an academic conference paper or article. I encouraged one of my dissertation students to present her findings at the annual British Association for the Study of Religions (BASR) conference.

To sum up, the three most important elements to include when supporting undergraduates engaging in participant observation or research involving human participants are a secure understanding of research ethics, a clear rationale for the research, and the inclusion of critical analysis based on scholarly research.

See also: Assignments; Critical Thinking; Experiential Learning; Group Work; High-Impact Practices; Professionalization; Readings; Transferable Skills

44

Writing

K. Merinda Simmons

"Writing" is one of those giant categories that might seem so broad as to either make little sense as a specific chapter in a book like this, on one hand, or warrant entire volumes in its own right, on the other. After all, doesn't every college student write? What does a discussion on writing entail beyond the finer points of crafting a research paper (about which there are many volumes indeed—the one I dog-eared as a college student was the first edition of Anthony Weston's *A Rulebook for Arguments*, a 30-year-old artifact now in the conversation on craft)? Well, like any social or institutional phenomenon, "writing" refers not only to the contents of a freshman composition class but also to structural elements that a lot of colleges and universities use in building an undergraduate curriculum. A savvy teacher certainly considers the former in navigating the latter, but the latter too often remains mystified behind a curtain of administrative bureaucracy, with little guidance on how to approach writing as a curricular designation rather than as solely a vessel for argumentation.

The university where I work offers upper-level undergraduate courses that carry a "W" or "writing" designation. In the Core requirements currently in place, all students must take six hours (typically two courses' worth) of W-designated classes. These are not housed in any one department or discipline, but they all share some syllabus elements that have been deemed both necessary and sufficient for a course to carry the writing designation. Here are those elements:

- Course description includes the following statements, verbatim: "Writing proficiency is required for a passing grade in this course. A student who does not write with the skill normally required of an upper-division student will not earn a passing grade, no matter how well the student performs in other areas of the course."

- Course syllabus indicates that written assignments require coherent, logical, and carefully edited prose. These assignments should require students to demonstrate higher-level critical thinking skills, such as analysis and synthesis.

- Course syllabus indicates that at least two written, individual assignments are required.

- Course syllabus indicates that one of the written assignments will be graded and returned by mid-term.

- Course syllabus must state that rubrics are available for each assignment.

How exactly and by whom are these required criteria chosen? Well, different institutions have different levels of transparency, of course, suffice it to say that safe money is on the answer's lying as much if not more so in structural needs and priorities than in pedagogically driven compositional best practices.

That is not to suggest that administrators are entirely uninterested in enhancing undergraduate writing proficiency (though, I should add, our school's new requirements, implemented in a couple years, do drop the two W courses down to just one). It does, however, cast kindly skepticism on the notion that said proficiency will cohere with only two upper-level (often elective) courses, potentially on very different topics taught by very different professors with very different priorities. Taking just that last element as an example, some teachers will approach the W designation with the level of investment necessary to fill out a form correctly: they have been assigned a class that requires the elements listed above, but they don't see writing as what the class is *about*. Others will take the designation incredibly seriously, seeing their course as potentially the last real chance to instill a skill they consider to be fundamental to a liberal arts education. Whether institutional decisions like common curricular requirements happen to be made with purist sensibilities on writing at heart or whether they're made with the begrudging but practical need to tick certain boxes in mind, the work of someone teaching a class with a formal writing element is to make their own meaning of this vague designation.

That meaning lies on a spectrum, of course, and does not conveniently fall into the binary described above of a teacher ignoring or caring deeply about student writing. I have taught several W courses at my university, and my approach has changed over the years. So as not to bury the lede, I'll go ahead and say that my takeaways from those experiences are:

1 Compositional rigor is not necessarily the same thing as sound compositional pedagogy. To wit: sometimes less is more.

2 Process is its own progress.

3 Confident argumentation > eloquent articulation.

Some context first: In my university, and in many others, students sign up for a W course to take care of their requirement and/but look for which class among the offerings is about something they find at least moderately interesting. And because everyone has to have a couple of these designated seminars regardless of their major, the chances of having at least half the class populated by students from disciplinary contexts outside the humanities or social sciences are pretty good. Large departments may be able to allow only their own majors to take their W seminars, but many religious studies departments are small enough that they open those seats to students throughout the Arts and Sciences (or even throughout the entire university, depending on how these requirements shake out) in order for the courses to fill.

To the first two or three experiences teaching a W course, I brought my own brand of writing purism. I have a PhD. in English, so my training in writing as its own craft and research as its own formal genre was scrupulous. The grammarian who lives in my head and who diagrammed long sentences in college for fun (true story) showed up to the writing party with gratuitous resources on how to pursue clarity and avoid comma splices. I seemed compelled to include in my comments on paper drafts copious line edits, and I was determined to see students climb a writing mountain. Never mind the fact that many of them didn't have the proverbial gear or that they didn't particularly care to pursue mountaineering. They'd achieve something huge and thank me later, I told myself. To that end, my culminating paper assignment was 20–30 pages long and went through a meticulous writing process with multiple draft stages. At the same time, however, there was still course content outside that process to teach—in my case, "Religion in the American South" or "Religion and Literature." What ensued was a complicated balancing act wherein I attempted to present the course topic and a substantive focus on writing in equal measure.

In those early experiments, I fell into the trap that ensnares a lot of early career faculty: I was trying to "do it all," as if, in making rigorous demands of my students, I'd demonstrate my own capability as a scholar and teacher. I wasn't thinking about it in that way consciously, of course. At the time, I just hadn't yet made the shift from showing what I know to teaching what students need. Over time, however, what became as clear as the writing I wanted them to produce was that I was not best serving my students in their various professional tracks and goals by showing them how to avoid split infinitives and misplaced modifiers. What they needed was not an exercise in writing long essays with superfluous schooling on the finer points of grammar along the way. No, they needed some training in the craft of locating, exploring, and articulating their own ideas. Across the board, regardless of major or degree program, they all needed to start thinking of themselves as people with something to say—something from which their particular professional world would benefit.

As my colleague Mike Altman put it recently in conversation, we need to rethink what we mean by "rigor" in the classroom. Too often, we define it as a set of exacting requirements, a gauntlet of specific tasks to perform. But especially in classes that draw students from multiple disciplines, that definition leaves too many students with the ability to repeat certain scripts or conform to certain conventions but without the ability to translate those scripts and conventions into their own future professional contexts. So instead, what if we treat rigor instead as challenging our students to ask certain questions about their own intellectual priorities and processes? With that shift in perspective, I came to see the W designation as a chance to sharpen (or introduce, in some cases) the tools necessary for academic writing. The course now emphasizes the writing *process* more than the writing *product*. We take a bit more time discussing strategies for each stage of the writing process—brainstorming, planning, drafting, editing, revising, and proofreading. Along the way, my hope is that students develop and learn more about their own writing habits: what works for them and what doesn't, what context or time of day sees them at their most productive, what their blind spots are and how to avoid them.

Talking about not only *how* to do something but also *why* it matters is often as much a process of unlearning for students as it is of acquiring new skills. Suddenly a three-point thesis is not *the* way to nutshell a claim unless there are indeed three main sections of a paper, and there is little reason to avoid using personal pronouns when addressing one's own authorial ideas. The new questions they are invited to ask are about what they think and why, and how they might best explain that to others. In this way, confidence in argumentation takes on greater importance than eloquence. That can always come later if needed. I try to intertwine these different questions and emphases as much as possible throughout our discussions about the course topic itself, allowing us to explore directly the strategies scholars use to describe or analyze their object of study. These layers of reflection—on published authors, sure, but even more importantly on themselves as thinkers and writers—are very much at the center of the learning outcomes that are possible in a class formally concerned with writing.

See also: Critical Thinking; Professionalization; Seminars; Transferable Skills

Afterword

The Introductory Course: Less is Better[1]

Jonathan Z. Smith

Better fewer but better.

V. I. LENIN

In a sense, I prefer the topic I was first invited to speak on: "The Role of Courses in Religion in the Liberal Arts Curriculum... Including an Assessment of the Current State of the Liberal Arts" to the topic I discovered I was expected to speak on when the program arrived in the mail: "How I would Teach an Introductory Course in Religion." But, no matter. You cannot think about the one without the other. The second topic presupposes the first. That is to say, to think about an introductory course—any introductory course—is to think about the nature of liberal education. The least interesting term in the title is "religion."

I am delighted that such a topic has been proposed. If taken seriously, it marks the beginning of our potential for maturity as a part of the profession of education. Because of this, I note with sadness that this conference is the result of independent entrepreneurship (as was Claude Welch's pioneering

---

[1] This brief essay—originally a lecture—first appeared in Mark Jurgensmeyer's once well-known edited volume, *Teaching the Introductory Course in Religious Studies: A Sourcebook* (Atlanta: Scholar's Press, 1991), 185–92. Although the book continues to be available for sale from Duke University Press, neither Duke, Oxford University Press (which took over Scholar's Press titles once the publisher was dissolved upon the break-up of the AAR/SBL), nor the American Academy of Religion continue to assert any ownership of that title. It therefore appears here with the kind permission of Jonathan's widow, Elaine Smith.

work) rather than being a major focus of our putative professional society, the American Academy of Religion. Note the contrast to a mature discipline such as history which, as early as 1899, had a committee of the American Historical Association reporting to a national meeting in plenary session on the teaching of history in secondary schools. In 1905, the same was established for the first year of college work in history. (Both reports, published by the Association, still merit reading.) In 1967, an important refereed journal, *History Teacher*, was founded. In 1976, the Association sponsored a major national conference on "The Introductory Course," hotly debated at subsequent annual meetings. In June, 1982, the Association devoted the bulk of its scholarly journal, *The American Historical Review*, to a "Forum" on the Western Civilization course. A rapid reading of the Association's *Annual Reports* reveals that a significant proportion of presidential addresses have been devoted to issues of education.[2]

I report these matters not entirely by way of invidious comparison, but rather to suggest, on the one hand, how far we have to go as a profession, and, on the other, to signal my delight that you have gathered to take this initial step.

There is nothing necessarily sinister in our lack of an articulate consensus on such matters. We are, after all, in many ways in our infancy. Until the 1960s, it would have been almost impossible for anyone doing doctoral work in religious studies to be trained by graduate professors who, themselves, regularly taught undergraduates. I suspect that the majority of present members of the AAR were so trained. In influential fields, such as biblical studies, the pattern persists to this day. That is to say, if graduate education as a whole is notorious for its irresponsible lack of interest in educational issues, in religious studies this is compounded by sheer ignorance. Perhaps this is why our conveners phrased the topic for these evening sessions in the diplomatic subjunctive, "How I would teach. . ." rather that the reportorial indicative, "How I do teach introductory courses." In my case, I do. It is an activity which is not just indicative but imperative. For almost a decade I have taught nothing but introductory courses in my college. Most are designed for first- and second-year students, no course is designed specifically for majors or, for that matter, for potential majors. In a typical year I teach in the Social Sciences Core, I teach a year-long sequence in Western Civilization, and I

---

[2] I have taken the next four paragraphs, with minor alterations, from Jonathan Z. Smith, "No Need to Travel to the Indies: Judaism and the Study of Religion," in Jacob Neusner (ed.), *Take Judaism, For Example* (Chicago: University of Chicago Press, 1983), 216–17. For another version, see Jonathan Z. Smith, "Why the College Major? Questioning the Great Unexplained Aspect of Undergraduate Education," *Change* (July–August, 1983): 14–15.

teach some sort of introduction to religion. My remarks will be based in part on this experience, in part on my other career. Since 1973, I have worked, spoken and written as much on liberal education as I have on religion, serving in a variety of administrative roles in the college at Chicago and on national commissions on undergraduate education.

I take as my starting point the proposition that *an introductory course serves the primary function of introducing the student to college level work*, to work in the liberal arts. Its particular subject matter is of secondary interest (indeed, I suspect it is irrelevant). All of my remarks this evening aim at unpacking this proposition from several vantage points.

First, it is necessary to step back and reflect, briefly, on the nature of the liberal arts curriculum. As I have written elsewhere, as one surveys the more than three thousand institutions of higher learning who, together, offer 534 different kinds of bachelor degrees, it becomes apparent that there are a multitude of spatial arrangements, the ways in which the blocks of courses are organized: general requirements, major requirements, prerequisites, and the like. Each is appropriate to the peculiar institutions. What remains more or less constant are the temporal arrangements. Whatever we do we must do it in the equivalent of four years. Regardless of the academic calendar, there is almost always less than four full days of teaching time in a *year-long* course, less than one hundred hours of class meetings. And, there is no reason to presume that any student who takes one course on a given subject will necessarily take another one. Less than one hundred hours may represent, for a significant number of students, at best, their sole course of study in a particular subject matter. It is at this point—with the introductory course—and not with the major that curricular thought must begin. For within such a context, no course can do everything, no course can be complete. The notion of a survey, of "covering," becomes ludicrous under such circumstances. Rather, each course is required to be incomplete, to be self-consciously and articulately selective. We do not celebrate often enough the delicious yet terrifying freedom undergraduate liberal arts education affords the faculty by its rigid temporal constraints. As long as we do not allow ourselves to be misled by that sad heresy that the bachelor's degree is but a preparation for graduate studies (a notion that is becoming pragmatically unjustified; it has never been educationally justifiable), then *there is nothing that must be taught*, there is nothing that cannot be left out. A curriculum, whether represented by a particular course, a program, or a four-year course of study becomes an occasion for deliberate, collegial, institutionalized choice.

I take as a corollary to these observations that each thing taught is taught not because it is "there," but because it connects in some interesting way with something else, because it is an example, an "e.g." of something that is fundamental, something that may serve as a precedent for further acts of interpretation and understanding by providing an arsenal of instances, of paradigmatic events and expressions as resources from which to reason, from which to extend the possibility of intelligibility to that which first appears to be novel or strange. Whether this be perceived as some descriptive notion of the "characteristic," or some more normative notion of the "classical," or some point in-between, matters little. These are issues on which academicians of good will can responsibly disagree.

What ought not to be at controversy is the purpose for which we labor, that long-standing and deeply felt perception of the relationship between liberal learning and citizenship.

I would articulate the grounds of this relationship as follows. From the point of view of the academy, I take it that it is by an act of human will, through language and history, through words and memory, that we are able to fabricate a meaningful world and give place to ourselves. Education comes to life at the moment of tension generated by the double sense of "fabrication," for it means both to build and to lie. For, although we have no other means than language for treating with the world, words are not after all the same as that which they name and describe. Although we have no other recourse but to memory, to precedent, if the world is not forever to be perceived as novel and, hence, remain forever unintelligible, the fit is never exact, nothing is ever quite the same. What is required at this point of tension is the trained capacity for judgment, for appreciating and criticizing the relative adequacy and insufficiency of any proposal of language and memory. What we seek to train in college are individuals who know not only that the world is more complex than it first appears, but also that, therefore, interpretative decisions must be made, decisions of judgment which entail real consequences for which one must take responsibility, from which one may not flee by the dodge of disclaiming expertise. This ultimately political quest for fundamentals, for the acquisition of the powers of informed judgment, for the dual capacities of appreciation and criticism must be the explicit goal of every level of the liberal arts curriculum. The difficult task of making *interpretative decisions* must inform each and every course.

If I were asked to define liberal education while standing on one leg, my answer would be that it is *training in argument about interpretations*. An introductory course, then, is a first step in this training. Arguments and interpretations are what we introduce, our particular subject matter serves merely as the excuse, the occasion, the "e.g."

This may seem a bit airy-fairy to you, so I shall begin again. An *introductory course* is not best conceived as a first step for future professionals, nor is it best conceived as an occasion for "literacy," for initial acquaintance with some aspects of the "stuff." *An introductory course is concerned primarily with developing the students capacities for reading, writing and speaking*—put another way, for interpreting and arguing. This is what they are paying for. This is what we are paid for. We are not as college teachers called upon to display, obsessively, those thorny disciplinary problems internal to the rhetoric of professionals (e.g. in our field, the autonomy and integrity of religious studies). Our trade is educational problems, common (although refracted differently) to all human sciences. So, there are formal tests for an introductory course: it must feature a good deal of *self-conscious* activity in reading, writing, and speaking, because it is not enough that there be required occasions for such activities. In my own courses this means weekly writing assignments on a set theme which requires argumentation. Each piece of writing must be rewritten at least once regardless of grade. Please note: this requires that every piece of writing be returned to the student with useful comments no later than the next class period. In addition, there should be written homework. (Examples: take pages 21–25 of Durkheim's *Elementary Forms* and reduce his argument to a single paragraph using no words not in Durkheim; or, Here is a list of 33 sentences from Louis Dumont, state the point of each in your own words.) At least once a quarter, I call in all students' notebooks and texts. After reading them through, I have individual conferences with each student to go over what they've written and underlined and what this implies as to how they are reading. But this is insufficient. It is not enough that there be all this activity. Both the students and we need help. We need to provide our students with models of good writing. Wherever possible, beyond its intrinsic interest, each text read should be exemplary of good writing and effective argument. We also need to make available to our students the sort of help others provide. For example, in my introductory courses I regularly have the students buy Jack Meiland's little book *College Thinking: How to Get the Most out of College* and discuss portions of it with them.

Even more, we need help. At the most minimal level, most of us do not know how to write a proper writing assignment so as to make clear to the student what is expected of them. Most of us can recognize mistakes in writing and poor argument, we can circle them or write a marginal comment, but most of us do not know how to correct the mistake. We do not know how to help our students improve in the future, how to prevent the problems from recurring. These are not matters where sheer good will or pious wishes help. For example, circling spelling or grammatical errors has been shown, from a pedagogical point of view, to be a waste of time. We need to go to competent professionals and be taught how to teach writing. This is the *basic requirement* for a teacher of introductory courses.

This raises a larger question: the professional responsibilities of college teachers. Bluntly put, *we have as solemn an obligation to 'keep up' with the literature and research in education and learning as we do in our particular fields of research*. Even more bluntly, no one should be permitted to teach an introductory course who is not conversant, among other matters, with the literature on the cognitive development of college age individuals, with issues of critical reasoning and informal logic, and with techniques of writing instruction. While there is some art in teaching, it is, above all, a skilled profession. To move to the particular question, "How I Teach Introductory Courses in Religion?" I have taught introductory courses in all three modes described by this project: the survey, the comparative, and the disciplinary. From a pedagogical standpoint, there is no difference between them. They all require explicit attention to matters of reading, writing and speaking, to issues of interpretation and argument—to that most fundamental social goal of liberal education, the bringing of private adherence to the pedagogical rule that "less is better." For example, my year-long survey, "Religion in Western Civilization," is organized around a single issue: "What is a tradition? How are traditions maintained through acts of reinterpretation?, and three pairs of topics: kingship/cosmology; purity-impurity/wisdom; voluntary associations/salvation. Note that the first member of each pair is preeminently social; the second, ideological. This allows a modest introduction of theoretical issues into a course which consists, essentially, of reading "classic" primary texts.

All three modes require explicit recognition of the educational dilemma of breadth and depth. Each of my introductory courses divides each topic into two parts. The first, usually entitled "the vocabulary of x" features the rapid reading of a wide variety of little snippets simply to get a sense of the semantic range of the topic and to experiment with what clusters of relationships can be discerned within the vocabulary. The second part features the slow and careful reading of a few exemplary documents. Each section of each introductory course is preceded by a lecture in which the topic is introduced; but, of more importance, in which the syllabus is "unpacked." The students need to know what decisions I have made, and why? What have I included? What have I excluded? They also need to hear some cost accounting of these decisions. That is to say, I want my students to use the syllabus as an occasion for reflection on judgement and consequences, to be conscious of the fact that a syllabus is not self-evident, but (hopefully) a carefully constructed argument.

Beyond these generalities, I have two, and only two, criteria which govern the selection of the example and the organization of the syllabi: one has more to do with the form, the other with content.

Each of my introductory courses is organized around the notion of argument and the insistence that the building blocks of argument remain constant: definitions, classifications, data, and explanations. If we are reading second-order texts together, we have to learn to recognize these in others; if we are reading primary religious documents, we may have to construct them for ourselves. In some of my introductory courses, we devote the first week to explicit attention to these matters, thereby building a vocabulary by which we can identify and discuss these elements in subsequent readings. In other introductory courses, the courses themselves are organized around these rubrics and we spend the entire term exploring them. For example, any introductory course must begin with the question of definition ("What is civilization?" "What is Western?"—I have my students take out a piece of paper and write their answers to these questions within the first five minutes of the first day of the course. We spend the rest of the period classifying their answers, discussing them, and discussing what makes a good definition); or a unit of a course might be designed to display the question of definition (in one introduction, I use as readings: H. Penner and E. Yonan, W.C. Smith, R. Otto, P. Berger, M. Spiro and R. B. Edwards).

The second rule is more central: *nothing must stand alone*. That is to say, every item studied in an introductory course must have a conversation partner. Items must have, or be made to have, arguments with each other. The possibilities are manifold; the only requirement is that the juxtaposition be interesting. For example, in what you have termed disciplinary courses, I search very hard for readings which contain two representative scholars who employ identical data (e.g., Piddocks vs. Orans; the Kronenfelds vs. Levi-Strauss); or for a striking juxtaposition which reveals hidden implications in a given position (e.g., showing Leni Riefenstahl's "Triumph of the Will" after reading Durkheim's *Elementary Forms*; reading the classic pornographic novel, *The Story of O* after reading Eliade and others on initiation).

Congruent with a concern for the relationship between the enterprise of liberal education and citizenship and with the observation that critical inquiry as often taught ("there's always another point of view") too frequently results in cynicism, the students must not be left with mere juxtaposition. There must be explicit attention to the possibilities and problems of translating, of reducing, one item in terms of the other. And, there must be explicit attention to consequences and entailments. What if the world really is as so–and–so describes it? What would it mean to live in such a world? What acts of translation must I perform? What would be gained? What would be lost?

Finally, if possible, there should be a "laboratory" component in an introductory course. The students should have to do something which fosters reflection on all of the above. It can be based on observation (for example, in the unit on purity/impurity I have my students describe an actual meal, determine the rules which governed it, and attempt to reduce them to a system. This is in no way the same as the ancient rules; but, it provokes thought). It can be based on a real research, for example, in my Bible and Western Civilization sequence, each student chooses a Bible printed before 1750 from our rare book collection and attempts to determine the significance of the format. The text is in each case the same; but the Bibles look very different. Why? It can be explicitly argumentative (for example, I have my students write a "tenth" opinion, employing some particular perspective, on some recent Supreme Court decision involving religion after reading the transcript—e.g. What would Durkheim have ruled in the Rhode Island crèche case?).

In sum, there is nothing distinctive to the issue of introducing religion. Its problems are indigenous to the genre of introductory courses. The issues are not inherently disciplinary. They are primarily pedagogical. This is as it should be. For our task, in the long run, is not to introduce or teach our field for its own sake, but to use our field in the service of the broader and more fundamental enterprise of liberal learning.

Extended Glossary

Russell T. McCutcheon

All items addressed in main entries of this volume are summarized below, in succinct, primer-style, but with a large number of related topics not covered in the main chapters also included. Although this glossary clearly reflects mostly a North American university teaching experience—and, more specifically, a typical U.S. context—my thanks goes to Steffen Führding, Suzanne Owen, and Teemu Taira for their comments on an earlier draft along with their suggestions for ways to make it more broadly applicable to those working in other settings.

Nine-Month Faculty Contracts

It is not uncommon in U.S. colleges for full-time faculty (including tenure-track and tenured professors) to work on what is called a nine-month contract, thereby paying them a salary only for the fall and spring (in places also known as winter) semesters—meaning that any summer school teaching is considered additional income (and thus deriving from a different budget). In such cases, a faculty member may be paid their monthly salary "9 over 12," i.e., for each of the nine fall and spring semesters' monthly pay checks the college would hold back a portion of the gross salary such that over the course of nine pays a sufficient amount of money remains to then be paid out during the summer months. A "9 over 9" college implies that the faculty member receives all of their income during the nine months of the fall and spring semesters, requiring them to set aside funds on their own for whatever income will be needed throughout their summer months. Although the research these faculty carry out throughout the summer is more than likely essential for their individual career progress (some faculty, with heavy teaching loads, many set aside summers as the main time in which their research takes place), the normalization of nine-month contracts are best understood as a cost-cutting strategy on the part of employers; they clearly convey that colleges finance faculty to teach, research, and carry out service duties only during just the fall and spring semesters (i.e., that the work for which faculty are remunerated does not include whatever they choose to do all summer—nicely playing into the longstanding assumption that teachers at all levels of schooling are just on holiday when not in the classroom). Technically, although employed full time, a nine-month faculty member is therefore free to work for other employers in the summer, usually without needing to submit a supplemental pay request (but here the question of time vs. money likely enters for many faculty trying to advance their research agenda). Those faculty for whom external grants are relevant will often build into their budgets their own summer salaries to carry out the work of the grant. Often, Chairs of larger Departments along with all senior administrators are appointed "12 over 12," thereby meaning a significant raise (to account for being seen to work for three additional months each year—again, at least as work is defined by the university) but this also comes with tracking their sick time while also submitting holiday time requests. Chairs who are "9 over 9" or "9 over 12" will likely receive a small stipend and reduced teaching duties in exchange for their administrative labor during the fall and spring as well as a stipend in the summer to continue to be the Chair after the end of the spring semester.

Academic Freedom

Linked to the once strong sense of faculty members joining with the senior administration to participate in so-called shared governance of a campus (with an assortment of faculty committees contributing to decision-making at a college), the value of academic freedom—closely associated with the institution of tenure (or a permanent contract in the UK), which faculty members have traditionally worked over the initial several years of their careers to attain—could be said to have declined on a number of current campuses (perhaps depending on the region or national setting). With the dramatic rise in non-tenured, contingent instructors over the past decades, the stake of the faculty in long term decision-making on a campus (let alone the traditional institutions whereby this participation took place) has, understandably perhaps, diminished greatly in many places. How this impacts the classroom varies from place to place, with administrations, accreditors, and governments more easily being able to dictate a variety of things related to teaching, from assessment initiatives and mandatory elements to an instructor's syllabus to the once strong ability of the faculty to govern the curriculum being undermined by the practical interests of other bodies.

Academic Misconduct

The term is commonly used to name a series of behavioral challenges among students that pertain directly to their performance in the classroom and thus in relation to the expectations and requirements of a course—sometimes also known as Academic Integrity (a term with a different valence, i.e., the goal to be achieved as opposed to the more punitive "misconduct"). Examples would include plagiarism (copying, without credit, the work of another), the many different ways to cheat on tests, completing assignments for someone else, purchasing completed assignments from so-called paper mills, falsifying results, submitting AI-generated essays, etc. Penalties for students found guilty of committing such misconduct (which is usually distinguished from student misconduct associated with a campus's broader codes of conduct) can vary—all depending on the nature of the infraction, from a penalized grade on the assignment in question to being failed in a course. Universities generally have closely prescribed ways in which accusations of academic misconduct are handled and adjudicated (given that these can sometimes result in legal proceedings), with students having an opportunity to hear and answer for the charges; faculty members are therefore well served by acquainting themselves with their campus's policies and procedures and then following them closely. Instructors would also be wise to be proactive to encourage integrity in student work via a variety of assignments in which such things as proper citation practices are learned well before possible infractions take place.

Accessibility

Usually enshrined in law, equal access for students who have some form of documentable disability or other sorts of challenges is an item of importance in all universities—whether this refers to, for example, ease of access to buildings (perhaps necessitating the installation of ramps and elevators) or the ease of access to all course materials (e.g., requiring that, for instance, screen reader programs, for the visually impaired, to be able to work with materials posted online or that closed captioning be available for images or videos used in classes). Of importance to note is that this applies not just to materials for students but often to the general public as well, such as so-called web accessibility for public-facing material on a school's website. Often the focus of a specific office or service on a campus, ensuring all course materials are accessible in a class is also among the instructor's responsibilities, sometimes involving resources or training from a disabilities office or a tech center on campus. Currently, debates around accessibility even intersect with attitudes on the part of instructors or fellow students that may impact another person's ability to feel like a fully participating member of the class (i.e., implicit bias).

Accommodations

Often a term of legal consequence—i.e., reasonable accommodation is the term of preference in U.S. law, by way of 1990's Americans with Disabilities Act (ADA)—defined as the necessary revisions to a course's format or requirements that will allow disabled students to have equal access to the course's materials and thus the ability to succeed in the course. Usually determined by an office of disabilities on a campus, in consultation with the student (who will submit documentation of their disability to that office as part of this process), the accommodations legally required—not merely recommended—for a student are confidentially communicated directly to the instructor and, although they can and likely should be discussed by the instructor privately with the student in question, they are not items of negotiation with the student; the instructor is asked to implement them (e.g., extended time for tests and exams, examinations taken outside class so as to minimize distractions, a note taker, closed captioning for any films watched in class, etc.) in the service of the student's learning needs. Such accommodations must be "reasonable," however, and thus not require the modification of elements of the course that are fundamental to the instructor's goals or material. Instead, such accommodations are best understood as adaptations that assist all students to access and understand the course material and fulfill its various requirements.

Active Learning

A couple decades ago, or so, a shift took place in higher education whereby conversations on and attempts to assess teaching shifted to learning, i.e., emphasizing not the *delivery* of class material but it's *reception* and *retention* by students. Closely aligned with the so-called assessment initiative across campuses, this more student- or learner-centered approach is often linked to measures of student performance that are finer grained than final grades in a course or even performance on a specific exam, and part of what many administrations now refer to as continuous quality improvement, i.e., determining ways to ensure that more students perform better on future assignments and/or implementing continual increases in standards coupled with greater attention to student success. That this initiative is not difficult to see as a response, on the part of universities, to the possible disengagement of students in increasingly large classes (especially in the natural sciences), associated with a variety of funding issues on many campuses and the rise of contingent labor among instructors, should likely not go without notice.

Add/Drop/Withdraw

There is usually a deadline by which students can add a course for the current semester/year or drop a course in which they are already enrolled (sometimes with or without penalties [e.g., if paying tuition, was the course dropped in time for it to be refunded?]). Add deadlines are usually near the start of a semester but nonetheless provide students with a week or two to decide on their courses, such that new students can appear unannounced in a course, having missed all prior material. During the opening week(s) of each semester instructors would be wise to routinely check their class roster to determine if students have added or dropped the course. Some campuses will distinguish a withdrawal later in the semester from dropping a course in the initial weeks, with different rules possibly applying to the former and thus with such student names remaining on a course roster though with a "W" in their status column. A late add, well into a course, is sometimes also possible, often with the permission of an instructor or maybe even the students' advisor. In such cases the student will need some special attention to assist them to cover much past content.

Administration/Executive

Typically university employees are divided between the administration or the members of a campus's executive, the faculty, as well as the staff, with the first usually comprising positions from the Dean upward, including, starting from the top, such position names as Presidents, Chancellors, or Principals, followed by a variety of Vice Presidents or Vice Chancellors (with the Vice President for Academic Affairs, the Provost, or the Pro-Vice Chancellor usually heading up the academic side of the college) along with a series of more specialized Associate and even Assistant Provosts/Chancellors as well as Associate and Assistant Deans. While Deans typically administer Colleges or Faculties (sometimes these are interchangeable designations, e.g., the

Faculty of Engineering or the College of Arts and Sciences), a Provost's responsibilities involve the operations of all degree programs on a campus. (Staff is also internally divided, such as clerical or clinical staff working in academic units versus those working for facilities, e.g., maintaining buildings or the grounds; faculty are also internally divided, whether by rank/seniority or by type of appointment, i.e., tenured and tenure-track or a permanent or open-ended contract and temporary contracts in the UK, versus contingent—whether full-time or part-time.) While there was a time when onetime faculty members constituted much of the administration, i.e., professors accepting limited-term administrative appointments and then, at their completion, returning to the so-called faculty ranks, today a professional administrative class largely runs many universities; as such, the senior administration, even if many of its members had once held faculty positions of their own, now rarely return to faculty positions and usually engage in little to no teaching or research of their own. Traditionally, Department Chairs (members of the faculty) are not considered part of the administration, though their job does require them to represent to faculty the administration's wishes and initiatives, while also requiring them to represent faculty desires back up the chain of command. In some settings a professional managerial class has now risen throughout the administration's ranks, either with non-faculty managers comprising its members (often bringing to the university a business model more at home in for-profit corporations) or onetime faculty members who aim to progress through the administration's ranks instead of ever returning to a faculty/teaching position.

Advising

All depending on a campus's policies, academic advising, or what is sometimes known as tutoring in places, for all students may take place within a centralized advising office in the college or faculty or within a student's specialty department (sometimes leaving only incoming first year students and those whose major or specialty is undeclared seeking advising in a central office). When happening within the department, models for advising students vary, from one faculty member serving in the role of advisor or tutor (such as when a unit does not have many majors, making this a manageable task) to either all faculty sharing in these duties (with students assigned to a faculty member in various ways) or the unit hiring a professional staff member for this role. Such advising often takes place prior to students registering for the coming semester's classes, as a way to ensure students are on track toward satisfying all requirements, either for the major or for the degree as a whole. Another form of undergraduate advising on many campuses happens in the career center, where students are assisted with their search for employment either before (e.g., internships) or after graduation. Career centers, however, often emphasize careers in the professional schools, where there is presumed to be a straighter line from university to career, with the skills and potential employment for Humanities students sometimes being greater challenges for career counselors to understand. In the study of religion, for example, many career centers use standardized materials that presume the degree is linked to futures in Christian theology, thereby (mistakenly) assuming that Religious Studies graduates will either become ordained clergy or go into one or another of the so-called helping professions (e.g., social work, guidance counselor, etc.).

Artificial Intelligence (AI)

Although efforts to employ computers for increasingly original integration and presentation of information are longstanding, only recently, with the advent of open source tools being posted online, has AI had a clear (and, for many, a worrisome) impact on the undergraduate classroom. For example, ChatGPT (chat + Generative Pre-Trained Transformer, a particular type of Large Language Model [LLM] by which computers are "trained" on large data sets) was first available to users beginning in November of 2022; queries (e.g., What is the academic study of religion?) produced what many found to be convincing and surprisingly thorough responses that would be suitable as possible test answers or even essays. (The responses, of course, are only as strong as the data sets on which such computers are trained, i.e., a data set filled with stereotypes about a group will invariably produce AI-generated responses that repeat and thereby reinforce such clichés.) In response, software claiming to be capable of detecting AI-generated writing along with revised academic misconduct policies concerning AI assignments were introduced on many campuses (e.g., Turnitin, a software that has long been in use on some campuses to detect plagiarism by searching online for related word usage, recently had an AI-detection feature added—though such detection is merely based on statistical probability). While some faculty and administrators now worry even more about the future integrity of student writing assignments, AI capabilities at present seem unable to create a convincing reply to a highly specific writing prompt of relevance only to a particular course; accordingly, AI-generated submissions to vaguely worded, general essay prompts are more likely to present instructors with grading challenges in the near future. Accordingly, AI advances will more than likely challenge faculty members to be more creative and precise in the writing topics that they assign to their students (instead of recirculating past, overly broad topics), possibly relying more on the once common practice of brief, in-class writing assignments.

Assessment

Over the past two decades or so, increasing attention has been given on campuses to reporting data to confirm that students are indeed learning what a course sets out to teach to them, let alone that everything from Core Curriculum or General Education courses to entire degree programs are accomplishing their stated goals—and if not, to chart a plan for how to address failings and improve performance. This assessment initiative (closely associated with the learner-centered model), which can impact whole academic units and colleges as well as individual faculty (notably early career and contingent faculty who will need to show attention to this in their own courses), can be seen as an effort on the part of universities to prevent greater intrusion by outside bodies (e.g., governments and credentialing associations) by developing methods of self-policing and reporting (even though, in some settings, such central bodies—whether from within or outside of the discipline—already play a considerable part in establishing guidelines or benchmarks for course goals, assessment instruments, achievement standards, etc., along with establishing boards of examiners that ensure such standards are being met). The assessment initiative reinvents the sometimes lofty or even somewhat ethereal course goals, usually listed near the opening of any syllabus, as more discrete, empirically measurable outcomes while also devising rubrics to govern the assessment process itself (e.g., the specifics on how an essay will be graded by the instructor, and thus what the student needs to address in order to earn a B or an A). Among the goals of this initiative is to confirm that goals are being met but also to ensure so-called continuous quality improvement. While there are those who argue that assessment initiatives are, at the end of the day, a process to be undertaken mainly for the sake of being seen as undertaking it, campuses have nonetheless invested significant resources in this initiative (i.e., whole offices, with staffs of their own, to ensure all aspects of the curriculum are regularly assessed) and individual faculty careers can be hampered if rubrics are not created for their courses and properly formatted assessment reports regularly submitted at their completion each semester.

Assignments

While there are an array of ways of modeling or applying the content and skills acquired in any given class—from essays to group projects and oral presentations and seminars—taken together they would be known as the assignments in a course, or the tasks given to and therefore required of students to be completed, to the satisfaction of the instructor, by specific dates. Based on such performance an overall grade for the courses is usually determined—though it is not unusual to find schools or courses that invite students to self-assess or which avoid formal grading altogether. In most cases, however, an overall course grade of some sort (e.g., a percentage or a letter grade, such as B+ or C-) will be assigned to each student based on their completion of the course's various assignments. While some courses (notably upper-level, more senior courses) may result in one major assignment due near the end of the semester and on which the majority of the overall grade is based (e.g., a final research essay or final examination), in other classes (e.g., an introductory course) there may be quite a number of different sorts of assignments required of students throughout the semester, such that the final grade is not excessively impacted by a poor performance on any one. Taking into account the various ways in which many students learn (not all do well on standardized tests, for example), utilizing a variety of assignments in a course, along with ways of assessing them, is more than likely in the favor of students.

Attendance

While there are those faculty members who treat university students very differently from those still enrolled in high school/secondary school, thereby seeing their regular attendance in lectures as a decision to be made by each student and thus not something to be tracked in detail by the faculty member (knowing full well that their performance in the class will be impaired by their absences), there are also those who will instead take regular class attendance and then base a portion of the final grade in the course on the degree to which students were or were not absent from class (an approach that, in turn, requires a stated policy concerning classes missed for what the instructor sees as legitimate reasons). Given the greater in-class demands often placed on upper-level students in a seminar, which will more than likely be a far smaller class than a large lecture (of 100 or far more), some faculty approach attendance in such venues differently than their introductory courses. Regardless of a faculty member's sensibilities on this, governments (due to student loan programs where tuition is required of students) will sometimes need to know the "last class attended" for a student dropping a course, a requirement that may encourage some to take attendance regularly. In yet other settings, where passing a final standardized examination is the sole mark of successfully completing a course, attendance at daily or weekly lectures may be far more voluntary, resulting in no attendance ever being taken by the instructor and some students mainly reading and studying the required course books.

Auditing/Non-Degree Students

Many campuses have a mechanism for students to be formally placed in a course but not for credit, often called auditing. Students therefore may periodically make a request of instructors to audit their course, doing so for a variety of reasons (e.g., to familiarize themselves with the subject matter while enrolled for credit in other courses that count toward their degrees). Others, enrolled for credit, may not be seeking a degree (traditionally also known in places as non-matriculating or non-degree students), such as a student who has already earned an undergraduate degree but who wishes to go on to graduate school in a different discipline, thereby possibly enrolling initially in a year of upper-level classes in their new field but not enrolling in a degree (doing so to gain experience in the discipline). In the latter case, these students are enrolled just like any other student, but in the former case, those auditing a course may only attend lectures and not complete any assignments or they may wish to complete assignments but with no grade being recorded—a conversation with such students, if the instructor allows them to audit a course, to determine what they hope to gain, is likely required.

Benchmarking

Along with rubrics, an initiative that discloses to students the progressive goals that they are expected to meet in a course. The term is also often used for institutions as a whole, for the standards that they aim to implement and meet, often developed in comparison to peer institutions or so-called aspirational peers.

Blackboards/Whiteboards

With the advent of routinized multimedia installations in classrooms over the past decades, the traditional chalk blackboards that once lined a lecture hall's walls may have been removed (to minimize on chalk dust affecting the electronics, it is said), with dry erase markers and so-called whiteboards replacing them (or even so-called smartboards in some cases—a choice often limited by a campus's technology budget). Regularly utilizing a classroom's multimedia as part of a lecture (e.g., showing PowerPoint slides, videos, visiting websites, etc.) sometimes leads to situations in which an instructor rarely uses the whiteboards (with the classroom's projector screen often blocking them); this is all contrary to a time when a professor would have filled the blackboards with notations throughout the lecture. While the practice of recording or working out/through aspects of a class on either a blackboard or whiteboard will vary from instructor to instructor, effective student notetaking is likely assisted by an oral lecture or presentation being accompanied by key notations for the class that summarize or stand in for more elaborate class comments, thereby signally visually to students a reinforcement of information presented to them orally. Erasing these at the end of a class session is a service to the incoming instructor. With visually impaired students enrolled in a class, let alone those with possible auditory challenges, both spoken lectures and whiteboard notations may have to be rethought (or augmented) in the interests of accessibility.

Campus Calendars

There are a variety of calendars in effect on a typical university campus, from the academic calendar (that governs the key moments in a semester (which themselves carry different names in different regions, like designating a spring semester instead as a winter semester), such as the deadline by which a course must be added or dropped, when midterm grades must be reported, or when final exams must take place), the fiscal calendar (which determines when budgets go into effect or come to an end), the productivity reporting calendar (when faculty annually report their teaching, research, and service accomplishments for the past year), etc.—but none of these calendars necessarily overlap. Becoming acquainted with all of these and then understanding how each does or does not impinge on an instructor's role and duties as a teacher, is incumbent on each faculty member.

Canceling Class

Traditionally, faculty have felt free to cancel periodic classes due to illness or conference travel (this is separate, of course, from the university itself canceling classes due to such factors as extreme or dangerous weather conditions); whether a department chair or department administrative staff needs to be alerted of such cancelations depends upon local habits on each campus. (Faculty should be aware that in some settings such absences may be tracked and recorded.) With the advent of remote teaching technology the need to cancel an in-person class may, in some cases, now be supplemented by a virtual class session. Canceling a class may also be avoided by the instructor devising beneficial projects or assignments on which students work (either in or outside of class time) in the instructor's absence, thereby progressing through the syllabus despite the faculty member's departure for a class period.

Carnegie Classifications of Institutions of Higher Education

In the U.S., universities are classified based on their type and the extent to which they emphasize teaching or research. In the early 1970s the Carnegie Commission on Higher Education (founded in 1905 as part of the philanthropic enterprise of the wealthy steel industrialist Andrew Carnegie [1835–1919]) developed a scale and criteria (frequently revised since then) as part of its effort to assess American higher education, resulting in colleges being designated as either: an R1 or R2 Research University, a D/PU Doctoral/Professional University, an M1, M2, or M3 Master's College and University, a Baccalaureate College, a Baccalaureate/Associate's College, an Associate's College, a Tribal College and University, or a Special Focus Research Institution. The level of research activity (as judged by such things as the annual grant dollar expenditures and portion of the college's budget dedicated to research activities) and the size of the programs are among the criteria distinguishing among some of these designations. This system is used by universities (many of which have aspirations for the coveted R1 classification), granting and accrediting agencies, and government to distinguish among and rank all accredited colleges when, for example, looking to make comparisons among schools. At present, there are about 150 colleges designated as R1 universities in the U.S.—the rankings are updated every three years.

Center for Teaching and Learning

Although training in pedagogy is not often included in many graduate programs throughout the disciplines, the importance of teaching once hired into many faculty positions has prompted a number of colleges to institute their own centers for excellence in teaching—units that are usually devoid of their own faculty lines (often a mark of what may be known as a center on a campus, as opposed to a department or an institute) and which are therefore staffed either by cross-appointed faculty from other academic units or staff members with teaching experience. Such centers usually offer regular workshops for faculty and provide resources to assist teachers. The value of such units likely differs from place to place, often depending on the estimation and teaching experience of each faculty member. Familiarizing yourself with the resources offered, if such an office exists on your campus, can be helpful by making instructors aware of assistance should they require any.

Class, Course, Module

For some, these are interchangeable terms while, for others, a class names a discrete daily or weekly appearance of students in a classroom or lecture hall (e.g., "I missed class today"), the sum total of which, across a semester, is known as a course (e.g., "What courses are you taking next semester?"), with an entire curriculum sometimes designated as a course of study. In this usage, a course of study is comprised of a number of different courses, all on different topics and each of which is constituted by multiple daily class meetings across a semester or an academic year. In yet other settings and regions, the term module has replaced course (or sometimes even naming a grouping of related courses, i.e., a pathway, concentration, or track), indicative for some of a certain managerial or professional ethos that has recently come to dominate aspects of higher education. Sometimes, in colleges that still regularly use the designation course there will nonetheless be a tendency to refer to the discrete units of an online course as modules.

Class Participation

Closely aligned with attendance, faculty may base a portion of the course grade on the degree to which a student provided evidence that they were engaged in the material and, during class, showed evidence that they have prepared for the class and were integrating and applying the material. For faculty unwilling to take attendance, including a score for class participation is assumed to be a roundabout way of also assessing attendance. However, due to the various ways in which students learn and do or do not participate verbally in class, judging preparation and engagement merely on the degree to which a student speaks can prove to be an insufficient, even disadvantaged, measure of the extent to which any given student has prepared for the class and has also integrated past material. Also, what can amount to an imprecise, even arbitrary, judgment of preparation and retention/application is likely among the reasons why universities now prefer empirically measurable assessment techniques.

Collaboration

Whether among students, working with an alum, or a faculty member, learning can often be enhanced when cooperating with another person(s) whose content expertise and skills either complement or motivate and therefore enhance one's own. Although it can risk one student relying on another far too much (and thus we arrive at a common complaint among some students concerning the downside of group work), working with a partner or as part of a team, on a task that's designed for and thus well-suited to such an exercise, can result in shared goals, shared work, and a shared sense of accomplishments. For some, such classroom collaboration better models so-called real world work environments.

Compliance

Especially noteworthy in public, as opposed to the somewhat lessened role it might play in private, universities, whole offices are often devoted to ensuring that the school is in compliance with a wide variety of laws let alone policies, expectations, and requirements of government, credentialing or granting agencies. Compliance Offices are also often the site that manages the increasing amount of in-house training expected of a university employee, ranging from annual workshops or online training on harassment policies to handling hazardous chemicals (especially relevant in some disciplines).

Contingent Faculty

An increasing number of those teaching undergraduate students on a university campus are now neither tenure-track nor tenured (i.e., are not permanently contracted faculty) but are, instead, employed on a limited term contract of some sort, whether as a graduate student funded annually as a teaching assistant (but listed as the instructor of record for a class, as opposed to merely running discussion, recitation, or tutorial sections for another faculty member who is in charge of the course) or a part-time instructor, lecturer, sessional or visiting lecturer (the terms differ in different settings) teaching even just one or up to several courses, along with a retired faculty member teaching a course or even a full-time instructor working on a three or five etc., year contract. In fact, so normalized have such appointments become that universities are now developing long-term contracts for non-tenure track/non-permanent lines or positions that are, however, also eligible for promotions and modest pay increases (sometimes called teaching professors or any number of other terms). All of this is related to, at least in many regions, declining funding from the state for public education and thus a series of budgetary pressures placed on a school (sometimes by its own administration, given each campus's own budgetary priorities) and which in turn impact the way a school finances its instructional costs (i.e., salaries and the number of available teaching positions—with fewer positions often meaning larger class sizes). That the rise of the broad group of non-tenure-track instructors now known collectively as contingent faculty impacts both those doctoral students and recent graduates who are themselves hoping to enter tenure-track positions (which are now increasingly few in some sectors of higher education) as well as the job security of those few remaining in tenured positions (inasmuch as the institution of, and thus protections of, tenure and academic freedom are not necessarily extended to all those who are teaching undergraduate students) suggests that both parties share common interests; however, in many cases, currently tenured or tenure-track faculty can be somewhat disengaged from the plight of their contingent colleagues, even those working in the same department with them.

Continuous Quality Improvement (CQI)

Some variation on this term is often heard today in academia, usually linked to credentialing associations and assessment initiatives, as a way to convey to those outside a college that its members are not satisfied with the status quo and, instead, seek to implement ongoing improvement in all areas of its operation. In the classroom, this can involve demonstrating to outside bodies that the department and faculty members continually reassesses outcomes and standards, so that it can be demonstrated that students continue to be challenged more and then also continue to improve on their performance from year to year. Often, this is something faculty naturally and consistently do, though they may not sufficiently represent this to those outside their classrooms; thus, CQI initiatives may be approached less as a substantive and more as a reporting initiative.

Core Courses/Modules

Although this may refer to courses that are part of the Core Curriculum (i.e., a campus's General Education program, particularly in the U.S.), it may also refer simply to modules or units of a degree program that are key or especially central to a topic and thus required as part of a program of study.

Core Curriculum/General Education (Gen Ed)

A specific feature of much U.S. undergraduate degree programs, so-called Gen Ed or simply the Core, is part of a long tradition in which a Bachelor's degree was in part assumed to prepare students for eventual participation in citizenship, by ensuring that they had a breadth of understandings, from an acquaintance with history, the arts, writing and reading skills, language training, as well as some exposure to the natural sciences. Many U.S. colleges therefore have what some call a Common Core, whereby a portion of each undergraduate student's degree (up to one third or more of it, perhaps, i.e., something common to all students regardless of their specialty subject or major) is spent familiarizing them with subjects well outside that concentration. As professional colleges moved into universities, starting in the mid-twentieth century (i.e., onetime autonomous Business Schools, Nursing Schools, Teachers Colleges, etc., becoming colleges or faculties within the university), pressure rose to minimize the time that it took to earn an undergraduate degree (i.e., time to degree) and thus to decrease the number of courses required outside the major. This, in turn, has often weakened the onetime influential College of Arts and Sciences, which had been the traditional home to the vast majority of Core courses offered on a typical campus, while the ability of professional schools to begin to offer courses that also satisfy Gen Ed requirements strengthens them (by allowing them to retain a far great proportion of the credit hours generated by their own majors, such as those who may no longer need to go elsewhere to satisfy, say, a campus's math requirements). Moreover, the traditional Gen Ed distribution model (i.e., enrolling in a prescribed number of Natural Science, Social Science, and Humanities or Fine Arts classes—with each discipline working to ensure some of their courses satisfy these requirements, thereby bringing students to their departments—making evident that the Core is also a way to subsidize enrollments in various units) has lately been either supplemented or outright replaced with not just fewer required Core courses but also with required courses in such other areas as critical thinking, diversity, research, and so-called high-impact practices as internships or study abroad courses. In settings without a required Core, undergraduate students tend to enroll in far more courses in their undergraduate major or specialty, opening the debate on the relevance of a Gen Ed curriculum. Throughout most of Europe, for example, pretty much all of the courses that constitute a student's Bachelor's degree are earned within their concentration, resulting in students focusing on their specialty in far greater detail than a comparable student in the U.S. (who may take no more than a total of ten courses in their major [i.e., 30 credit hours]); thus, when Gen Ed courses are part of an undergraduate degree, more specialized focus on a topic often does not take place until a student enrolls in a graduate degree.

Co-Teaching

If allowed by their unit(s), instructors can collaborate and share in the teaching of one course in a variety of ways, from planning the course together and being in each class together to each devising discrete units of the class and then taking turns as the instructor on any given day. The pairing can signal a mentoring relationship between experienced and less experienced faculty or constitute two viewpoints on a subject for the benefit of the students enrolled in the course. The degree to which the course is experienced by students as coherent and beneficial surely depends on the extent to which co-teachers share in planning and offering the course. Whether the course counts fully (or only as half effort if two faculty shared in the teaching), when it comes time for faculty to submit annual productivity reporting, is something that will more than likely vary campus to campus, depending on their departments' policies.

Credentialing Associations (Accreditation)

Although there are certainly private universities (notably in the U.S.), higher education in many settings is directly funded by public tax dollars, with the sometimes significant percentage (which varies across universities) of a school's operating budget directly dependent on state funding. Government, therefore, has a vested interest in how education works—whether standards, practices (in our outside of the classroom), spending, etc. In some settings this is delegated to a series of non-governmental agencies that accredit entire schools or even specific programs, whose purpose is to ensure that colleges comply with regional or national standards. In yet other settings, some universities themselves determine the accrediting of other colleges. In the cases of the professional schools (e.g., Engineering, Nursing, etc.), national professional associations can also be involved in accrediting the degree program, to ensure its graduates are prepared for work in that field. In all such cases the credentialing association will either annually or periodically assess a program or perhaps an entire campus, doing so in detail, to ensure that it remains in compliance, and to identify any infractions. Falling out of compliance can risk a school's ranking, its ability to attract certain students (such as, in some settings, risking whether students receiving certain sorts of loans and funding can even attend), let alone the school's ability to place their graduates within the professions for which they've trained. As part of this work institutions themselves will often have internal accrediting processes of their own whereby entire departments or degree programs are routinely assessed internally, possibly by a specific committee within the institution that is more than likely comprised of faculty from within the college (but outside of the department) and perhaps joined by an outside expert from another university.

Credits/Credit Hour Production

Often students are required not just to pass a certain number of courses but, more generally, to also obtain a certain number of credits or credit hours in order to graduate, thus not measuring their progress simply by the number of courses that they have passed, since not all courses require the same time commitment and thus amount of work. In most cases, a course or a module that meets for class approximately three hours per week (either 50 minutes per day three times a week or 75 minutes per day twice a week [leaving time in the schedule for a change of classes]) might be considered to be a three credit hour course. Natural science or foreign language classes which usually also require a weekly lab in addition to the lectures may be classified as a four credit hour course (with the lab hour per week added to the total count). This variation then also requires, as part of the curriculum, the creation of far shorter and less demanding one credit hour courses, simply to help students add up the correct number of expected credits in order to earn their degrees.

Critical Thinking

Although often named as a skill to be acquired in a Humanities class, critical thinking is surprisingly ill-defined in most cases, as if it somehow speaks for itself. While different definitions of it will likely be offered by different instructors (or departments, if the term is used in their recruiting materials), it is likely best to think ahead concerning what one means by this plastic and omnipresent term. Although there may have been a time when it implied objective and dispassionate analysis, the now widely shared critique of past efforts at attaining neutrality surely necessitates that the term be reconsidered, such as emphasizing instead contextualization of the claims or situations under study, both in terms of historical precedents and contemporary issues (so as not to allow any claim to stand alone or be seen as self-evidently significant), let alone the skills of comparison and explanation (to establish both similarities and difference between items as well as to offer an account for why such overlaps or divergences may exist) as well as self-reflexive critique (which includes scholarship itself among the items to be in need of study).

Cross-appointments

Although departments, organized around traditional disciplinary differences (e.g., the Department of Anthropology, the Department of Religious Studies, the Department of History, etc.), are the primary academic organizational unit on most campuses, and thus the unit to which a faculty member is assigned and through which their salary is budgeted (i.e., home to their faculty line), in some cases an incentive exists to share a faculty member's appointment across more than one unit, resulting in a cross-appointment. In such a case, varying percentages of the faculty member's time (usually meaning their teaching and service duties) will exist in each of the units. For example, a faculty member teaching three courses per semester may regularly teach two in one unit and one in another because their appointment is 33 percent in one while 66 percent in another. That service expectations can sometimes be a challenge, with both units expecting all of the faculty member's time (e.g., two monthly Department meetings to attend, two search committees on which to serve, etc.), is something of which a cross-appointed faculty member needs to be aware. Usually all cross-appointed faculty still retain one unit as their home department or their so-called tenure home, meaning that for the purposes of tenure or promotion applications as well as annual productivity reporting and raises, the procedures and standards of one unit will always take priority, with the other unit perhaps just submitting recommendations or reports to contribute to the home unit's assessment of the instructor's performance. Having all of this clearly spelled out in writing, ahead of accepting a cross-appointment, is recommended. In some cases an administration may suggest a cross-appointment as a cost-cutting strategy (somewhat akin to hiring contingent faculty), thereby relying on one faculty member to teach in two or more units, saving the university from funding more full-time faculty hires; although there are faculty who may value such appointments, given the manner in which some professors' work emphasizes cross-disciplinarity, it can be a strategy bound in many ways to fail given the insufficient amount of time and energy that the instructor might be able to put into more than one unit.

Curriculum

The overall structure and progression of courses in which students enroll to eventually earn a degree is generally known as a curriculum, sometimes also known as a course of study. Whether an undergraduate degree has a curriculum or, instead, a list of courses that do not necessarily build upon one another in order to attain some overall effect in students, is something to consider when looking at a program's requirements for its majors or specialists. In many cases, first year classes are broad surveys with subsequent courses narrowing the focus so that by the end of a degree students are looking in detail at a very small aspect of what, in their survey course, they had passed over all too quickly. Contrary to this model, there are curricula in which skills and not content are emphasized, such that a level of familiarity with the details are, of course, still acquired by students but always in service of using such skills as definition, description, comparison, interpretation, and explanation. The extent to which an undergraduate curriculum's requirements include (or maybe simply recommend or have the option for) such things as prerequisites, a certain sequential distribution of courses by level or subject matter, as well as such things as experiential learning, honors theses, or senior seminars varies. In many cases, the curriculum is merely inherited from past iterations of the department (often linked to the faculty who once taught, and their specialties), since revising a curriculum may either be seen as considerable work or be an exercise that makes too evident longstanding disciplinary disagreements among the faculty.

Curriculum Map

As part of recent assessment initiatives (focused not on individual classes, in this case, but instead on an entire degree program), the administration will sometimes require that the department demonstrate how the individual courses that together make up a curriculum each achieve one or more of the goals (i.e., outcomes) of the degree itself. For example, if the department claims that among the things it will train students to do is to engage in cross-cultural comparison (in order to find unexpected similarities and differences) then, or so it may be asked, in which course does this happen and, drilling even deeper, on which assignment within that course can the extent to which students learn this skill be measured and confirmed. Creating such curriculum maps—for each degree program offered by a department—may be required or merely recommended, and might need to be completed in a standardized manner, by means of a third-party software to which the university may subscribe for its assessment initiative.

Digital Humanities

Increasingly, scholars in the Humanities are using computing technology to produce their research, doing so in a manner long associated with the Social Sciences and especially the Natural Sciences. Such scholars may either use programming created by others or write their own programming, in order to do such things as, for example, analyze large bodies of data that defy an individual merely reading and analyzing it all for themselves. Whether the product of this work appears in a traditional publishing venue (peer review print articles or books) or lives online, let alone the scholarly product being the software itself that the faculty member develops to carry out a research task (and which can therefore be of use to others), the move to digital work in the Humanities more than likely requires departments to reconsider what they mean by scholarship, peer review publication, etc., as well as the standards that they employ to help assess career progress and that they use for hiring.

Directed Readings/Independent Study Course

Often seen as additional to a faculty member's regular teaching duties—and thus carried out voluntarily and therefore at the discretion of the instructor (i.e., an unpaid overload course)—most curricula include course numbers that allow a student to enroll in an individualized course of readings with a faculty member who is interested/qualified in the topic that engages the student. Most schools do not specify how this course must meet or proceed (with some not even requiring it to have a syllabus), leading to a variety of forms taken by directed reading courses, from a student being given a reading list to work through, with scheduled weekly meetings to discuss the material with the instructor, to a student pursuing a topic as they see fit, only in periodic consultation with a faculty member, and doing so at their own pace, to produce a final assignment due at the end of the semester. Depending on a faculty member's willingness to enroll students in such courses, they can be a very positive experience for a student, who gets to pursue an interest that is not represented in the regularly offered courses (making such courses an example of so-called high-impact practices).

Diversity, Equity, and Inclusion (DEI)/Equality, Diversity, and Inclusion (EDI)

A now widely adopted and broader designation than even just a few years ago, DEI Offices and Officers (e.g., a Vice President or Associate Dean for DEI), as it is known in the U.S. (EDI in the UK) are now standard in universities (along with many other institutions and corporations) and home to a variety of initiatives to ensure all students and employees feel welcome, safe, and represented on a campus. It would therefore be an error to assume that such initiatives are mainly about race or ethnicity and national origin (once the main focus of such initiatives); instead, they are just as much about gender, sexual identity, disability, and indigenous identity. Given the place of these issues in the laws of many nations (i.e., discrimination of members of protected classes being illegal), coupled with the fact that a DEI initiative can touch on all aspects of campus life (from the residence system and the classroom to the campus as a workplace), a campus's DEI staff work closely with a wide variety of other offices, from Academic Affairs (which is sometimes the designation for the senior academic office on a campus) to professional and clerical staff associations and Student Life. DEI initiatives have direct impact on the classroom as well, where teaching methods and especially class content can be seen as either promoting or inhibiting this work (now often known as inclusive pedagogy). Ensuring that each student feels welcome to participate in all aspects of a class and that classes include in their course material not just work produced by an array of scholars representing an academic discipline's diversity but also work focused on a variety of sectors and groups within any given population are important initial steps in this direction.

DWF Rate

The rate at which students either drop, withdraw, or fail a particular class is known as the DWF rate, used as an indicator of at-risk students. A variety of strategies have been developed by universities to identify and then reach out to and engage, and thereby retain, such students before such as time as a course needs to be dropped or a student earns a failing grade. While it is likely inevitable that a variety of students will not complete any given course, for a wide variety of reasons, the rate at which, say, first generation students have difficulty in a specific gateway course will impact the number who go on to careers in that discipline, suggesting that there may be something that a university or a department can do to address trends that include high DWF rates in certain disciplines or specific classes. Thus, working to reduce a college's or a department's DWF rate is among the common outcomes that units will now often set for themselves.

Electives/Options

Courses that are not required by either an undergraduate degree or a major are often designated as electives or as options, in which student can choose (i.e., elect or opt) to take a course for reasons other than their degree's requirements (though degrees often dictate a minimum or even a maximum number of electives or options credit hours in which a student must enroll, often linked to courses at the upper level).

Engaged Learning

Using as the model the large natural science lecture, much higher education today is concerned with increasing the engagement among potentially alienated undergraduate students, both to improve their learning as well as to retain and, eventually, graduate them. Much attention has therefore been given, over the past decades, to how engagement among students—both inside and outside of the classroom—can be enhanced, from devising so-called high-impact practices in the classroom (e.g., problem-based learning, internships, group work, not to mention offering new and timely courses, etc.) to providing an array of extracurricular options on a campus (e.g., student clubs, recreation facilities, etc.). That lower enrollments in all courses would likely be among the ways to systematically increase engagement with students is, for obvious reasons perhaps, not among the options at many schools, such as those whose operating budgets require a high degree of tuition revenue. For some, initiatives to implement new ways to increase student engagement could therefore be said to coincide with colleges trying to lower their instructional costs.

Exam, Quiz, Test

Traditionally the designation of exam (short for examination) has been limited to cumulative or comprehensive evaluations of an entire course's worth of material, upon which a large portion of the course's final grade was probably based. Tests, on the other hand, usually cover the information for a discrete unit within the course, take place periodically throughout the semester, and are usually worth a smaller percentage of the course (though, cumulatively, all tests in a course could be worth a very large percentage of a course's final grade). Quizzes or so-called pop quizzes, itself a rather older designation, usually implies unannounced and very brief in-class tests, perhaps consisting of just one question that can be quickly answered and then submitted to the instructor by students (sometimes accomplished by means of electronic devices [i.e., clickers] or even smartphones), and which are therefore worth a rather small portion of a course's final grade (functioning, in some cases, as a way to take attendance on any given day or as evidence that students prepared for the class by doing the required readings).

Examples Approach

A way of teaching that makes use of content or data but always or eventually in the service of wider or more general issues that reach beyond the specifics of the content has come to be known, for some, as the examples approach; it is an approach in which items are not studied due to their inherent interest (itself a longstanding model in the Humanities) but, rather, they are studied always in a comparative manner so as to shed light on broader social issues. For instance, one might study the plays of Shakespeare because they are self-evidently classics deserving of our careful attention (a position some traditionalists might adopt) or, instead, because they provide an opportunity to investigate a variety of topics of relevance elsewhere in history or the world, such as ways in which gender relations are represented and negotiated. In this way, *Hamlet* might be an example of something also seen elsewhere, ensuring that the play serves as a detailed instance of something also evident on other occasions and in other situations. In the study of religion this means that any datum traditionally at home in a religious studies course is now understood as evidence of a practical human situation that can also be seen elsewhere—whether involving religion or not—so that one might now study, for instance, origins narratives as but one example of how storytellers and writers use discourses on the distant past for purposes of contemporary relevance to them and their listeners/readers.

Experiential Learning

Critics of traditional college lectures have long argued that learning can be enhanced if students understand firsthand the so-called real world application of the information that they acquire in their classes; as a result, a wide array of practical applications for classroom skills have now developed, in which students are said to experience, for themselves, the relevance of and applications for their classroom work—whether this extends to something as detailed as a semester-long internship related to their specialty (which, in some cases, can lead to future employment) or even just working on practical case studies as part of a class or completing weekly labs where students engage in hands-on activities that apply the content of their lectures.

Extra Credit

Although disallowed on some campuses (for the unfair advantage they may provide to some students, let alone ways in which it can be misused), some faculty elsewhere allow students to complete additional work, apart from the course requirements as defined in the syllabus, for additional credit or points in a course, thereby turning a class worth a total of 100 possible points into one in which a student might be able to earn 105 or more points. Such extra credit assignments may vary from additional items directly relevant to the course, that a student voluntarily completes in order to earn additional points (more than likely to compensate for their poor performance on some other course requirements), to a faculty member identifying campus events, such as public lectures or performances, at which extra credit students are expected to attend and either sign an attendance sheet at the event or perhaps submit a brief report on the event. Whether extra credit is fair to those students who are already excelling in the course, and thus is an abuse of a course's requirements, or is instead a way to encourage especially lower-level students to become more involved in campus life, is an ongoing debate. If an instructor opts to include extra credit work in a course then an important point is that it is offered equitably, in a way that will benefit or is at least available to all students, should they opt to take advantage of it (including those who, for whatever reason, are unavailable to attend campus events outside the course's regular meeting times), and described in detail in the syllabus.

Faculty Lines

Referring to the horizontal lines of a traditional leger or, today, spreadsheet, a faculty line is the budgeted position of a faculty member that extends into future budget years, such as a permanently contracted or tenured faculty member for whom the college anticipates paying a salary well into the future (i.e., until their retirement). Debates have long taken place on campuses concerning who retains the line, i.e., the funding that finances a faculty position, should a faculty member depart from the university for whatever reason, with Departments and programs arguing that they ought to be able to search to replace the person while administrative levels above the Department usually attempt to regain the line and possibly repurpose it, whether leaving it unfilled for a period of time (and thereby using the budgeted salary for that period of time for other purposes on a campus—a strategy long-used on university campuses to finance some program or even operating budgets) or giving the position to another Department whose hiring needs are seen by the administration, for whatever reason, as more pressing. Given that authority over budgets is usually wielded by the senior administration or the campus's so-called executive office, the resolution of debates over who owns faculty lines is usually not in doubt.

Faculty Governance

Traditionally the notion of shared governance signaled the way in which the senior administration and the faculty at large cooperated in determining the direction of a college, with such elected bodies as a representative Faculty Senate sometimes comprising the faculty members' contribution to a university's governance. More specifically, the notion of faculty governance has also applied to the curriculum and course/class content, with faculty members once being considered to be the sole authority on these matters (i.e., under the longtime banner of academic freedom). With increasing input into the daily operations of a campus from governments, credentialing associations, and senior administrations, coupled with declining budgets and greater reliance on untenured contingent labor (notably in the Humanities), the once taken-for-granted idea of faculty governance, and even shared governance, has become an item of debate in many settings, with faculty members now often feeling like they exercise less control over basic elements of the job (e.g., requirements for what must be included in a syllabus) than previous generations of professors would have taken for granted. In those settings where it is legal for faculty to organize and form unions or faculty associations, this sense among faculty will, of course, vary.

FERPA/HIPAA

Specific to the U.S., 1974's Family Educational Rights and Privacy Act (FERPA) and 1996's Health Insurance Portability and Accountability Act (HIPAA) directly impact student information on a university campus, with instructors and colleges disallowed by federal law from sharing a student's academic or health information with third parties—unless the student has signed a waiver and signified to whom such information can be released. In an effort to increase retention of incoming students, some colleges now invite them to sign such a FERPA waiver so that specific parents/guardians have routine access to their grades so that students feel accountable and thus more inclined to excel in their classes. While being courteous, instructors should therefore not disclose any information about a student's standing in class or performance/attendance if ever contacted by a third party, such as a parent phoning or emailing a professor, and first determine if the student has authorized such queries. Contact your department chair if you have questions.

Films

How to use feature-length films in a course is always a challenge, given that they most often run far longer than class times (unless one is teaching a three-hour class that meets once weekly). Seeing it together as a class is often a key element of the pedagogical utility of the film, though some courses will require students to view a film on their own, outside class time. Although many films of relevance to a course are now easily streamed it is unwise to assume that all students have equal access to such online services, though many campus libraries now subscribe to online video services, such as Kanopy, which allows students to watch a wide array of titles online inasmuch as they can login as students registered at the university. Key to making the inclusion of one or more films in a syllabus relevant to the class is the pre- and post-film discussion and any assignments in the class based on the film and discussion.

Final Examinations

Some years ago, the final grades in many courses were largely determined by a student's performance on a cumulative final test, though such comprehensive instruments were often called examinations (or exams for short), which might take up to three hours to complete, comprising short or long answer questions as well as fill-in-the-blank and/or multiple-choice questions. Over the recent decades, the role of such exams has become more limited in some disciplines, due to a variety of reasons, from an increasing awareness that they may instead be measuring a student's ability to perform in such settings rather than their retention or application of information to calculations of final grades increasingly emphasizing a wider variety of work and assignments completed throughout the semester. It is now not unusual to have courses in which there is no final exam but, perhaps, either a final test merely on the last semester's unit or a culminating writing assignment or project.

First Year Seminars

Whether or not they are part of the so-called Gen Ed or Core curriculum, some universities (notably in the U.S.) have required courses for incoming first-year students, often called something akin to first year seminars or, perhaps, a common book experience. Such classes are intended to provide new students with, as the term makes evident, a shared basis via a common syllabus. The topics of such courses can vary widely, from one credit hour classes, sometimes largely taught by staff who work in campus advising offices (or other student services offices) that are devoted to initiative students into the life of the university (covering such topics as study habits and campus resources), to three credit hour courses that meet more frequently and are devoted to an academic topic—though one necessarily of broad appeal, given that students from across the campus's majors will all be enrolled. Depending how a campus offers such required courses faculty in departments may never teach such courses or may have an opportunity to teach them as either a paid or unpaid overload.

Full-time Equivalency (FTE)

A numeric system to represent the extent to which different instructors contribute to or are valued by a university. With a full-time tenured or tenure-track faculty member often considered a 1, for example, full-time graduate teaching assistants might be designated as a 0.5. It is also a system that can be used to represent the portion of a faculty member's workload that is devoted to the traditional three areas of teaching, research, and service (i.e., committee work), such as the FTE being reported as 40/40/20 for a person who spends approximately equal time on teaching and research but only half as much of that time on various service obligations; someone going on sabbatical, with no teaching or service duties for an entire semester, would therefore report an FTE of 0/100/0. A faculty member cross-appointed equally between two units would have 50 percent of their FTE reported in each unit.

Grade Book

Each instructor will have a record of student accomplishment on all assignments, which, at the end of the course, will allow them to calculate each student's final grade. Often made and managed throughout the semester by the faculty member themselves (though sometimes varying portions of this work is delegated to a Teaching Assistant), the grade book or grade sheet contains confidential information and must always be carefully maintained. In some settings school policy requires a faculty member to retain such documentation for a specific number of years, in case a past student returns to contest their grades. For those using learning management systems in their courses, such online tools may offer their own grade book features, automatically adding to it and tabulating a student's standing in the course—information available to each individual student.

Grades/Marks

The type of grade or mark—designations that vary from region to region—that an instructor is able to assign to a student as an assessment of their performance on an individual assignment or in the course as a whole can vary from campus to campus. Although some settings, such as universities in the UK, may rely on a system that includes such designations as First Class Honors, Upper Second Class Honors, Lower Second Class Honors, and Third Class Honors, the letter marking system is now common in many places but is certainly not the only option available. But even if letter grades are preferred, whether there is an option to assign a plus or a minus (e.g., A+ or C-) is not universal, and neither is the significance of a letter grade. (Is a failing grade [F] awarded for grades below 60% or below 50%?) Sometimes a Pass/Fail option (or even the further designation of a High Pass) is possible and sometimes also a grad of I or Incomplete, which usually comes with a specific deadline, after the completion of the semester, by which time the late work in the course must be finished, submitted, and graded, with the correct final grade then replacing the I—which implies that a change of grade is also possible, at the instructor's discretion, though a rationale for the change is often required (e.g., due to a mathematical error in calculating a final grade or the completion of outstanding work). In some settings student loan programs require that student attendance be reported, such that a failing grade will need to be distinguished, i.e., did the student "earn" the F by their poor performance or did they stop attending class and cease completing assignments—and, if the latter, then when was their last day of class attendance.

Grading/Marking

Known as grading in the U.S. and often marking elsewhere in the world (notably school traditions more connected to the UK), it is a commonly adopted practice throughout schooling systems and levels to assess student performance by ranking their accomplishments in a course, usually judged in comparison to each other, either using a numeric or letter system (sometimes, as in the U.S., later converted to a so-called Grade Point Average [GPA] on a standardized scale, e.g., a 4.0 GPA which is equivalent to an A, which is itself often equal to a performance of 90% or better). While a passing grade can vary widely, across a spectrum of abilities and results, an F often symbolizes an insufficient or failing performance. Course planning therefore requires an instructor to decide which assignments to use, when to use them, and also to consider how they will each culminate in a final grade in the course (i.e., what weight to place on which assignments, with some counting for either a larger or smaller portion of the final course grade [i.e., weighted grading]). Debates over the purpose and efficacy of grading have a long history, with some programs either opting to have students assess each other, or even themselves (in light of parameters provided to them by the instructor), on either all or a limited number of assignments, while yet others might instead choose to provide only substantial qualitative comments to students as the primary means for assessment, comparing them, perhaps, to their own past performance and capabilities.

Grading on a Curve

Likely not a widely adopted practice in Humanities courses today (and sometimes forbidden, in efforts to better compare marks across institutions), there are yet other courses in which the distribution of grades among students are still normalized by the instructor, under the assumption that a classic bell curve's distribution ought to result, representing what statisticians would consider to be a normal distribution among a random sample. Among the various methods of doing this would be taking the best student performance on any given assignment and designating it as an A+ or 100 percent (regardless what the student might have actually earned) and then increasing all student grades in the course by that same amount, to normalize the scores across the class, in relation to the best performance. Whether or not this is desirable to an instructor, looking at the distribution of grades for an assignment does help them to quickly determine if any individual question on the test might have been unfair, vague, or poorly written, let alone whether the overall test was far too difficult or not sufficiently demanding, since one would expect a bell curve (and sometimes the distribution strikes an instructor as being weighted much too heavily toward one or the other end of the grading scale). That yet others do not concern themselves with the distribution of grades indicates that there are most certainly still debates around whether or not students should be graded on a curve.

Graduate/Postgraduate Students

Depending on the region, students who have completed their Bachelor's degree may be known as either graduate students (grad students for short, especially in North America) or postgraduate students (e.g., in the UK), which is not to be confused with those holding certain sorts of brief fellowship positions (one or two years) after completing their PhD, i.e., postdoctoral fellows (i.e., postdocs).

Graduation Rate

Although the days of a four-year undergraduate degree in North America are long behind many schools (for a wide variety of reasons, among which are the rising costs of education and the extent to which many students must work in order to finance their schooling), the rate at which students graduate with their Bachelor's degree in four, five, or six years is tracked by universities and often used in comparing (i.e., ranking) colleges. In yet other parts of the world, where higher education is still financed far more by the government (and which sometimes lack any tuition from the student), standardized three- or four-year Bachelor's degrees are still common, with only part-time students there taking longer than this to complete their program of study. The ability to retain a student from their first to second year has proven a strong indicator of the likelihood of a student completing their degree but the rate at which they end up completing it can be impacted by a larger number of factors, from the student's own performance and capabilities in the classes, of course, to how quickly they can find and then focus on a discipline in which they are interested and especially also their financial situation (i.e., will they need to drop courses in order to work either part- or full-time to support themselves or even their families?). On a pragmatic level, successfully moving students through their various years at college, and thereby graduating them efficiently, can be said to have an impact on the rate at which new incoming students can be recruited and enrolled into seats vacated by the most recent graduates, indicating that improved graduation rates can be connected not only to enhanced student learning but also to a school's overall business model.

Group Work

While collaboration is likely an essential skill to acquire during an undergraduate career, inasmuch as it is often a fundamental component of many workplaces, the variation in student abilities and motivation means that required group work in a course can be met with a less than enthusiastic response on the part of some students—notably those who feel that past groups in which they worked on assignments benefitted far too much for their own individual contributions. If challenging student to develop collaborative skills is important to an instructor then it is important to devise ways for students to self-assess and to engage in peer assessment, as part of their group work, as well as to work on some individualized components of the assignment, all with clear expectations.

Handouts

There was a time when hardcopy class handouts (mimeographed many years ago, possibly made on a Gestetner machine [named after its inventor, David

Gestetner] but, beginning in the 1970s, more than likely photocopied or, now, laser printed) were an essential component of teaching in a university, with students retaining handouts distributed during the lecture, taking notes on them, studying from them, etc. But with the advent of decreased photocopying budgets in some schools, increasingly large classes, the arrival of learning management systems, PDFs that are easily distributed to students via email, not to mention PowerPoint slides and notes (which can be sent directly to students before or after a class), along with recordings of lectures that are sometimes made available to students after the class, the need for tangible in-class handouts has diminished dramatically.

Harassment

Due to the legal nature of such charges, harassment accusations and adjudications of such are more than likely the purview of a specific office and staff on a university campus, whether the accusations involve students, students and faculty/staff, or are exclusively between employees of a college. A broad definition of harassment would include behavior that creates an unwelcome environment for someone at the university (whether in a residence, cafeteria, recreation center, classroom, faculty office, etc.), and which involves any of the protected classes of individuals, such as abusive or hostile behavior (everything from overt actions to insulting jokes and slurs) exhibited toward someone due to their religious identity, gender, national origin, race, age, etc. Questions concerning the process by which complaints are made and then assessed on a campus, as well as the various appeal procedures and eventual penalties than can be instituted, should be directed to a department chair who can then assist the instructor with navigating the process on each campus. Given the legal ramifications of employees engaging in harassing actions, many colleges have instituted required annual training (whether a workshop or an online tutorial) to educate all employees, including Teaching Assistants or perhaps even student workers hired for clerical work in departments.

Hard Skills/Soft Skills

A longstanding distinction between practical and measurable knowledge acquired in college, that can presumably be applied directly in specific careers (e.g., practical know how acquired in computer science, nursing, business, chemistry, etc.), and those social or cognitive skills that are widely applicable across careers but which are generally more difficult to assess (how to work well in groups, how to manage time or disagreements, creativity, oral and written communication, description, comparison, interpretation, analysis, etc.). Traditionally, the argument is made that in the Humanities—widely seen, correctly or not, as lacking the practical knowledge that employers desire—the latter, soft or core skills, are taught. That these might be the far more important transferable skills to acquire in college is often overlooked, given that many employers will train new workers in the specific so-called hard skills needed for their specific job, while depending on employees to already arrive with the tools to be creative, contributing members of teams. If so, training in the Humanities may be far more effective and beneficial for diverse futures than some have assumed.

High-Impact Practices (HIP)

A term used for a variety of teaching approaches and initiatives that are said to deviate from traditional and rather passive large lectures and which, instead, engage students far more and more actively, thereby assumed to assist with more effectively retaining and graduating students. Among the approaches included would be: experiential learning, internships, portfolios, collaborative classroom projects, study abroad courses and student exchanges, living/learning communities, service learning, first year seminars and senior seminars, individualized reading courses, undergraduate research, etc. From even just this brief list it is apparent that HIPs can be stand-alone initiatives, which may or may not involve an instructor (i.e., studying abroad for a semester or a directed reading course), or one among other pedagogical strategies that an instructor incorporates into a course or class period (e.g., collaboration, a service learning project, or portfolios). Although there was a time when this designation did not exist, the increasing size among some lecture courses as well as increased competition among schools for tuition revenue (where tuition is charged of students) could be understood to have helped to establish conditions in which explicit attention needed to be given by various colleges to developing strategies to distinguish a student's educational experience at their institution.

Higher Education

A clearly ranked term often used to name a broad grouping of degrees and programs of study (from the BA to the PhD) that one can earn after completing what is often known as secondary school, gymnasium, or simply high school in some places (in distinction from what is sometimes known as primary or elementary education, which includes the schooling of children up to early adolescence). In some settings, so-called middle school signifies a separate school attended by older adolescents prior to enrolling in secondary school. Often, some sort of qualifying or standardized exams must be completed as part of a competitive application process to gain admission to higher or postsecondary education (i.e., college or university).

Honors

Whether part of a campus-wide unit (such as housed within and thereby governed by an Honors Program or Honors College [usually headed by a Dean]), and thus a designation that appears on a degree and transcript, or some form of delimited additional work within a department and thus a major, the honors designation in some regions can signify higher achieving students or students that completed additional work, such as an undergraduate thesis (usually supervised by a faculty member and, in most cases, constituting an additional research paper that might be defended orally, akin to graduate programs). In yet other parts of the world, the honors designation is attached to a degree, e.g., one earns a BA Honors or a BSc Honors, having been admitted into a final year of an undergraduate program based on merit, with those not admitted simply earning a BA or what some might designate as an ordinary degree. Honors Programs or Colleges can take a variety of forms, some requiring faculty from units across campus to teach courses in that college (as overloads or as part of their regular duties) or others hiring their own faculty (whether tenure-track or not), though honors students will likely still be required to declare a major in a discipline just as any student is. In some cases Honors Colleges are mainly a recruiting and thus marketing devices but in others they have a rigorous curriculum that more advanced students complete in addition to the requirements of their major or specialty discipline(s). Within departments and thus majors, however, the honors designation can operate free of an Honors College's requirements and governance, leading to a rather unregulated economy as to just what honors within a discipline might mean. On some campuses departments can offer honors courses recognized by an Honors Program or College, which often takes the form of smaller enrollments, enhanced discussion, and additional requirements—courses that, in some cases, prove to be ideal sites from which to recruit motivated students to a major or minor. Teaching such courses may be seen by some faculty as a benefit, and thus something possibly shared among the faculty.

Humanities

A traditional division within the university (along with the Fine or Performing Arts, the Social Sciences and the Natural Sciences), that groups together what is usually a fairly routine number of disciplines that are thought to all investigate the so-called enduring human spirit, with each studying a discrete site where it is sometimes said to be expressed or instantiated, and thus sites or expressions that are open to interpretation or even appreciation. Sometimes thought to be coterminous with the liberal arts, the Humanities usually is a narrower term, however, and often includes English Literature, Philosophy, Religious Studies, foreign language study, Art History, etc., with History once also being considered a standard element of the Humanities though it is now sometimes designated as a Social Science in some settings. It is not difficult to imagine the study of religion taught in a classical humanities fashion (given that the field often is represented as studying "manifestations of the sacred," or so it might have once been phrased) but it is also not hard to see the field practiced rather differently, not only in a traditional social scientific manner (hence the more quantifiably-based sociology and psychology of religion, even the anthropology of religion) but also in a way that does not presume an enduring and uniform human nature to be animating the various cross-cultural and trans-historical situations and artifacts studied in its courses.

Inclusive Pedagogy

This is the term now preferred for efforts in the classroom to ensure that all students feel welcome to participate fully in a course and that they are studying topics widely representative of our complex societies, whether that means the ones in which they themselves live or those past or present groups they may be interested to study. This initiative therefore impacts the topics under consideration in a course but also the resources used to pursue these topics as well as the methods used to teach the material and to assess student learning. For a typical university classroom contains a wide variety of students, from those who are first generation, and who may have little familiarity with some aspects of academia or class expectations, to those who, for whatever reason, may see themselves as being on the margins of a dominant demographic (whether in terms of such designations as their gender, race, orientation, age, or physical abilities). Inclusive pedagogies are a sub-set of wider efforts to engage and involve all students actively in a course, making it an initiative very much in line with a variety of student-centered teaching styles. Apart from treating all students respectfully, other key elements of an inclusive classroom are: touching base with students frequently, in a variety of ways (sometimes anonymously), to elicit feedback on their experience of the course (while also being ready to revise the class's material or methods in light of these comments); presenting class content in a variety of ways so as to engage a wide array of students who each may learn differently; offering a variety of assignments to students to assess their learning in the course, such that no one mode of assessment is emphasized or relied upon exclusively, thereby ensuring that all students have the opportunity to document their learning satisfactorily.

Inquiry-Based Assignments

Another example of a so-called high-impact practice (HIP) and possibly an instance of undergraduate research, creating assignments in which students must engage in research to complete the task or solve a problem. While such assignments comprise a broad range—with virtually all assignments being inquiry-based in some way—instructors can craft assignments in which students are presented with a new situation in which information and skills from class must be applied in novel ways, along with incorporating new information the students must source from resources introduced during class.

Internships

An example of a so-called high-impact teaching practice (HIP), as well as experiential learning, students enrolling in an internship that complements and applies their disciplinary specialty can be a beneficial experience for a student—sometimes even leading to a career. While some campuses have a central office that arranges and manages such experiences—whether or not they are for credit toward a degree—on others they are arranged more informally, though always involving a department if they are to be for course credit (in such cases departments likely have a specific course number that is used for internships). While the internship may take place on campus, there's a rather good chance it will be off-campus and not necessarily in the same city, with students sometimes spending a semester elsewhere in order to work (whether paid or not) in an internship.

Introduction vs. Survey

"Introduce the yeast into the flour," as might be heard on a cooking show, is a good example of a technical use of the term, inasmuch as it means to initiate something into a novel setting (think of a onetime "letter of introduction" provided to someone new to a city or social circle, written by one already familiar with their new setting and intended to be read by their new acquaintances, as assistance to the newcomer hoping to join a new group). Thus, in this technical sense, the introductory course is not to be confused with a survey course, inasmuch as the latter is a broad summary and generalization. Thus, a Survey of World Religions is more than likely a rather different course than an Introduction to the Study of Religion (with disciplines and specialties easily interchangeable in this example), although, to their loss, both of these terms are more than likely synonymous for most instructors and students.

Large Lectures

Although they risk alienating students who may feel lost in a large venue, many programs have had to implement large lecture courses—enrolling 100 or even far more students in a single course, all attending a common lecture—in order to meet student demand when new faculty lines are not forthcoming from the administration. Such courses are a double-edged sword: while they can considerably enhance a unit's overall credit hour production (undoubtedly an important metric to assess departmental viability in many universities) they can also be a rather poor setting in which to recruit new majors, given their lack of personal attention and the general inability to encourage class participation. Teaching Assistants assigned to work with the instructor can enhance contact time with students, to be sure, and properly chosen class assignments can also help to moderate the effects of such large classes, though they should not be confused with the clear benefits of a small seminar in which the instructor routinely interacts closely with all students.

Learner-Centered Initiatives

Over the past two decades increasing attention has been paid to assessing the degree to which students obtain and then retain information acquired in class as opposed to simply polling students for feedback on the instructor's teaching via surveys at the end of the semester. Such initiatives focus on the reception and not the delivery of the material and, in some cases, has resulted in rather fine-grained analysis of where and how in the course its various goals, now known as outcomes, are achieved or at least measured. This initiative is also linked to the increasing role played by credentialing agencies on a university campus and their desire to obtain empirical data to better judge the performance of an entire college or even a specific course.

Learning Management Systems (LMS)/ Virtual Learning Environments (VLE)

As part of the declining number of faculty, increased teaching duties for some, and the increase in class size over recent decades—all linked to ongoing challenges to university budgets and, in many cases, declining government support for higher education—most schools have by now contracted with third party vendors to implement a variety of online systems (whether used by the instructor synchronously [students and instructor meeting live though remotely] or asynchronously [students each accessing recorded material at a time of their choosing]) that can be a resource to the instructor and students alike (both distance learners, of course, but also on-campus students as well), offering a site where the course can live online, integrating discussion boards, grade books, supplementary text/audio/video content, recordings of lectures, as well as a variety of assessment tools that allow online testing (from short and long answer to multiple choice and fill in the blank questions). No contemporary instructor can therefore be unaware of a school's LMS or VLE (e.g., Canvas, Blackboard, Moodle, etc.); although some faculty will not be enamored with what they offer, others will quickly adopt them in appreciation for what they allow the faculty member to now do in a course. Case in point: during the global COVID-19 pandemic, it is fair to say that LMSs saved higher education, whether that meant offering entire courses remotely or enabling faculty and students to continue with their schooling despite sometimes mandated classroom absences.

Lectures

Although now frowned upon by some (for the manner in which it can encourage passive participation by students because of the material sometimes simply being read verbatim by the instructor from their lecture notes), there is still a place for the traditional lecture, though one that is now revised so as to ensure that it engages students and thereby encourages their learning. Whether accompanied by visuals, regularly broken up by the insertion of different teaching modes (e.g., small group work, discussion, etc.), or involving the instructor physically moving throughout the class while lecturing (so as to create a more intimate sense with those students nearby at any given moment), the traditional lecture can be an effective teaching technique if done properly and dynamically, notably in those large classes where it more than likely remains a basic aspect of most classes.

Lesson Plans

With the advent of assessment initiatives there is now a degree of routinization to planning a university course (i.e., instructional design) that previous generations of faculty might not have experienced. Despite this, formal lesson plans, at least as associated with those teaching in either elementary schools or high schools—i.e., written in advance of a class meeting and detailing the topics to be covered on any given day and which, taken together, represent the material or topics covered in an entire course—are, as of yet, generally not expected in most university classes. This does not mean, however, that they are not considered part of course design on some campuses, perhaps being the topic of voluntary or mandatory faculty workshops, following standardized formats, or even expected to be included in a faculty member's evidence of their teaching effectiveness (notably among earlier career or junior faculty). Even if one thinks of them as an intrusion on faculty governance of the curriculum, determining an organized way to offer a class, one that moves the students through a new topic in a manner that allows them to understand, retain, and apply it, does not just naturally happen and therefore deserves careful consideration by any faculty member hoping to be an effective teacher—whether or not formal lesson plans are expected on their campus.

Liberal Arts

A now somewhat dated terminology, if only for some, implementing a classical and therefore longstanding model in which so-called higher education was meant to "liberalize" students (from Latin for freedom, honor or ample and generous [i.e., being served a liberal portion at a meal], and therefore used in a sense rather different from many contemporary political uses of the term), thereby contributing to their individuality, supposed fulfillment, as well as future role as citizens. The collection of disciplines with whose methods the student was presumed to be in need of familiarization—dating in part to antiquity—came to be known as the liberal arts, ranging from rhetoric, logic, mathematics, etc., to, in more recent iterations, English, History, the natural sciences, and foreign languages. The so-called Core or Gen Ed (general education) curriculum has become the vehicle, at least in the U.S., whereby a prescribed sampling of undergraduate courses from across the disciplines generally known as the Humanities, Social Sciences, Natural Sciences and Mathematics was made mandatory for all university students, regardless of their major or specialty. Thus, the liberal arts and the so-called Core are, at least traditionally, closely overlapping.

Library Resources

Often, university libraries employ specific librarians to be liaisons to academic units on campus, and among the services that they offer are often such things as creating and posting guides to using library resources in each of their disciplinary areas as well as offering sessions with individual faculty and meeting with their courses and students, to provide either an overview on using the library or tailored assistance with specific class assignments or projects that will benefit from library research. Familiarizing yourself with these resources and making full use of them to assist students in your classes is a wise investment of time—either when first arriving on a campus or anytime the library staff member assigned to your area changes. Today, many libraries no longer stock hard copy academic journals and hardcopies databases, having moved all such resources online. It is therefore difficult to imagine producing scholarship on a modern university campus (whether as a faculty member or student) without becoming thoroughly acquainted with not just what a campus library offers—including its interlibrary loan services, whereby a network of libraries routinely share print resources among all of their patrons—but also how its various online resources are made available and navigated.

Living-Learning Communities

As a specific subset of experiential learning and another example of a high-impact practice (HIP), over the past decades some residential colleges have moved toward implementing an arrangement where students pursuing common studies may also live together in the same part of a residence system (something often limited to a required first year dorm experience), aiming for a more integrated learning setting in which students with similar interests not only take their classes together but also reside and even socialize together. The residence system may therefore also plan programming that is thought to enhance the students' learning. To whatever extent such initiatives impact their learning, they are also linked to systematic and sustained efforts on the part of colleges to increasingly engage and thereby retain students beyond their first year, something that takes on increasing importance given the always present challenges associated with incoming undergraduate students who are, at least in many cases, away from home for the first time and who thereby risk alienation, loneliness, and even mental health crises.

Lower/Upper Division

Many undergraduate programs will distinguish more introductory or survey courses—a distinction often glossed over but one that retains importance, with the former performing an initiatory role for those new to a discipline whereas the latter a generalizing, summary role—from subsequent classes in which a student might later enroll, which will probably be more specialized or focused. Regardless the numbering system adopted by a university, the first courses in an area will often be known as lower-level classes whereas the classes in which students enroll who are more experienced in a subject matter may be designated as upper-level classes, with specific rules and requirements pertaining to each (e.g., a degree requires a certain number of upper-level courses).

Majors/Minors

A distinction often adopted, especially in the U.S., to name the specialty or concentration in which a student has trained as part of their undergraduate career, with a greater number of courses/credit hours required to earn a major as opposed to earning just a minor in a discipline. Colleges—in an effort to produce so-called well-rounded students, notably in the U.S.—sometimes have requirements that students must demonstrate a degree of breadth throughout their studies, whereby they must declare both a major and a minor (or sometimes opting to complete two majors, i.e., declaring a so-called double major in two subject areas, or even a triple major), with the second major often being in a subject thought to complement their major area of study or, perhaps, seen as something in which the student is interested and thus quite apart from a first major which may be linked to their career hopes. The viability of an academic unit in such systems can be linked directly to the number of majors that graduate (sometimes measured annually or as a rolling annual average), although overall credit hour production (and thus tuition revenue) is also a criterion of importance in the modern university.

Mandatory Reporting

All depending on the local or national laws in your setting, college instructors may be bound by law—as opposed to just university policy—to report to the relevant authorities (whether to the relevant office on campus or to law enforcement itself) certain sorts of personal disclosures that a student may make to them, such as in a meeting during offices hours or some other time outside of class, and perhaps offered by the student in explanation for their absence or performance in a course. The sorts of disclosures involved can vary, of course, but would likely always include students showing evidence of being at risk for self-harm or harm by another (i.e., various forms of abuse, whether past or current). Settings in which faculty are designated as mandatory reporters—a role often placed upon those working with minors—often include required training (often annual) to ensure all employees are familiar with these requirements. Although such mandatory reporting is intended as a way to ensure that students in various forms of possible jeopardy do not slip between the cracks, as they say, and that a variety of possible crises do not go unaddressed, it can also risk a student's privacy, inasmuch as they may, for whatever reason, wish this information not to be known by authorities. Instructors should be thoroughly familiar with such reporting requirements in their setting and, if they sense a conversation with a student going in such a direction, be prepared to empower the student by briefly familiarizing them with the requirements placed upon faculty, so that a student is informed and can then decide if they wish to proceed with making any disclosures. Knowing the limits of one's expertise and role, as an instructor, means being prepared to involve the relevant support offices that populate modern university campuses, for the benefit of your students.

Matriculate/Matriculation

Now an older, less frequently used term that signifies a student being admitted to or enrolling in a college degree program or perhaps even a course. In some settings it may be retained but redefined to mean ways of initiating new students into the practices and traditions of a college, via entry-level orientation programs or even formal events or convocations.

Midterm Grades

In an effort to institute a means by which students are well aware of their standing early in a course (so they can adjust their performance, to improve, or consider dropping a course instead of failing it) some universities may mandate faculty to have offered and graded some sort of test or assignment prior to a specific early date in the course, that will then enable them to provide each student with an indication of their performance in the course. These midterm grades are often approximations of performance, sometimes based on meagre assessment information; students should be made aware of this.

At some colleges a uniform date is in place when midterm exams are offered in most courses, comprising a more formal (and potentially weighty) assessment of student performance—in such cases the syllabus should ensure that an assessment of some sort has been given to students before that reporting deadline.

MOOC

Massively Open Online Courses (MOOCs) were very much a topic of conversation and implementation about a decade or more ago, when such large enrollment online courses (possibly free of charge to students and, when asynchronous, highly adaptable to student schedules) were heralded as a way to level the playing field in higher education, by enabling far more students to attend classes and earn degrees (e.g., Ivy League MOOCs would increase access to elite faculty, we were told). However, the speed with which MOOCs, which could enroll hundreds or even thousands of students, were linked to the profit-motive, either by colleges or for-profit education businesses, dramatically lessened the anticipated impact of this initiative.

Multimedia

Once known as audio-visual, multimedia equipment and internet connections are now so standard in many university classrooms and lecture halls as to go virtually unnoticed and simply expected by faculty and students, especially a younger generation from both groups which might now take such things as PowerPoint presentations (especially popular for some time in large Natural Science lectures) for granted as a basic element of any lecture. As demonstrated by research on student learning, 50 or 75 minutes of uninterrupted lecturing by an instructor can be less than engaging, whether or not one takes into account the role that social media and more limited attention spans has increasingly played with university-aged students. However, an entire lecture of PowerPoint slides that are read verbatim by an instructor hardly constitutes an engaging class. For a variety of reasons, then, judiciously employing visuals and audio in support of the information presented by an instructor—if for no other reason than to reinforce the points being made, to provide brief examples to which the lecture's material can be applied, to provide periodic key summaries of points under consideration in the lecture, etc.—can be a basic element of any class (always taking into consideration, and therefore being prepared for, the admittedly infrequent but inevitable glitches that can attend technology, such as incompatibility of file formats, project bulbs burning out, computer systems failing, etc.). What's more, the ease of students drawing upon material of their own to show during presentations via the classroom's multimedia system means that instructors can now craft assignments and individual or group presentations that are far different from what was possible just an academic generation ago. The degree to which reliance on multimedia can minimize accessibility for some students enrolled in a course is, however, a factor to keep in mind when using such resources.

Note-taking

It is an acquired skill to listen during a lecture and take notes that serve as both a summary of the lecture as well as a memory prompt for later (e.g., during preparation for an eventual test on the material)—and not all students are necessarily equally adept at doing this. If we add to this the need for students to integrate readings that they may have done in preparation for a lecture (again, class preparation is not something equally tackled by all students in a course) into the notes that they take during a lecture, then note-taking is an activity that can have a considerable consequence for a student's success in a class. Much like writing skills, then—which an instructor should not just assume to be already established, and in equal representation, among all of their students—so too note-taking may need to be a topic of explicit focus in a course, especially (but not only) in a lower-level course with students who may be relatively new to the university. While some ambitious instructors may periodically require students to hand in their class notes, to provide professors with a sense for how students understand their lectures (perhaps leading either to feedback to students on note-taking or, possibly, a revision to the lectures themselves), this is obviously not practical in large enrollment classes. Instructors can assist students in these and other settings by regularly delivering their information in certain routinized ways, providing verbal or visual prompts to students for whom note-taking is a new or an under-developed skill, thereby signaling to them something in need of referencing for future use. Further, inviting students to exchange notes at some point in the course may be an exercise in which peers can assist each other with developing this skill, though this too likely needs to be done under supervision since there is no guarantee that the notes received will be useful to a student. With their permission, an instructor may occasionally share notes with the class from someone enrolled in the course who has mastered this skill, likely doing so anonymously, accompanied by a commentary on why the notes strike the instructor as useful. This provides an opportunity to review these notes with the class as a group, to look for the traits that make them particularly useful to a student, as a way to model for others in the class this skill.

Office Hours

The weekly days and times when a professor or Teaching Assistant will be available for unscheduled drop-ins from their students. Although many students may opt to make an appointment in advance, colleges often require faculty to post (outside their office or on their syllabi and course websites/LMS pages) their office hours. All depending on the college, students can be eager to attend such hours, in order to obtain additional assistance in their course or even to meet and chat with a faculty member about a variety of topics, or they can rarely stop by—there is a considerable range of experiences on the part of faculty when it comes to the utility of posted office hours. More often than not, the office hour visit can be about things other than class content, providing an instructor with an opportunity to learn more about their students—their career aspirations or present challenges that may impact their performance in class. Some instructors therefore build in a course requirement for students to visit their office hours at least once during a semester, perhaps doing so within the first few weeks of the semester.

Online/Remote/Virtual Courses

Pre-pandemic online courses were largely the modern successor to what was once known as correspondence courses or, more recently, what is termed either continuing education or distance learning, and thus a vast improvement on the onetime textbook and hardcopy course guide/question booklet mailed to students who lived off-campus but who were enrolled in a course nonetheless. Using Learning Management Systems (e.g., Canvas, Blackboard, Moodle, etc.), virtual courses became much richer over the past decade or so and were offered either in real-time (synchronously) or were recorded and viewed by students at times that suited their schedule (asynchronously). A recent development included so-called hybrid or blended courses, in which on-campus and/or in-person students would complete a portion of the course using remote/online technology, such as viewing a pre-recorded lecture or answering quizzes on the readings, in preparation for an in-person task/discussion during the class meeting time. (During COVID-19 we saw this strategy used to minimize in-person attendance by regularly rotating all students enrolled in a course through face-to-face and then remote instruction.) During the recent pandemic, remote technology became the primary means by which universities, let alone other levels of schooling, delivered classes for approximately two years, thus immersing all faculty and students, regardless of their acquaintance with online courses, in remote learning. Post-pandemic has therefore seen a greater ease with using remote teaching, perhaps employing it in a fashion akin to hybrid or blended teaching, although the challenges not just of creating engaging remote courses but of completing a degree wholly immersed in an online environment remain, ensuring that some students (let alone their families) now bristle at the idea of not having a consistently in-person experience during their classes.

Outcomes

Formerly just known as goals, i.e., the course goals that often are listed near the opening of a syllabus, the now widely adopted designation of outcomes betrays the current emphasis on accomplishments in a course that can be measured empirically and then reported as part of a college's assessment initiative. Accordingly, the outcomes associated with a specific course, or perhaps even an entire degree program, must now be specific and tangible, so that they can be assessed, to determine whether an individual course or an entire degree program is delivering what it promised in advance to provide to students.

Overloads (Paid or Unpaid)

Apart from the regular teaching duties assigned to a faculty member (i.e., what in many settings is known as their teaching load), some will opt to teach additional courses, whether voluntarily for no income or, with the agreement of their chair and/or Dean, for additional income (usually paid either as a flat rate per credit hour/course or as a percentage of gross income—a supplemental pay request more than likely must be submitted for the administration to consider). Whether such overload teaching can involve working one-on-one with a lone student (e.g., an independent study or directed reading course) or teaching a fully enrolled course (perhaps in the instructor's own department or elsewhere on campus, such as in an honors program that lacks a faculty of its own), the way this work does or does not enhance the faculty member's work conditions and career progress always needs to be taken into account. In some settings, unpaid additional teaching can be "banked" to lessen a future semester's teaching duties, though this is not a uniform practice across all departments or colleges. Should research/publishing and grant productivity be important to a college, and thus an instructor's career path, then the rate at which a faculty member engages in each may be a factor weighed by a chair or Dean in determining whether an increased portion of an instructor's time is best devoted to additional teaching (whether paid or not). In many settings, summer school can operate via a separate budget (especially in cases where faculty are hired on a nine-month contract) such that summer teaching is not considered overload teaching.

Peer Grading and Self-Grading/ Peer Assessment and Self-Assessment

Longstanding debates on whether to grade students—i.e., reward them based on their class performance, calculated in relation to that of their peers—have resulted in some schools adopting practices of either peer grading (students assess each other's work) or students assessing their own work, whether on specific assignments or for an entire course. For such practices to be effective, considerable attention is required from the instructor, both to explain the rational to students but also to provide them with (or create along with them) rubrics to guide their assessments. Some instructors find that students in such situations will have much higher expectations of others and even themselves; if done properly, the grading of assignments, and discussions around assessment itself, becomes part of the learning process rather than a rote operation performed by an authority when the learning is thought to be completed.

Peer Tutors/Peer Learning Mentor

Usually a voluntary role, students either currently registered in a course or module or those who have recently completed it successfully, can be called upon to mentor other students in the same course, providing experience for the mentors and an additional resource for students who may be having difficulties in the course. Implementing such a program requires forethought and support for the peer tutors/mentors, so that they are not expected to play the role of a paid and trained Teaching Assistant. Although often an unpaid position (though many campuses have such things as student success offices that likely employ student tutors), colleges may still consider such roles as authority figures who must be properly trained in how to work with other students, perhaps requiring tutors to go through some sort of compliance training (e.g., training to address the possibility of harassment or conflicts of interest).

Preparations (Preps)

Although a faculty member might teach two, three, or four (or even more) courses per semester, sometimes they repeat courses in the same semester, offering one section of a class from, let's say, 10:00–10:50 a.m. and another section of the very same course from 1:00–1:50 p.m. (This can be a way of meeting student demand for an introductory course, for example, but without opting for a large enrollment lecture.) Thus, preparing the first lecture is thought to also count as preparation of the second, thereby lessening a faculty member's workload. As such, while a faculty member may report having a 3/3 teaching load (i.e., they teach three courses each fall and three courses each spring), by repeating one course in two different sections each semester the number of "preps" they have would be 2/2 (i.e., although teaching three courses per semester, each semester they repeat a course so that they are only teaching two different classes each semester, each requiring its own preparation). Although minimizing preps is often desired by faculty, teaching two sections of the same course during a semester can be surprisingly different with challenges of its own, largely due to the varying classroom dynamics of teaching different students.

Prerequisites

Service departments, i.e., those whose existence is premised more on serving the needs of other disciplines' majors by offering courses that satisfy the requirements of a campus's Gen Ed or Core curriculum than on the number of their own majors that they recruit and graduate, often cannot afford to institute many requirements within their own major. As such, a precise sequence of courses that must be taken, in the correct order, is a luxury that such departments cannot afford to institute. Prerequisites can therefore be relatively uncommon in such programs (notably in the Humanities), since it can discourage enrollment in upper-level courses because students have not taken a required lower-level course first. (Often, a campus has an expectation of a minimum number of enrollees in order for a course to run or, as is sometimes said, make.) Of course, this leads to a situation in which even more advanced seminars can be somewhat akin to the tone or content of an introductory course (even if only for the first few weeks, to bring everyone up to speed), given that it might be the first class in the specialty for some of the students who have enrolled. However, given that more advanced undergraduates are often known to become disillusioned with their first major, and, midstream, may later change their degree focus or at least add a second major, their presence in more advanced courses can, in some cases, hold the promise of recruiting a student to the major. Thus, prerequisites are a double-edged sword, for while they may increase the level of discourse within upper-level classes, helping to create an environment in which students specialize more successfully, they may also diminish enrollments, which itself can undermine a unit's long-term viability.

Presentations

Among the many ways to further engage students and have them apply class material is to include classroom or student presentations into the requirements of a course. Although the enrollment of a class will determine the likelihood that this is practical or not, even in large lectures group presentations scattered throughout the semesters can be an effective way to accomplish a number of outcomes of relevance to the course, such as honing oral presentation skills, promoting collaboration, etc. These presentations can vary, from presenters making use of technology to students reading a brief paper—though all of which likely need prior meetings with the instructor to develop their presentation and hone their presentation skills. For novice presenters who have good reason to feel nervous in front of their peers, a well-defined and delimited presentation is likely best, allowing small enrollment courses, such as seminars, to incorporate more than one presentation throughout a semester, enabling the student to build on past experience and tackle more ambitious presentations the course. Although sometimes difficult to grade (just having some novice students complete this task can sometimes be enough of a gain), instructors should be clear in advance with students concerning the aspects of this assignment that will be assessed.

Primary/Secondary Sources

A longstanding distinction between the data or content on which scholarship is carried out, on the one hand, and, on the other, the work of other scholars on that same material, which we may consult in producing our own commentaries or analyses. A problem with this distinction, however, is that, upon closer inspection, it is apparent that the so-called primary source is itself a product of what is usually designated as past secondary scholarship, since it is the commentary tradition that more than likely creates a discursive object that only later seems to be in obvious need of study. While this distinction may be of heuristic use in lower-level courses it likely needs to be unpacked in subsequent courses, to help students problematize the widespread impression that certain aspects of the world are self-evidently distinctive and therefore in need of study. Moreover, studying secondary scholarship (i.e., an interpretive or scholarly tradition or school of thought) can itself legitimately occupy a scholar, making it their primary sources—demonstrating that the two terms are slippery at best.

Problem-Based Learning (PBL)

Among the strategies associated with so-called high-impact teaching practices (HIP), PBL is a pedagogical approach that consistently explores and applies classroom information by formulating specific practical "real world" scenarios in which the class material can address what is considered to be a social problem. It is an approach often championed in the professional schools, one which is thought to engage students more than straight lectures, but which is sometimes difficult to implement in subjects that are considered to be part of basic science research (though labs in the natural sciences could easily be considered a longstanding example of PBL). Although it is an approach that presupposes a consensus on what situations even count as problems in need of solving or correcting it is not difficult to imagine a PBL approach to explore highly invested disagreements about what in a particular society does or does not need fixing.

Professionalization

Although some in the Humanities might contest this as being a goal of our courses—associating it instead with the work carried out in the so-called professional schools, e.g., business, engineering, social work, nursing, etc.—others might interpret it more broadly, to imply timeliness and consistency but also adaptability, respectfulness, a certain sort of work ethic and dedication to a task, an understanding of the expectations of a specific setting and an ability to meet or exceed them, etc., and thereby see it as among the things that we are hoping to attain for our students in all of their courses. Given the number of Humanities students who do not go on to careers in the discipline of their undergraduate degree (e.g., many English majors do not become English teachers and many History majors do not become historians), but who instead take the skills acquired in their classes and use them in a wide array of careers (from education to business, medicine, law, government and non-governmental settings, etc.), then among the goals of Humanities classes likely should be broad-based training in professionalism that students can draw upon regardless the situations they enter after they leave these classes.

Public Humanities

Especially in the disciplines commonly collected together as the Humanities (e.g., English, Modern Languages, Philosophy, Religious Studies, etc.), there is sometimes a question of their relevance to the so-called real world, a question that involves a set of issues linked to the modern university in which the professional schools (e.g., Business, Nursing, Engineering, Social Work, Computer Science, etc.) often dominate campus life, which includes campus budgets and a university's PR apparatus. In response, an initiative has begun in which students in these fields are now often trained to communicate more effectively with wider audiences, as a way to convey the relevance of their research for those who are well beyond the academy—often using computer-based/internet publishing skills. In their research assignments in courses, such students can also be invited to address topics that they believe to be of contemporary import to their societies. This broad initiative, which takes many forms in a variety of courses and disciplines, is now collectively known as the public humanities.

Reading Aloud

Although there was a time when it might have been routine to ask students, in smaller classes, to take turns reading aloud from an assigned text during class (i.e., as a way to focus on a specific passage for discussion, whether or not the reading was pre-distributed), today this practice is seen by some to unfairly single out students who, for a variety of reasons, may not wish to, or may not benefit from, such a practice. Whether due to varied reading abilities, lack of preparation, or any number of learning challenges, such a practice is now understood by many to put students on the spot in unproductive ways (especially in settings where students come to class with wide variation in their levels of preparation for college). Should reading aloud be an important element to a class, then there are ways that an instructor can accomplish this, either by asking for volunteers in a manner that is not high stakes or by reading the passage themselves with students following along.

Readings

In preparation for a specific class, let alone during the research phase for a presentation or piece of writing, students are often asked to become familiar with information by means of a variety of assigned texts (some of which might be required in a course while others are merely recommended)—in fact, this longstanding means of acquiring information likely still dominates in higher education (whether the reading is from a hardcopy book or article or an online/portable source); although required textbooks were once widely preferred, in many cases their now high cost, as part of the rising costs of higher education in many national settings, has prompted some instructors to provide a course's readings through portable documents (PDF) that are distributed to students by, in many cases today, being posted on the course's learning management system. (Such an approach also requires the instructor to be rather more intentional about course design, rather than more passively relying on a textbook author's choices.) In such cases, accessibility to a course's daily or weekly readings is not limited by income in the same fashion as are courses with a variety of expensive required books, although continuing technological challenges for some students, let alone possible learning disabilities, can certainly still present impediments for some of those who are enrolled in a course. Along with such issues, the frequency, volume, and difficulty level of assigned readings is also worth an instructor's consideration, especially depending on the level and enrollment of the course (and whether it is a service course or a course for specialist students). Finally, the degree to which each reading is integrated into class time, via discussions and various assessment instruments (i.e., tests, essays, etc.), is crucial to also consider, so as to convey to students a direct, rather than arbitrary or even merely tangential, relationship between the reading and the course's daily overall goals, to help persuade them to complete these readings in advance of class.

Recitations/Tutorials

Some large enrollment Humanities courses, especially those making use of teaching assistants (TAs), may include required recitation sections (somewhat akin to a weekly lab in the Natural Sciences), also known as tutorials or even seminars in some places, where the class's lecture content is reviewed, reinforced, applied, and elaborated upon. Often run by a teaching assistant (who may lead several of these per week), and ideally overseen by the instructor (who may provide the course material to the tutors and/or meet with them in preparation for each week's tutorial), they can often be the first teaching experience gained by a graduate student while also being an important opportunity for undergraduate students to review and reinforce class content. Unlike weekly office hours, which are voluntary for students to attend, recitations can be included in the syllabus's requirements making attendance and participation mandatory and possibly worth grade points, though the portion of the final course grade that is dedicated to the tutorial may vary.

Recruiting

A term commonly used to name a series of activities either to bring students to a university or even to declare a particular major/specialty. In cases of U.S. Humanities programs, where a large investment is made in serving other discipline's needs through offering Gen Ed or Core courses, such courses are often also the place where prospective specialists first meet the field of study, making so-called service courses (which may be many students' only exposure to a field) also courses that recruit majors and which are therefore what some call gateways into the discipline (i.e., gateway courses)—sometimes a tough balance for an instructor to manage when both types of students are enrolled in the same introductory or survey course.

Registrar

On many college campuses the office that retains control over registering students for classes, assessing new course proposals, recording and tracking student academic performance (e.g., issuing transcripts of their cumulative, completed course grades), listing all degree requirements in the so-called catalogue or catalog, as well as managing the academic calendar is often known as the Registrar's Office, with an individual usually appointed as the Registrar for a campus (in some cases with a series of Associate or Assistant Registrars also working in the office). On large campuses this role may be split between an Undergraduate Registrar and a Graduate Registrar, sometimes with colleges or faculties having their own registrars with delimited duties.

Retention

A term commonly used to name a series of activities to continue to engage and thereby keep students once they have either enrolled at a university or declared a particular major or specialty. Universities have found that the rate at which first year undergraduate students return to their second year is a very strong indicator of the likeliness of them completing their Bachelor's degree, and so the term "retention rate" has come to name the rate at which first year students successfully enroll in their second year at a college. Among majors, however, devising ways to retain those who have declared an interest in a subject—from offering engaging and timely classes to rewarding experiences outside class time, e.g., student associations, special departmental events, active social media, etc.—is something that requires attention on the part of a department and its faculty.

Rigor

A term often used in the context of standards for student performance (i.e., "the course is very rigorous"), which has recently been linked to complaints that certain courses or assignments are now not insufficiently demanding (i.e., they lack rigor). For yet others, however, such criticisms are linked to expectations that are closely associated with specific subgroups (either their presumed abilities and level of preparation or their interests) and which are therefore inappropriately universalized to govern how the accomplishments of all students are understood and measured. Accordingly, at least for some, rigor is no longer understood as an objective measure but, instead, a subjective quality or gatekeeping effect.

Roster

Whether distributed in hardcopy or, as is now more likely the case, via an online student information system to which faculty members have access, each instructor receives or can generate for themselves a list of all students enrolled in their course. A course roster is dynamic (requiring it to be periodically updated), inasmuch as students will often add or drop/withdraw from the course. Much of the information on such rosters may be confidential (e.g., a student's home address, their student ID number, etc.), so an instructor is wise to take care with how such information is stored and managed. Based on this roster a faculty member will likely create their grade book/sheet for the course.

Rubrics

As part of the larger assessment initiative across universities, faculty (when it comes to their individual courses as well as each course's various assignments) and even entire departments as a whole (when it comes to their various degree programs) are now often required to develop clear and explicit rubrics with clearly stated and distinguishable criteria that formalize and systematize how essays, projects, presentations, let alone entire courses or overall degrees are evaluated. Perhaps distributed to the students, or even used to record and return the results of grading to the students, a rubric is said to assist with establishing uniform and thus fairly applied grading practices by making explicit the common factors that establish the differences between various levels of accomplishment (i.e., grades). Among the many criteria for assessing an essay, for example, might not just be the ability of a student to cite a source properly but, moreover, to select an appropriate source as well as quotations from such a source that, in turn, are properly integrated into the piece of writing so as to support the essay's own argument; thus, demonstrating all of these skills would distinguish an essay from one that merely cites sources—improvement of the student's grade on future assignments is then premised on addressing the itemized shortcomings in previous essays. Faculty (especially probationary faculty, such as those whose employment is contingent or those who are tenure-track, or those mid-career faculty aiming for their final promotion to the rank of Professor [now often called Full Professor, to better distinguish it from other professorial ranks]) must often provide for the administration samples of their grading rubrics as part of the application for retention or promotion. Debates continue, of course, concerning the degree to which non-specified and even idiosyncratic criteria yet remain in the practice of grading.

Scaffolding

Term used to describe larger tasks or projects that, in a classically analytic manner, can be broken down into a series of interrelated sub-tasks or problems, each of which can be mastered in a progressive or developmental manner, so that the larger task then becomes more possible to complete. Case in point: writing a traditional research essay requires students first to master a series of what eventually become connected practices, from reading critically and writing well to knowing how to formulate a problem, hypothesis, or thesis to investigate, conduct original research, use and cite sources, etc.

Scholarship of Teaching

In the early to mid-1990s, a trend began in which some colleges began to prioritize the so-called scholarship of teaching (now sometimes called the scholarship of teaching and learning, so as to emphasize not just the delivery but also the reception of information and skills), in which schools began to credit more explicitly such things as faculty teaching innovation and classroom labor, publications on pedagogy, and attendance at teaching workshops and conferences, somewhat akin to how traditional research and publication had long been credited toward faculty career progress. A number of practical publications then also began to appear on the scholarship of teaching. While the manner in which the importance of teaching (especially undergraduate, and even introductory, teaching) has, in many colleges, been diminished in comparison to research—with many faculty still seeing their teaching as taking time away from their research and few of them ever being trained, as graduate students, in pedagogy, under the longstanding assumption that it would somehow "just come naturally" to them sooner or later—equating teaching with research and publication seemed ill-fated, what with productive researchers often teaching no less than those colleagues whose careers sometimes almost exclusively emphasize their role as teachers. That these two faculty roles (creating and then conveying new knowledge) should be seen as mutually reinforcing seems the more beneficial approach to adopt.

Seating Plan

Perhaps in an effort to better learn the names of students enrolled in a course, over the years some faculty have opted to use a seating plan, either assigning seats to students or, after students have chosen their own seats, to record this and require students to retain the same seat in the classroom throughout the semester. However effective this might be in mid-sized classrooms (i.e., 25–50 seats), it is likely not necessary in small seminars and of little use in large lecture courses. For a variety of reasons, students tend to remain in the same seat through a semester, whether or not they are asked to, making seating assignments redundant in many cases. At some colleges photo class lists are now available to instructors, utilizing students' ID photos, and can instead be used as a prompt for learning names.

Sections

Each discrete topic taught as part of a curriculum is usually called a course, such as Introduction to the World's Religions (a still common course found in many department, though sometimes going by various names); sometimes a course is repeated in the same semester, with the same or perhaps different professors teaching each. Thus, while the course is the same, each section is discrete and meets on its own days and times. A department's class offerings in any given semester might therefore list several different sections of the same course, each distinguished by having its own section number (e.g., REL 100 might have section 1, 2, 3, and so on), location, meeting times, and even instructor.

Seminars

Traditionally, there is a distinction between a lecture course and an upper level seminar (which usually enrolls far fewer students), with the latter shifting some or even much of the burden of class time to students themselves, by means of presentations and discussion throughout the semester, as opposed to the more passive reception of information characteristic of a lecture that is delivered by the instructor. In some settings the term seminar may instead be synonymous with tutorial.

Senior Seminars/Capstone Seminars/ Integrative Seminars

Departments will sometimes offer a final, culminating course that is required of its own graduating majors and specialists (i.e., seniors in the common designation of U.S. schools), in which the students are expected to reflect and draw upon and then integrate what they have learned throughout their entire degree, with such integrative seminars sometimes required by a Gen Ed/Core Curriculum (indicating a pedagogical rationale to offering them). For some, the existence of such courses, and the logic that drives their creation, indicates the disparate nature of the rest of the degree, where its various courses may have no obvious or evident relevance to each other (this being left to the senior seminar to establish).

Service Courses

Given Gen Ed/Core Curriculum requirements common in most U.S. universities, students in assorted majors must still also complete a broad variety of courses outside of their specialty, such as an Engineering student needing to take an English or a History course. In this way, such departments are "serving" the needs of students in other parts of the university and not just their own majors. In some cases, Humanities programs can be at risk given that they are often called upon to play this role to the benefit of majors in the professional schools across a campus, with fewer students opting to declare the major in the Humanities area itself.

Service Department

Academic units in which the main, or perhaps sole, teaching focus is on serving the needs of students enrolled in other majors, to enable them to complete a university's Core Curriculum's requirements, are often known as service departments (especially in the U.S.). In some cases such departments have a small cohort of specialized majors of their own, while in other settings the department may have no major or minor degree program and therefore only exists to teach introductory or survey courses to students from other disciplines, so that they can satisfy, for instance, a college's Humanities or a Writing requirement. Faculty working in such units may infrequently teach upper-level courses or be involved in classes with students who already have a grounding in the field.

Service Learning

Another so-called high-impact practice, service learning can either be a component of a course or an entire course experience (somewhat akin to an internship), in which students draw upon classroom knowledge and skills to the benefit of (i.e., serving) a group outside of campus, perhaps a local group in need of the services that students in a specific discipline can offer. Ideally, such courses involve preparing and then debriefing with an instructor, a self-reflexive component that enhances the learning that can be taken away from such "real world" settings (demonstrating that the service learning initiative over the past decades is highly critical of traditional, passive lecture courses). For students in the Humanities, who may lack a direct or obvious professional setting in which their skills can be practiced, identifying service learning opportunities can sometimes be a challenge, unlike, say, a business student majoring in accounting who offers their services to a local nonprofit organization. Given the way students in such courses are placed in the community, the PR value of service learning courses to a college cannot be overlooked, what with some colleges now working hard to ensure that local or regional and even national governments understand their impact on the economy.

Small Liberal Arts College (SLAC)

In the U.S. this designation identifies a type of private college or university which is contrasted from a public state school, with the former being rather smaller in terms of the number of students admitted (sometimes less than 1,000) as well as the number of faculty and staff employed. There are a large number of SLACs in the U.S.—a subset of about 100 would also be known as HBCUs (historically black colleges and universities, established prior to the Civil Rights Act of 1964)—with some considered rather prestigious to attend (in which the S might also stand for selective or even highly selective). Students may opt to apply to a SLAC versus a much larger state school for a wide variety of reasons (e.g., the student–teacher ratio, the reputation of the school, the student is a legacy [i.e., a relative of an alum], etc.). Given the religious and denominational history of many SLACs—inasmuch as they may have first been founded to train ministers or, as private institutions, to educate students who were members of a specific Christian denomination)—there are still times when religion programs benefit from longstanding assumptions that all students need a grounding in the study of religion (sometimes equated with ethics, studies of the bible, or overt theological instruction).

Student Athlete

Especially in the U.S., where some college sports have a remarkably close relationship to the professional leagues (i.e., in which college athletes comprise the main pool from which the professional leagues recruit the vast majority of their players), the designation of student athlete is relied upon to navigate the sometimes tricky distinction between being a full-time student and a high performance athlete. Often said to have been devised in the early 1960s by the founding executive director of the still influential National Collegiate Athletics Association (NCAA)—a body in U.S. higher education that, with the agreement of colleges, governs college sports, sanctioning programs or schools that run afoul of its various rules—the term is read by critics as a way to ensure that the athletes whose talent and labor finances a college's sometimes exorbitant athletics budget (often premised on multi-million dollar broadcast rights for certain sports) are not considered employees and thus are not eligible for salaries, labor protections under law, etc.; it is therefore a designation of fundamental importance to debates over the distinction between amateur and professional sports. That this distinction has somewhat eroded is evidenced in U.S. college athletes now—since a unanimous U.S. Supreme Court decision against the NCAA in July 2021—being able to profit modestly from such things as the sale of their likeness (i.e., appearance in sports video games). For supporters, the term recognizes the importance of tuition and food/housing scholarships that enable these students to earn a degree while pursuing their sport. For instructors on such campuses, dealing with some of their students' training, practice, and game or meet schedules (absences that cannot count against such students) and working with the sometimes elaborate tutoring services that often support student athletes (e.g., tracking and reporting attendance and grades for these students) can bring additional layers to their classroom management.

Student Conduct

Student behavior on a campus is often governed by some sort of code of conduct, which applies to their actions across campus, including within the classroom. Student disruptions in a class can therefore be addressed, through the appropriate channels on a campus, as student conduct issues; each campus has its own process for assessing and penalizing code of conduct violations, making the department chair a wise first point of contact for a faculty member in need of understanding the process.

Student Evaluations of Instruction

Each semester most colleges invite students to assess a course and it's instructor via a standardized form (now often online, and therefore usually completed by the student outside class time, unlike past years when the hardcopy form was distributed during class, with the faculty member usually leaving the room while it was being completed by their students), consisting of scoring aspects of the course as exceeding, meeting, or failing to meet expectations. Such forms generally also provide students with the ability to offer comments or anecdotes about the class. Instructors see the anonymous/cumulative results of such evaluations and institutions often use these evaluations when assessing a faculty member's annual job performance. That such an assessment instrument can easily turn evaluating a course into a popularity contest is well known by universities but no widely agreed upon alternative has yet to be devised.

Student Life/Student Affairs/Student Services

Each campus likely employs one of a few different nomenclatures for the office and staff—sometimes housed within each college or faculty and sometimes operating across all colleges or faculties—that act as resources to students, whether for advising, degree checks prior to graduation, or even financial, emotional/mental health, or academic challenges. While many campuses will certainly have a specific financial aid office as well as a counselling center, where specialists in each of these areas are resources to students, the student life office (once widely known as student affairs) can be the place where a variety of extracurricular activities are planned or hosted, to which student organizations within departments, residences, or across campus can apply for funding to assist with the events that they may host. Student services offices can differ, in that they may be more focused on the academic side of the student's life on campus, thus housing a registrar, managing enrollments, transcripts, advising students on degree progress and on semester-to-semester classes (sometimes only the undeclared will gain advising from such central offices, with students who have declared a major or a specialty perhaps gaining their advising within their home departments). All of these offices can be a resource to an instructor when confronted with a student missing too many classes, or a student who approaches them with difficulties or challenges that exceed the instructor's competencies. A department chair should be a handy resource to instructors to help them navigate the various services available on the campus to support the success of all of their students. While being mindful of each student's privacy, making recommendations to the student concerning services they can seek on a campus can sometimes be the most important help an instructor can offer.

Student Success

This has by now become a bit of a branded designation—including such other initiatives as engaged or experiential learning, high-impact practices, etc.—that, in some cases, names not just campus initiatives but also offices on campus that are devoted to such things as advising students on their degree progress and tutoring students via volunteer or paid peer mentors and even full-time staff members who are hired to work either in groups or individually with at-risk undergraduate students, all in an effort to retain and eventually graduate them. Thus, degree completion within a specified period of time (thereby impacting a college's four-, five-, or six-year graduation rate) and gaining employment in the area of their major is more than likely the main metric for assessing student success today, at least according to senior administrators on many campuses. That there are a variety of other ways to assess student success goes without saying, of course, such as finding a major that motivates them and in which they can excel, improving grades and acquiring/using discrete skills, learning to live away from home, etc.

Student Union

Although in some settings this now simply refers to the site where certain elements of shared student life are housed (akin to a student center, i.e., where there may be a bookstore, coffee shops, cafeterias, the offices for student clubs, tutoring services, and even, at least in some settings, student pubs, etc.), student unions once referred, and indeed still can refer, in a more traditional sense to collective associations that represent and advocate for student interests on a campus. In settings where unionization is frowned upon, this once prominent tradition on a college campus has likely been replaced by representative student government.

Student Wellness

A term now widely used to include assessments of a student's physical and mental health as well as such related factors as their social life or their housing. Although faculty interact regularly with students—along a continuum, from close contact in small classes to relatively little direct contact in large lectures—they are not trained professionals in this area. Instructors should therefore become acquainted with Student Life and counselling resources on a campus, along with the resources of Student Services offices, and be ready to refer students to such office.

Summer School

On many campuses the academic year begins in the fall and includes the spring (sometimes also known as the winter semester, depending on the region) and the summer semesters (along with what is sometimes termed an interim semester, whether during the winter break or again after the spring and prior to the start of summer school; however, the interim and summer semesters' budget models, especially in the U.S., are often separate from the fall and spring, with faculty working on a nine-month contract earning additional income for summer teaching—whether as a flat rate (which is often the case for part-time instructors) or as a percentage of their gross salary (sometimes common for tenure-track or tenured faculty). For this reason, summer courses often depend upon a sufficient number of students enrolling so as to earn revenue for the college while also covering the costs of the instructor's salary. In fields like the study of religion this means that the more dependable summer enrollments may come from lower-level core courses that broadly appeal to students on campus throughout the summer, regardless of their major. In some settings, where the rate of monthly retirement benefits may be linked to a faculty member's highest earning years, there can be an appeal for near-to-retirement faculty to teach summer school, so as to increase their final years' earnings.

Syllabus

Understood in some colleges as the so-called learning contract between the instructor and the students (and maybe even known, notably in the UK, as a module or even program handbook), the required course elements listed in a syllabus can vary from campus-to-campus, with the days of a brief, one-page list of topics to be covered, provided to students by the instructor, well behind us. Generally speaking, syllabi are now fairly detailed (and sometimes surprisingly lengthy) documents which not only provide a course description, schedule of topics and required books and readings, along with a description of the course's various assignments (and their value), but also a series of required policy statements mandated by the university (e.g., a severe weather policy, the absence policy, the academic misconduct policy, etc.). Some schools now rely on centralized online tools where syllabi are created by faculty and posted (thereby allowing the college to insert a variety of standard, required statements into the template that is used by all faculty) while others still defer to individual faculty to make and distribute hardcopy documents of their own on the first day of class (the day many faculty continue to use to go over/read through the syllabus in detail). Being aware that unanticipated events throughout the semester may change a faculty member's plans for a course should ensure that the schedule of syllabus is always listed as tentative, with students receiving sufficient advance notice if changes are required.

Teaching vs. Learning

A distinction primarily based on the delivery of information and skills as opposed to the reception, retention, and application of both.

Teaching Assistants (TA)

Many instructors teaching large undergraduate courses in settings where graduate students are also enrolled in degree programs may have one or more teaching assistants, or TAs, assigned to them to assist with the logistics of the course. This is an ideal mentoring opportunity, to provide graduate students with classroom experience while it is obviously also a chance to distribute some of the workload of teaching (e.g., grading, taking attendance, weekly office hours, tutorials, etc.). The manner in which TAs are used in a course must therefore be thought through clearly by an instructor, aiming to provide them with a beneficial experience while also being mindful of their own workload as graduate students. Ironically, perhaps, a well-planned and implemented course that involves a TA can be more work for an instructor—or at least a different form of work for them, inasmuch as the instructor may also regularly meet with the TAs, to ensure uniformity of message and approach with all of the students enrolled in the course (notably if TAs run weekly discussion sections or tutorials of their own that complement the course). Many campuses now offer training, or at least an initial orientation for new TAs, often focusing not on pedagogical topics but on legal issues, such as the campus's approach to charges of academic misconduct among students (thereby ensuring the college's liability exposure is minimized).

Teaching Philosophy

Considered a required element of some faculty job or promotion applications, a succinct (i.e., one or two pages) teaching philosophy is a statement that conveys an instructor's view on the purpose and process of university education. Such statements are, of course, unique to each teacher (with the manner in which a hiring or promotion committee reads them no less unique to each member of the committee), but today they are likely also expected to demonstrate evidence of awareness and implementation of certain elements of or initiatives within higher education that, on many campuses, are required, such as diversity and accessibility in the classroom and the curriculum, assessment initiatives, student-centered/active learning initiatives, etc.

Theory

There are those who see a conflict between theory and content, or at least those who see the latter as coming first and theory, then, as something one only calls upon later, akin to a method, in order to manage or do something with the content after having sufficiently described it (e.g., to then interpret its meaning). Yet others understand theory to name the wider conditions, assumptions, and structures that allow something to seem to stand out as capable of being described, let alone understood or explained. Should the latter be one's sense of theory then theory—and, ideally, an ongoing and always explicit reflection upon it as part of the course—animates all classes while the former understanding leads to courses in which theory is sometimes thought to detract from the prior requirement simply to describe and compare the data. Many courses in the Humanities have traditionally opted for this approach, however, seeing their object of study as self-evidently in need of study, thus seeing theory as an inessential second step that can threaten the presumed autonomy of the datum.

Time Management

Effectively using the time allotted for a class is itself a skill to acquire, whether it is a 50-minute class that meets three times per week, a 75-minute class that meets twice a week, or perhaps a three-hour class that meets just once a week. From setting aside time for opening announcements and perhaps a brief review of the previous day's class content to pacing the class period by moving between different topics and/or different modes of instruction (i.e., traditional lecture, student presentations, open discussion, group work, etc.) and even planning for brief breaks during long class periods all impact how students experience the class and learn its material. A seasoned instructor—knowing how differently the time can pass on any given day—will often come to class with additional information, e.g. "in their back pocket," to draw upon during class if needed or to reserve for another day if time does not allow. Dismissing students early makes sense if the day's goals were accomplished but doing so too frequently will likely be frowned upon by various levels of the administration.

Transferable Skills

Considered by some to be the Humanities best argument for their ongoing relevance, the skills (sometimes known as soft skills) acquired in classes can have application in unexpected places, as long as students are intentional about what those skills might be and how they can be applied—something that can be modeled for them by their instructors. Such an approach implies that the content of a class is always understood by the students as an example, an illustration, and thus the site where an investigation is taking place that could also take place elsewhere (the transfer in transferable skills). Thus, comparing two versions of a text is not just an opportunity to find differences in the text or to illuminate something about its compositional history but it is also an exercise in identifying similarities and differences between any two items, something which then invites the student to consider the significance of each and their possible reasons or implications. In this way, a seemingly simple "compare and contrast" assignment, as they were once routinely called, provides an opportunity for the intentional instructor to help prepare students for a wide array of future settings in which such skills are crucial and valued. Successfully making this shift, of course, requires the instructor and students to relinquish the resumption that their objects of study are unique or self-evidently interesting, for they now become handy illustrations of wider situations or processes (the so-called examples approach), knowing full well that many of the students in our courses will not go on to careers in our discipline.

Trigger Warnings

A term that, over the past two decades, has increasingly been used for providing advance notice or cautions to students concerning upcoming course content that they may find to be personally problematic for a wide variety of reasons. Those instructors concerned with student wellbeing and who see the classroom as one more site at a university where this can be promoted will probably support informing students ahead of a film or reading, for instance, cornering content that some of them may find not merely objectionable but which may prompt (i.e., trigger) in them reactions based on, perhaps, past traumatic experiences of their own. The advance notice is aimed at preparing the student rather than having such information sprung upon them unannounced. Whether trigger warnings do in fact reduce adverse reactions to such material (or, instead, heighten anxiety in anticipation of it) is a matter of ongoing debate, with the inclination toward offering these warnings being the target of criticism by yet other faculty (who may see them as an unnecessary constraint on their teaching and academic freedom). Whether or not colleges have specific policies on offering trigger warnings, they may have developed advisory guidelines with which an instructor should be familiar.

Undergraduate

The term often used for the first university degree and thus a student's status after successfully completing secondary schooling (i.e., what is sometimes known as high school, A-levels or even Gymnasium). The Bachelor's degree (e.g., Bachelor of Arts, Bachelor of Science, etc.) is usually the degree program in which such students enroll, though they may instead seek what some schools designate as the shorter course of study resulting in an Associate's degree, a Foundational degree, or perhaps a Professional degree (and then, in some cases, moving on to earn a Bachelor's degree). Graduate or postgraduate study (e.g., as Master's degree or a doctoral degree) may then be pursued once an undergraduate degree is awarded.

Undergraduate Research

At a time when large lecture halls dominate some disciplines (notably, but not only, in the Natural Sciences), an emphasis on devising and implementing ways to increase student engagement (so as to improve their level of interest, involvement, class performance and, perhaps, to recruit students to a career in the discipline) has led to developing ways to involve undergraduate students in hands-on research (as a type of experiential learning or high-impact practice [HIP]). While it may be more easily accomplished in the sciences, where such students might get involved in a larger research lab, and thereby participate, under the supervision of a faculty member or a graduate research assistant, in a smaller aspect of a larger research project, undergraduate research also takes place in the Humanities, either by breaking down (scaffolding) the work of research into its constitute elements via course assignments, each of which must be mastered and later integrated with the others (e.g., formulating a problem that can be investigated, using research databases, creating an annotated bibliography, identifying and then surveying a body of literature, citation practices, writing and formulating an argument, etc.) or through supervised projects carried out outside class time, such as working with a faculty member on a portion of their own research. While the latter for Humanities scholars is likely more difficult than in some other fields, inasmuch as scholarship in the former often involves an individual faculty member reading and critically engaging the work of others—something they will more than likely need to do for themselves—co-writing or conducting various forms of primary research or analysis may, with the proper supervision, successfully involve novice students or more experienced majors in a discipline. Whether your campus has an ongoing initiative to promote undergraduate research, requires reporting and tracking of such opportunities, or operates with a precise definition for what counts as undergraduate research (i.e., can it be done for course credit or must it be outside class time?) is all something each instructor must determine. Also, the degree to which it adds work to an already busy faculty member's day is something to be considered, though the benefits of engaging students in this fashion can indeed be tangible.

Unessay

There was a time that the term "project" or "presentation" would have been used but today designating such non-writing assignments as an "unessay" has caught on among some in higher education. The unessay, as the name suggests, is a non-essay assignment in which students (whether working individually or in groups) can opt to creatively integrate and demonstrate their gains in knowledge in other ways. There are, after all, a wide array of skills that instructors hope students to acquire in their classes and only some of which are best conveyed by means of the formal writing and argumentation of a traditional research paper. Such unessays can range from something created using various forms of technology that are now widely available to many students (audio or video projects) to infographics, poster presentations, mobiles, dioramas, reconstructions and models, performances, oral exams, etc. How best to assess such alternative projects is something an instructor must consider when incorporating unessays into a course's requirements, especially given the range of approaches that might result when students are given such freedom for a particular assignment. And the amount that such an assignment is worth as part of the final course grade will be determined by the skills the instructor hopes the assignment to exemplify.

Ungrading

A term for a broad series of assessment strategies that avoids ranking students in relation to each other's performance and then grading or marking them along a uniform scale—a traditional practice still widely used in higher education, to be sure, but one critiqued by some nonetheless, for the way that it presupposes a standardized scale in a classroom where not all students come with the same preparation, support, interests, or abilities. Ungrading practices can therefore be more student-focused, rely more on qualitative input from the instructor than quantitative assessment (i.e., increased oral or written feedback to students), include self-assessment by students themselves along with assessments from their peers in the class (both likely requiring rubrics and guidance from the instructor), as well as a de-emphasis on cumulative or overall grades and, instead, an enhanced focus on individual assignments and, importantly, promoting progress across them. Ungrading, depending on how it is implemented in a course, can be considerably more of a commitment for an instructor than some traditional grading practices (such as, in the most extreme case, a 100% multiple choice final exam in a large lecture course graded automatically); opting for ungrading is therefore a broad spectrum of practices that an instructor may implement as their course's circumstances allow (i.e., it is more of a challenge in a large class but incorporating some strategies can certainly be done) and as a way to achieve something in the course that traditional writing assignments cannot accomplish.

Unions

Depending on where one works as a college instructor, one may be a member of a workers union or perhaps even a faculty/staff association that has varying degrees of collective bargaining power, such as the University and College Union (UCU) in Britain, which has around 120,000 members who, through collective action, endeavor to attain for themselves better work conditions. While about a quarter of U.S. faculty are reported to be either unionized or to work under the terms of a negotiated collective agreement of some sort, in American colleges without such bodies some faculty will opt to join the non-profit American Association of University Professor (AAUP, founded in 1915, with local chapters on campuses throughout the country), which, though not a union, nonetheless attempts to promote members' interests by exerting influence on higher ed institutions (e.g., sanctioning schools for breaching of their faculty members' academic freedom). Where faculty are unionized, then a number of factors having direct impact on the classroom will likely fall under their collective bargaining agreement with the college, e.g., determining salaries and teaching loads along with such matters as remote work policies, class sizes, salary scales, summer school policies, etc. Whether or not faculty should unionize (which, in some cases, may mean joining pre-existing, non-education unions) is a hot button issue on many campuses, linked directly to the degree to which faculty do or do not feel themselves to be protected by the institution of tenure and/or substantively involved in shared governance on their campus. In a November 2020 report from the U.S.'s National Center for the Study of Collective Bargaining in Higher Education and the Professions (located at Hunter College of City University of New York [CUNY]), between 2013 and 2019 there were 118 new collective bargaining organizations on American college campuses, with over 36,000 new members, suggesting to some that such factors as increasing cuts in higher ed funding, the continued rise of contingent labor, etc., have had an effect on the drive toward faculty unionization.

Writing Requirements

Sometimes as part of a larger General Education or Core Curriculum in the U.S., a college will have a requirement for students to be exposed to a certain amount of writing as part of their course of study. This might be distinguished from the so-called freshman composition (comp) course(s) in which incoming students in U.S. colleges must enroll, where they focus on basic writing skills that, today, can no longer be assumed to be evenly shared by all new students. In addition to this a school may require all students to have exposure to additional writing-intensive courses at the upper-level, possibly within their major area of study, to further ensure writing capabilities for all future graduates. Given that enrolling in such courses is often seen as taking time away from their major area of study there is a movement across campuses to lessen such requirements, possibly minimizing or even doing away with requirements for students to write more or even to study foreign languages as part of any undergraduate degree. In places where such requirements remain, however, the extent to which the students must write, and the kind and amount of writing they must complete, can be either precisely specified or only vaguely listed.

References

Direct quotations or paraphrases in the preceding chapters arise from the following sources.

"Abstract," *Web Content Accessibility Guidelines (WCAG) 2.1*, www.w3.org/TR/WCAG21/ (accessed June 12, 2023).

Bryant, Adam (2011). "Google's Quest to Build a Better Boss," *The New York Times* (March 12), www.nytimes.com/2011/03/13/business/13hire.html (accessed June 20, 2022).

"Curb Cuts," *99% Invisible*, https://99percentinvisible.org/episode/curb-cuts/ (accessed May 24, 2022).

"Defining Critical Thinking," The Foundation for Critical Thinking, www.criticalthinking.org/template.php?pages_id=766

Gilliat-Ray, Sophie (2016). "a," *Discourse: Learning and Teaching in Philosophical and Religious Studies* 4/2: 120–35.

Glaser, Edward M. (1941). *An Experiment in the Development of Critical Thinking*. Teacher's College: Columbia University.

"High Impact Practices," American Association of Colleges and Universities, www.aacu.org/trending-topics/high-impact (accessed May 28, 2022).

Lofton, Kathryn (2014). "Review Essay of J. Z. Smith's On Teaching Religion." *Journal of the American Academy of Religion* 82/2: 531–54.

McLuhan, Marshall (1967). *The Medium is the Message: An Inventory of Effects*. New York: Bantam Books.

Otto, Rudolph (1924). *The Idea of the Holy. An Inquiry into the Non-Rational Factor in the Idea of the Devine and its Relation to the Rational*. London: Oxford University Press.

Singer, Peter (2002). *Animal Liberation*. 2nd ed. New York: Ecco.

Smith, Jonathan Z. (2018). "The Dean's Craft of Teaching Seminar (2013)" in Willi Braun and Russell McCutcheon (eds.), *Reading J.Z. Smith: Interviews and Essay*. New York: Oxford University Press.

Storm, Jason Ā. Josephson, and Daniel Gorman, Jr. (2018). "From Static Categories to a River of Theories: The Myth of Disenchantment," *The Religious Studies Project*, https://www.religiousstudiesproject.com/podcast/from-static-categories-to-a-river-of-theories-the-myth-of-disenchantment/ (accessed May 20, 2022).

Contributors

Michael J. Altman is Professor of Religious Studies at the University of Alabama and the author of *Hinduism in America: An Introduction* (2022). He is also the Director of the American Examples program, a series of workshops on teaching, research, and public humanities for early-career scholars of religion. Currently, he is researching the intersection of religious studies and professional wrestling.

Emily D. Crews is the Executive Director of the Marty Center for the Public Understanding of Religion at the University of Chicago Divinity School. She earned her PhD in the History of Religions from the University of Chicago Divinity School and uses historical and ethnographic methods to make sense of the ways that religion, gender, and the reproductive body are entangled in the formation of personhood. In the classroom she loves to teach with everyday examples and confounds her students by answering most questions with the phrase, "It depends."

Steffen Führding is member of the research and teaching staff at the Institute for the Study of Religion, Gottfried Wilhelm Leibniz Universität, Hannover. He is editor of *Method and Theory in the Study of Religion. Working Papers from Hannover* and author of *Jenseits von Religion? Zur sozio-rhetorischen "Wende" in der Religionswissenschaft*. His areas of interest include the history of *Religionswissenschaft* and the study of the political significance of classification acts.

Khurram Hussain is Associate Professor of Religion Studies at Lehigh University, USA, and is a native of Pakistan. Hussain is broadly interested in exploring the possibility of a robust critical conversation across diverse cultures and traditions and has extensive training in comparative ethics, historical sociology, and modern Western philosophy. His second book, *The Muslim Speaks*, examines the tropes and discourses surrounding the category of Islam in modern Western public spheres.

CONTRIBUTORS

Rita Lester is Professor of Religion in the Philosophy and Religion Department at Nebraska Wesleyan University where she teaches all levels of undergraduate courses from the first-year seminar to the department research project capstone, including internships.

Craig Martin is Professor of Religious Studies at St. Thomas Aquinas College. He is the author of several books, including *A Critical Introduction to the Study of Religion* and *Discourse and Ideology: A Critique of the Study of Culture*. He also edits a book series with Bloomsbury, *Critiquing Religion: Discourse, Culture, Power*.

Russell T. McCutcheon is a University Research Professor and was the chair of Department of Religious Studies at the University of Alabama for eighteen years; he has continuously taught a wide array of undergraduate classes throughout his career, supervised graduate education, participated in a variety of program reviews, and has published widely on the history and politics of the field.

Richard Newton is Associate Professor of Religious Studies and Undergraduate Director at the University of Alabama. Newton is the author of *Identifying Roots: Alex Haley and the Anthropology of Scriptures*. He is Editor for the *Bulletin for the Study of Religion* and creator of the multimedia resource Sowing the Seed: Fruitful Conversations in Religion, Culture, and Teaching (sowinghteseed.org).

Suzanne Owen is Reader in Religious Studies at Leeds Trinity University, UK, where she teaches critical and anthropological studies of religion. She obtained her PhD from the University of Edinburgh and researches contemporary British Druidry and Eastern Canadian First Nations.

Steven W. Ramey is the Chair of the Department of Religious Studies at the University of Alabama. He received his PhD from the Department of Religious Studies at the University of North Carolina at Chapel Hill, where he focused on contemporary disagreements over identifications and practices in India, particularly through the experiences of Sindhi Hindus. His ongoing research and teaching focus on analyzing representations of religions related to Asia.

Leslie Dorrough Smith is Professor of Religious Studies and Director of the Women's and Gender Studies program at Avila University (Kansas City, MO, USA). She is the author of *Compromising Positions: Sex Scandals, Politics, and American Christianity* and *Righteous Rhetoric: Sex, Speech, and the Politics of Concerned Women for America*, as well as several other edited books, articles, and essays. She specializes in the impact of evangelical thought on sex, gender, and reproduction rhetoric in the United States.

K. Merinda Simmons is Professor of Religious Studies at the University of Alabama. Her areas of teaching and writing include identity theory and transatlantic southern studies. She is the editor of the series *Concepts in the Study of Religion: Critical Primers*.

Teemu Taira is Senior Lecturer in the Study of Religion at the University of Helsinki. He has published extensively on theoretical and methodological issues in the study of religion, religion and media, and atheism in public discourse, including *Taking "Religion" Seriously: Essays on the Discursive Study of Religion*, *Atheism in Five Minutes*, and *Media Portrayals of Religion and the Secular Sacred* (with Kim Knott and Elizabeth Poole).

Vaia Touna is Associate Professor in the Department of Religious Studies at the University of Alabama, Tuscaloosa. She is author of *Fabrications of the Greek Past: Religion, Tradition, and the Making of Modern Identities* and editor of *Strategic Acts in the Study of Identity: Towards a Dynamic Theory of People and Place*. Her research focuses on the sociology of religion, acts of identification and social formation, methodological issues concerning the use of the category of "religion" in the study of the ancient Graeco-Roman world, as well as the study of the past in general.

Index

academic freedom 226–7, 239, 250, 290, 293
academic misconduct, 8–13, 227, 231, 287–8 (*see also* time management)
    and note-taking 11
    as plagiarism 8–11, 32, 89, 160, 210, 227, 231
accessibility 14–16, 17, 19, 21–2, 227–8, 235, 268, 276, 288
    Americans with Disabilities Act (ADA) 17, 188, 228
    audio recordings and transcripts 19–20
    Office of Accessibility 15–16, 36, 228
    Web Content Accessibility Guidelines (WCAG) 16
accommodations 16, 17–22, 33–4, 228 (*see also* assessment; note-taking)
add/drop/withdraw 229, 246, 278
administration/executive 57, 61, 66–9, 109–10, 122, 134, 168, 178, 183–7, 213–14, 229–30, 235, 249–50, 270 (*see also* rubrics)
    initiatives of 6, 141–2
    requirements of 23–7, 82, 244
    student affairs (*see* student life/student affairs/student services)
advising 53, 56, 103, 110–11, 141, 154, 171, 193, 204, 229, 230–1, 251, 284–5 (*see also* majors/minors; recruiting)
    advisory guidelines 290
    as interventionist 104

African American religion 158–9
AI (artificial intelligence) 9–10, 64, 210, 227, 231
    ChatGPT 231
    Turnitin 231
Altman, Michael J. 216
American Academy of Religion (AAR) 217 n.1, 218
American Association of Colleges and Universities (AACU) 53, 57, 103, 181
American Religious Sounds Project 59
assessment 5, 9, 12, 19, 23–7, 51, 58–9, 80, 88, 95–6, 178–9, 193–6, 232, 237, 253–4, 259–62, 266–7, 270, 273, 276, 284–6, 291–2 (*see also* examinations; grading/marking; outcomes; rubrics)
    of faculty 183–4, 186, 243
    of higher education 55, 141, 178, 217, 236, 241
    initiatives 73, 125, 217, 228, 232, 239, 244, 263, 278, 288
    learning assessment 184–5
    mandatory reporting 23, 26, 265–6
    peer assessment 93, 98, 105–6, 255, 271, 292
    self-assessment 23–7, 93, 96, 135, 233, 255, 260, 271, 292
assignments 11–13, 20–1, 28–32, 232–3 (*see also* examinations; scaffolding)
    alignment and variety 29–31
    digital assignments 59–60, 87, 89, 137–8, 156, 159–61, 207

INDEX

Asad, Talal 40
attendance 21, 33–7, 78, 120, 125 233, 247, 253, 269, 276 (*see also* accommodation)
    and participation 94, 237 (*see also* class participation)
    taking/tracking 33, 121, 283, 287 (*see also* roster; seating plan)
auditing/non-degree students 234

Bass, Randall 103
Bayart, Jean-François 105
    "operational acts of identification" 105
Beauvoir, Simone de 55
benchmarking 93, 232, 234 (*see also* assessment; rubrics)
Berger, Peter 223
Bhagavad Gita 71, 148–51
bias 148, 205
    implicit bias 19, 45, 103, 228
    gender bias 184
    race bias 184
blackboards/whiteboards 234–5
Blum, Susan 106
Braun, Willi 115
British Association for the Study of Religions (BASR) 212
Brown v. Board of Education National Historical Park 153
Bryant, Adam 203
Buddhism 45–7, 64, 151, 163, 165
Buford, Bill 63

campus calendars 169, 188, 191, 219, 235, 277
canceling class 181, 235
Carnegie Classifications of Institutions of Higher Education 236
Center for Teaching and Learning 236
Civil Rights Act (1964) 66–7, 188, 282
class, course, module 237
    as fieldwork-based module 211
class participation 37, 38–42, 79, 94, 98, 136, 176, 228, 237, 246, 261, 276 (*see also* attendance)
    as active 120, 177, 259
    as passive 176, 262

classification 51–2, 114–15, 126, 128, 201, 222 (*see also* transferable skills)
cooperative learning (CL). *See* group work
collaboration 30, 38, 77, 103–5, 138, 141, 155, 179, 237–8, 240, 255, 257
    as unauthorized 8–9, 11 (*see also* academic misconduct)
College Thinking: How to Get the Most out of College (Meiland) 221
compliance 14–15, 67, 69, 188, 238, 241, 271 (*see also* accessibility; syllabus)
content management systems (CMS) 123
    Slack 123
    WordPress 123
Continuous Quality Improvement (CQI) 25, 229, 232, 239
Core Curriculum 43–7, 53–7, 58, 102, 112, 118, 168, 178, 184, 206, 232, 239–40, 251, 263, 272, 277, 281, 293
    core courses/modules 239–40, 277, 286
    degree requirements 104, 112, 202, 265, 277
co-teaching 240–1 (*see also* lectures; sections)
Cotter, Christopher R. 163
credentialing associations 6, 141, 232, 238–9, 241, 250, 261 (*see also* accreditation; compliance)
credits/credit hour production 242
Critical Race Theory 50, 66
critical thinking. *See under* transferable skills
curriculum 53–7, 243–4
    curriculum map 244

data 24, 28, 31, 49, 50–1, 53, 100, 200, 220, 222–3, 247–8, 273, 288 (*see also* examples; transferable skills)
    textbook as data 165

vs. theory 202, 288 (*see also* theory)
definition 46, 49, 51–2, 58–9, 68–9, 71, 89, 90, 114–15, 128, 152, 202, 222, 242, 244 (*see also* transferable skills)
   question of 223
digital humanities 58–61, 103–4, 125, 159, 179–80, 207, 244–5 (*see also* humanities; public humanities; transferable skills)
   digital literacy 53
   digital methods 59
   digital scholarly production 59
   and scaffolding 60 (*see also* scaffolding)
directed readings/independent study course 62–65, 110, 118, 179, 245, 257, 270
Diversity, Equity, and Inclusion (DEI) 56–7, 66–9, 245–6
Douglas, Mary 52, 201
Dumont, Louis 221
Durkheim, Émile 46, 52, 171, 221, 223–4
drop/withdraw/fail (DWF rate) 138, 246

Edwards, R. B. 223
electives/options 109, 146, 206, 214, 246
Elementary Forms of Religious Life (Durkheim) 221, 223
Eliade, Mircea 2, 223
Engaged Learning Center (Elon) 104
Equality, Diversity, and Inclusion (EDI). *See* Diversity, Equity, and Inclusion (DEI)
examinations (*see also* assignments; presentations)
   essay/written examination 28–9, 31, 60, 87–8, 92, 110–11, 118, 120–1, 160, 195, 232–3, 276, 278–9
   exam, quiz, test 23, 25, 35, 60, 73, 80, 95, 120–1, 125, 137, 185, 247, 269
   final examinations 60, 87–90, 95, 233, 245, 235, 251, 292
   oral examination 12, 28, 75, 88, 203, 232, 235, 273, 291–2
   unessay 291–2
examples 12, 70–3, 110, 114–15, 131, 161, 175–6, 197, 201, 204, 206, 210–11, 248, 289 (*see also* films)
   as "e.g." 219–20
   "nothing must stand alone" 223
extra credit 37, 78–82, 170, 248–9

faculty
   contingent faculty 26, 54, 57, 77, 102, 107, 125, 226, 229–30, 232, 238–9, 243, 250, 279, 293
   cross-appointments 236, 242–3, 252
   faculty governance 57, 125, 226, 249–50, 263, 293
   faculty lines 117, 155, 236, 243, 249, 261
   full-time equivalency (FTE) 1, 3, 45, 168, 170, 197, 225–6, 238, 243, 252
   nine-month faculty contracts 225–6, 271, 286
Felton, Peter 104
FERPA/HIPAA 188, 250
films 31, 71, 75, 83–6, 88, 120, 161, 190, 228, 250–1, 290 (*see also* examples)
   Kanopy 251
Finlay, Ashley 103
Foucault, Michel 11–12
Führding, Steffen 225

General Education (Gen Ed/GE). *See* Core Curriculum
Gilliat-Ray, Sophie 211
Glaser, Edward M. 49–50
Google 24, 41, 127, 206
   Project Oxygen 203
grade book 21, 123–4, 252, 262, 278
grades/marks 63, 80, 90–6, 133, 194, 252–4, 278, 283, 285 (*see also* assignments; examinations)
   cumulative grade 277, 295
   as final grades 36, 78, 81, 94–5, 123, 228, 233, 247, 251–3

INDEX

letter grades 253
   as midterm grades 95, 235, 266–7
grading/marking 90–6, 253–4 (*see also* assessment)
   grading on a curve 93, 254
   as ungrading 94, 106, 292
graduate/postgraduate students 7, 59, 118, 141–2, 180, 186, 193–4, 196, 201, 204, 238, 254, 276, 279, 287
graduation
   degree requirement 43, 54, 56–7, 104, 281, 284 (*see also* core curriculum; senior seminars)
   graduation rate 24, 254–5, 257, 285
group work 29–30, 88, 97–101, 105, 118, 238, 247, 255, 289
   small groups 262

handouts 255–6
harassment 187, 256, 271
Hegel, G. W. F. 149
high impact practices (HIP) 102–7, 257
   living-learning communities 264
   problem-based learning (PBL) 97; 274 (*see also* group work; learning)
higher education 257–8
Hinduism 45–7, 83, 148, 151, 163, 206
honors 45, 108–11, 171, 244, 253, 258, 279
Hughes, Aaron W. 84
Hulk Hogan 70–3
humanities 259 (*see also* digital humanities; liberal arts; public humanities)
   and humanistic inquiry 65
Hurston, Zora Neale 52

inquiry-based assignments 260 (*see also* assignments; HIP)
internships 55–6, 75, 103, 105, 155–6, 169, 179, 181, 207, 231, 240, 247–8, 257, 260, 282
inclusive pedagogy 246, 259–60

Institute for Teaching Diversity and Social Justice 105
interpretation v, 50, 115, 146, 151, 165, 206, 208, 219–21 (*see also* transferable skills)
introduction vs. survey 1, 3–5, 48–52, 70, 112–16, 158–9, 168, 173, 175, 197, 199–202, 205–6, 219–24, 260–1, 277, 281
Islam 45, 63, 84, 100, 146, 150, 163–6
   Finnish Muslims 100
   Muhammad 163

Jim Crow laws 153
Jurgensmeyer, Mark 217 n.1

Kant, Immanuel 165–6
Kolb, David A. 74–5
Khurramians, The 86

learning
   as active learning 73, 228–9, 288
   as engaged learning 247
   as learning vs. performing 21, 37, 158
Learner-Centered Initiative 24–5, 228, 232, 261 (*see also* assessment; learning)
Learning Management Systems (LMS) 20, 35–7, 60, 122–5, 262, 269 (*see also* Virtual Learning Environments)
   Blackboard 121, 123, 262, 269
   Canvas 37, 123, 262, 269
   Moodle 123, 262, 269
lectures 4, 28–9, 38–9, 88, 97, 141–2, 150, 187, 189, 193–8, 233–4, 242, 248
   as large lectures 117–21, 122–3, 125, 257, 261, 273–4, 286
   virtual/online 36, 137, 256, 262
lesson plans 204, 263
liberal arts 5, 8, 55, 109, 200, 202, 214, 217, 219–20, 259, 263
liberal education 103, 112, 217, 219–23
   "double sense of 'fabrication'" 220
   "training in argument about interpretations" 220–1

library resources 60, 126–9, 142, 153, 169, 264
Lincoln, Bruce 70
Loewen, Nathan R. B. 125 n.1
Lofton, Kathryn 48
Lusby, Stan 1

McCutcheon, Russell T. 39–40, 51
McKay, Bruce 3
McLuhan, Marshall 124
majors/minors 56, 110, 155, 178, 265 (*see also* recruiting)
matriculate/matriculation 234, 266
MOOC (Massively Open Online Course) 136, 267
Mars, Roman 19
Martin, Craig 156, 201
Marx, Karl 45–6, 201
Masuzawa, Tomoko, 40
Meiland, Jack 221
Money, Tay 160
Morris, Brian 3–4
multimedia 4, 159–62, 185, 234, 267–8
  PowerPoint 11, 28, 121, 234, 256, 267
myth 1–3, 39, 70–2, 170

narrative construction 2, 83–5, 149–52, 164, 248 (*see also* examples; films; transferable skills)
Norman, Ralph 1
normativity 84, 220
note-taking 3, 11, 18, 106, 131, 143, 175, 221, 228, 235, 256, 268

office hours 63–4, 130–3, 138, 186, 195, 269, 276, 287
online/remote/virtual courses 134–9, 269–70
Otto, Rudolf 52, 144, 150, 223
outcomes 25–7, 53, 55, 57, 77, 80, 87–90, 93, 95, 103, 119, 159, 161, 179, 185, 190–1, 201, 207, 212, 216, 232, 239, 244, 246, 261, 270, 273 (*see also* assessment; rubrics)

overloads (paid or unpaid) 245, 252, 258, 270–1
Owen, Suzanne 225

Pauha, Teemu 100
Paul, Richard 49–50
peer grading and self-grading/peer assessment and self-assessment 271 (*see also* assessment; grading/marking)
peer tutors/peer learning mentor 38, 98, 106, 140–3, 271, 285
Penner, Hans 223
Pfeifer, Geoff 106
preparations (preps) 86, 122, 138, 271–2
prerequisites 144–7, 165, 174, 219, 244, 272 (*see also* curriculum; majors/minors)
presentations 60, 75, 99, 110–11, 118, 156, 267, 273, 278, 280, 289 (*see also* assessment; examinations)
  digital skills based 161
  group 120–1, 268
  oral 12, 28, 75, 88, 203, 232, 235, 258, 273, 291
  video/film 86, 121
primary/secondary sources 53, 148–52, 164, 201, 273
professionalization 34, 64–5, 141, 153–7, 274 (*see also* transferable skills)
public humanities 59, 158–62, 274–5 (*see also* digital humanities; humanities)
  and public consumption 155, 160

Ramey, Steven 163
readings 2, 11–12, 14, 18, 41, 59–60, 75, 77, 79, 88, 96, 115, 123, 162–7, 191, 194, 201, 204, 223, 247, 268–9, 275–6, 287
  reading aloud 275
recitations/tutorials 81, 122, 141–3, 238, 256, 276, 281, 287
recruiting 106, 109–11, 118, 142, 168–72, 258, 272, 276–7

INDEX

(*see also* advising; majors/
minors; retention)
reflexivity 17, 40, 51, 54, 75, 94, 152, 211, 219, 222–3, 242, 282
registrar 18, 109, 188–9, 277, 294
Religious Studies Project, The (*RSP*) 19, 180
retention 24–5, 141, 172, 277, 279
    of knowledge/skills 124, 228, 237, 250, 287
    student retention 106, 124, 141, 172, 228, 250, 251, 277, 287
    (*see also* advising; majors/minors; recruiting)
Reynolds, Charles 1
rhetoric 7, 66, 69, 208, 221, 263
Riefenstahl, Leni 223
rigor 18, 24, 34, 109, 180, 185, 214–16, 258, 277–8
Robertson, David G. 163
Rocklin, Alexander 70
roster 46, 229, 278 (*see also* attendance; seating plan)
rubrics 5, 74, 89, 93, 96, 194, 214, 223, 232, 234, 271, 278–9, 292 (*see also* assessment; outcomes)

scaffolding 12, 55, 60–1, 65, 105, 160–1, 279, 291
    as critical scaffolding 40
scholarship of teaching xi, 279–80
Scriven, Michael 49–50
seating plan 174, 280 (*see also* attendance; roster)
sections 1, 45, 110, 117, 122, 125, 141–2, 193–4, 196, 238, 272, 276, 280, 287
seminars 62, 89, 109, 125, 135, 156, 173–7, 215, 232, 261, 272–3, 276, 280–1
    first year seminars 103, 106, 178, 181, 251–2, 257
    lower/upper division 1–2, 56, 80, 94–5, 104, 106, 112–13, 141, 147, 173, 181, 197, 199, 201–2, 205, 210–11, 213–14, 233–4, 236, 249, 265, 268, 272–3, 280, 282, 286, 293

online seminars (*see* online/remote/virtual courses)
senior seminars/capstone seminars/integrative seminars 103–5, 156, 178–82, 244, 257, 281
as tutorial 281
service
    courses 276–7, 281
    department 54, 77, 178, 272, 281
    learning 55–6, 103, 169, 257, 282
Singer, Peter 48, 50
small liberal arts college (SLAC) 43–5, 109, 125, 178, 282–3
    HBCUs (historically black colleges and universities) 282
Smith, Elaine 6, 217 n.1
Smith, Jonathan Z. 6–7, 40, 48, 51, 56, 89–90, 105, 114–15, 163–5, 197, 218 n.2
Smith, Leslie Dorrough 163
Smith, Wilfred Cantwell 223
Sommel, Jesse 106
Spiro, Melford 223
Stoddard, Brad 156
Storm, Jason Ā. Josephson 180
student athlete 35–6, 283
student conduct 283–4 (*see also* academic misconduct)
student evaluations of instruction 5, 82, 125, 183–7, 284 (*see also* assessment)
    evaluating teaching vs. assessing learning 185
student success 142, 229, 271, 285
student wellness, 17–22; 286, 290 (*see also* accommodation)
summer school 225, 270, 286, 293
Supreme Court (U.S.) 152, 224, 283
syllabus 78, 81, 89–90, 97, 105, 132, 160, 188–92, 213–14, 235, 245, 251, 269, 286–7
    as argument 4–5, 114–15, 189–90, 201, 222
    construction of 38, 41, 88, 102, 109, 113, 167, 188–9
    course goals/requirements 63, 232, 248, 267, 270, 276
    governance of 21, 250
    as standardized 142, 164, 251

Taira, Teemu 225
teaching philosophy 288
teaching vs. learning 4–5, 287
teaching assistants (TA) 81, 89, 118, 125, 193–8, 252, 256, 261, 269, 271, 276, 287–8
 graduate teaching assistants 2, 89, 122, 141–2, 199, 238, 252
theory 45, 50, 112, 114, 135, 138, 147, 158, 199–202, 210, 288 (*see also* transferable skills)
 experiential learning theory 74–7, 207, 244, 248, 257, 260, 264, 285, 290
 as set of specialized discourses 202
 theories of religion 5, 40, 138, 159
 theories of secularization 146
 theory courses/classes 11, 30, 45, 104, 115, 159, 211, 222, 199–202 (*see also* seminars)
 vs. data 202, 288 (*see also* data)
textbook 5, 16, 32, 149
 critical analysis of 149–50, 159, 164–5
 and pedagogical selectivity 83
 problematics of 156, 163–4, 276
time management 8–9, 12, 98–9, 288–9
Title XI (1972) 67, 188 (*see also* Diversity, Equity, and Inclusion)
transferable skills 30, 34, 47–8, 52, 53–4, 59, 87, 98–9, 113, 115, 124, 203–8, 248, 255, 274–5, 289, 293
 communication 87, 99, 114, 207, 273
 critical thinking skills 12, 17, 19, 24, 38–42, 48–52, 53–4, 75, 77, 85, 95, 103–5, 110, 114–15, 119, 150, 165–7, 176–7, 178, 194, 196–7, 199–203, 204–5, 210, 212, 214, 223, 240, 242
 language/methodology 145
 hard skills vs. soft skills 50, 115, 146, 150, 203, 243–4, 256–7, 289

professionalization 53–4, 103–4, 113, 140, 156, 181, 209, 237, 274–5
research and writing skills 10–13, 56–7, 166, 210–11, 240, 268
technology/digital skills 60, 156, 207, 275
trigger warnings 289–90

Uncivil Religion 59
undergraduate 5–7, 43, 46, 54, 56, 61, 62, 64, 83, 105, 113, 149–50, 152, 163, 178, 201, 219, 290, 293
 undergraduate research 51–2, 55, 103–4, 181, 209–12, 290–1
unions 250, 285, 292–3
 student union 285
University of Alabama 24, 39, 67–8, 126–7, 154–5, 171, 199, 207
University of Chicago 7, 128, 197, 219
Upanishads 149, 151

Vietnam War 66
Virtual Learning Environment (VLE) 64, 134, 136–8, 235, 262, 269
VR (virtual reality) 63–4, 86

Wabash Center for Teaching and Learning in Theology and Religion 105
Welch, Claude 217–18
Weston, Anthony 213
Whitehead, Dawn 53
World Religions Paradigm (WRP) 1–2, 4, 104, 114, 116, 145, 156, 165, 168, 196–7
 alternative approaches 163
 problematics of 156, 163–4
 survey vs. introduction 261
writing requirements 109, 213–16, 282, 293

Yonan, R. 223
Yoshi, Khyati Y. 105